## What People Are Saying About
### *A More Christlike Word*

A brilliant and compelling journey into reading Scripture as expounded by Christ himself on the road to Emmaus, gently exposing and correcting the weaknesses of many modern presuppositions and opening us up to the more wonderful mystery of a loving God. *A More Christlike Word* will be sure to touch the hearts of many.

—*Fr. John Behr*
Regius Chair of Humanity, University of Aberdeen, Scotland

Bradley Jersak has spent a lifetime immersed in the Scriptures. And now, with *A More Christlike Word*, he shares with us his hard-won insights on how to interpret the Scriptures as Christ himself did on the Emmaus road that first Easter. Of the many recent books on biblical interpretation, I find *A More Christlike Word* to be the most thorough and comprehensive. It is a gift!

—*Brian Zahnd*
Lead pastor, Word of Life Church, St. Joseph, MO
Author, *When Everything's on Fire*

Brad Jersak is a mapmaker, and *A More Christlike Word: Reading Scripture the Emmaus Way* is an atlas of sorts, a trusty guide for the journey ahead. This is a necessary book for our time, when so many people are experiencing crises of faith. For anyone who loves the triune God but has found the Bible problematic, this book feels like utter redemption. *A More Christlike Word* is an invitation to engage the written word through the living Word.

—*Felicia Murrell*
Author, *Truth Encounters*

For many of us who are conflicted between our deep respect for the Bible and legitimate questions which that esteem requires we address, Bradley Jersak has gifted us with this welcome companion, educating the mind and freeing the heart to harmonize Scripture with the revelation of God we see in Jesus the Messiah.

—*Paul Young*
Author, *The Shack, Cross Roads, Eve,* and *Lies We Believe About God*
Coauthor, with Bradley Jersak, *The Pastor: A Crisis*

Brad Jersak is a gifted storyteller, a wise scholar, a careful thinker and reader, and a compassionate human being. He brings these and other assets to the task of helping us rediscover the Bible. I dare to hope that every seminarian will be assigned this book as required reading and that Christians of all denominations and callings will let Brad Jersak reintroduce them to the Bible, a book he knows and loves contagiously.

—*Brian D. McLaren*
Author, *Faith After Doubt*

Memoricide is one of the besetting illnesses of our ethos, and a casualty of such an illness is a one-dimensional, literal-grammatical approach to biblical exegesis. *A More Christlike Word: Reading Scripture the Emmaus Way* is a portal into a more layered and classical exegetical tradition and, as such, both a way-finder to the fullness of the faith journey and an antidote for memoricide.

—*Ron Dart*
University of the Fraser Valley, Abbotsford, Canada

Have you ever felt that seemingly "toxic" texts in the Bible suffocate rather than strengthen faith? If so, then this book will help you find a way to hear the life-giving Word speaking through Scripture—even the tough parts. Bradley Jersak faces difficult passages head-on with honest, provocative, wise, and stimulating insights. Here is an accessible and informed guide to Christ-centered biblical interpretation.

—*Rev. Dr. Robin Parry*
Author, *The Evangelical Universalist* and *The Biblical Cosmos*

If you find the Bible heavy lifting rather than finding yourself carried *by* Jesus, the incarnate Word himself, and his indescribably good gospel of love, *A More Christlike Word* is for you. It will invite you to move from simply reading verses through an unexamined lens to always listening for the revelation *of* Christ, *by* Christ, who reveals what is true concerning the relentless, renewing love of God our Father, and, thus, what is true about us as his beloved ones.

—*Dr. Cherith Fee Nordling*
Sessional Lecturer, Regent College, Vancouver
Author, *Knowing God by Name*

Brad Jersak is passionate about reclaiming the Bible. Don't for a moment take that to mean that he's doubling down on the status quo. Instead, he's boldly inviting us to trade in the more recent glasses that have told us what the Bible means for a much earlier prescription—lenses that dare us to see the Bible through the image of Jesus stamped on our hearts and woven through its pages. Then, watch it come to life!

—*Gary Best*
Former National Director, Vineyard Canada
Author, *Where Joy Is Found*

In Bradley Jersak's *A More Christlike Word*, we see the author in *status viatoris*, on the way out of the idolatry that misplaced the living Word for the gift of Scripture, revealing the presence of the kingdom, precisely because the light of Christ illuminates the biblical text, turning our darkness and judgment to light and mercy, and our spiritual pride to the stance of humility through which the Holy Spirit makes all things new.

—*David Goa*
Founder, The Chester Ronning Centre for the Study
of Religion and Public Life
Augustana Campus, University of Alberta, Canada

What kind of book is the Bible? How should we read and interpret the Bible? How should we tell the Bible's story with our words and our lives? These are the questions at the heart of this marvelous book by Dr. Brad Jersak. In an era when each person, or each camp, views their own positions as thoroughly "biblical" and judges anyone who dissents as "unbiblical," *A More Christlike Word* serves as a powerful antidote to this hermeneutical disease. May God bless this wonderful book and help us all to read the Holy Bible in a more Christlike way.

—*Joe Beach*
Pastor, Amazing Grace Church, Denver, CO
Author, *Ordinary Church: A Loving and Longing Look*

*A More Christlike Word* is an extraordinarily fresh, yet remarkably ancient, vision of Holy Scripture. By placing the Bible in its rightful context of the incarnation of Jesus Christ, Bradley Jersak gives space to all its disparate voices—from the legalists to the mystics, from the priests to the common folks, from the prophets to the apostles. Here is an epic story that involves us all, and we are invited to follow Jesus as our Rabbi in community with the hungry. Brilliant, readable, visionary!

—C. *Baxter Kruger, Ph.D.*
Author, *The Shack Revisited* and *Patmos*

I can think of no more urgent task for the North American church than to rediscover her sacred scriptures via the "Emmaus Way"—that is, companioned by the illuminating person and counsel of the living, risen Christ. Brad Jersak's *A More Christlike Word* mercifully wrestles the scriptures from the gray, gripping fingers of modernity's literalists and inerrantists and places them back in the supple hands of Jesus.

—*Steve Bell*
Singer-songwriter

For years, I have been enriched by reading Brad Jersak's books. With *A More Christlike Word*, more than ever before, I have been both challenged and thrilled. Whether by digging deeply into issues like the fallacy of inerrancy, demonstrating how to read Scripture at multiple levels, or affirming the centrality of the gospel as the canon of our faith, Brad has shown that Christ—the Word—is the only sure guide for rightly reading the entire Bible.

*—Steve Stewart*
Founder and President, Impact Nations

Brad Jersak is a trustworthy, fair, good-natured, and generous guide who succeeds in presenting a high view of both Christ and Scripture, even if this means dethroning the latter from the right hand of the Father. If you've ever wanted to have an easygoing yet in-depth conversation with Brad Jersak about Christotelic hermeneutics over a beer (and who hasn't?), reading *A More Christlike Word* is about as close as it gets.

*—Dr. Andrew Klager*
Director, Institute for Religion, Peace and Justice

When Jesus spoke with Elijah and Moses on the Mount of Transfiguration, he gave us a visual icon for a new hermeneutic: Jesus as schooling the Law and the Prophets. Brad Jersak is urging us toward this ancient way of reading Scripture, in which Jesus is our true guide and interpreter. Laying aside unhelpful labels, such as "progressive" and "fundamentalist," Brad focuses on how Jesus actually opened Scriptures to us—and invites us to an Emmaus road experience ourselves.

*—Julie Canlis*
Author, *A Theology of the Ordinary*

Christians are people of the Scriptures. But what does that mean for those who've undergone "deconstruction"? What can we honestly still believe about these texts? How can we read them? Can we receive them as a gift? In *A More Christlike Word*, Bradley Jersak takes these questions seriously, handling them carefully and humbly. But he also answers them confidently, persuaded that because God is like Jesus, the Scriptures not only bear witness to the truth but also transfigure us into his likeness.

—*Chris E. W. Green*
Professor of Public Theology, Southeastern University
Author, *Sanctifying Interpretation: Vocation, Holiness, and Scripture*

The Bible is a troubling, mesmerizing library, at turns moving, brutal, complicated, and comforting. And almost no one in our time knows how to read it. Enter the first Christians. In *A More Christlike Word*, Bradley Jersak introduces us to their "Emmaus Way," a Jesus-directed predisposition that unveils the Bible's mysteries, helping us to smell the aroma, taste the goodness, hear the gladness, see the glory, and touch the wounds of the human God in every book of the Scriptures.

—*Fr. Kenneth Tanner*
Pastor, Church of the Holy Redeemer, Rochester Hills, MI

A MORE

*Christlike*

# WORD

# BRADLEY JERSAK

## A MORE
## *Christlike*
## WORD

### READING SCRIPTURE
### THE EMMAUS WAY

WHITAKER
HOUSE

## A MORE CHRISTLIKE WORD:
### Reading Scripture the Emmaus Way

ISBN: 978-1-64123-652-2 • eBook ISBN: 978-1-64123-653-9
Printed in the United States of America
© 2021 by Bradley Jersak

Whitaker House
1030 Hunt Valley Circle • New Kensington, PA 15068
www.whitakerhouse.com

LC record available at https://lccn.loc.gov/2021009777
LC ebook record available at https://lccn.loc.gov/2021009778

1 2 3 4 5 6 7 8 9 10 11 ⊔⊔ 28 27 26 25 24 23 22 21

For—and, in many ways, from—
my teacher
Fr. John Behr


and our Open Table "Gospel of John" panel:
John MacMurray
Cherith Fee Nordling
Kenneth Tanner
Paul Young
Jonathan Parker

# CONTENTS

## PART II: SCRIPTURE AS EPIC SAGA

# ON THE ROAD TO EMMAUS

¹³That very day, two of them were going to a village called Emmaus, which lay about seven miles from Jerusalem. ¹⁴They were discussing with each other all the various things that had taken place. ¹⁵As they were discussing, and arguing with each other, Jesus himself approached and walked with them. ¹⁶Their eyes, though, were prevented from recognizing him.

¹⁷"You're obviously having a very important discussion on your walk," he said; "what's it all about?"

They stood still, a picture of gloom. ¹⁸Then one of them, Cleopas by name, answered him.

"You must be the only person around Jerusalem," he said, "who doesn't know what's been going on there these last few days."

¹⁹"What things?" he asked.

"To do with Jesus of Nazareth," they said to him. "He was a prophet. He acted with power and he spoke with power, before God and all the people. ²⁰Our chief priests and rulers handed him over to be condemned to death, and they crucified him. ²¹But we were hoping that he was going to redeem Israel!

"And now, what with all this, it's the third day since it happened. [22]But some women from our group have astonished us. They went to his tomb very early this morning, [23]and didn't find his body. They came back saying they'd seen a vision of angels, who said he was alive. [24]Some of the folk with us went off to the tomb and found it just as the women had said, but they didn't see *him*."

[25]"You are so senseless!" he said to them. "So slow in your hearts to believe all the things the prophets said to you! Don't you see? [26]This is what *had* to happen: the Messiah had to suffer, and then come into his glory!"

[27]So he began with Moses, and with all the prophets, and explained to them the things about himself throughout the whole Bible.

(Luke 24:13–27 NTE)

# "INTERPRETING THE BIBLE IN FIVE WORDS"

Peter Enns

*A*uthor's note: Pete Enns is a popular, accessible, and humorous writer who has addressed issues of biblical interpretation, inspiration, and infallibility in many of his books and blogs. He also happens to be one of America's top-shelf scholars of the Hebrew Scriptures (what Christians usually call the "Old Testament") and has given much thought to how Christians should approach interpretation.

In lieu of a traditional foreword, I've asked Pete to share a brief introductory teaching on his "Five Words" to biblical interpretation, particularly because they align closely with my approach. Reading Pete's framework for interpreting the Bible will give you a clear sense of how and why I began to reconsider the way I read Scripture, and how I came to write *A More Christlike Word*. Indeed, I lean heavily on his groundbreaking notion of a "Christotelic reading" of the Bible. Over to you, Pete...

I was originally prompted to summarize my approach to interpreting the Bible to clarify what I was doing in *The Bible Tells Me So* and *Inspiration and Incarnation*, which is to say, I needed to address some remaining questions about our framework for reading Scripture.

Here are five words that I feel get at my approach to biblical interpretation.

## GENRE-CALIBRATION

(That's technically two words, but the hyphen makes it one.) The Bible, like anything that has ever been written, can be classified according to genre—many genres, in fact (letters, laws, wisdom, apocalyptic, prophecy, story, parable, rhetoric, etc.). Recognizing what genre you are reading is essential to sound biblical interpretation (i.e., don't expect a parable to relay historical information; don't read proverbs as if they were laws).

Recognizing the various *ancient* genres of our *ancient* Bible is greatly aided by our ability to *compare and contrast* the Bible with similar writings from the ancient world, i.e., by "calibrating" the Bible against ancient analogs and thus learning to adopt ancient expectations for interpreting biblical literature rather than imposing alien, modern conventions of reading.

So, Genesis 1–11 is best understood when compared to other ancient origins texts rather than expecting something along the lines of modern science; the Gospels are best understood alongside ancient Greco-Roman "biographies" rather than contemporary biographies.

## CHRISTOTELIC

*Telos* is a Greek word meaning "end" or "goal." The Scriptures (i.e., Old Testament) don't always flow easily into the New Testament, nor do its writers "predict" Jesus of Nazareth in any conventional sense of the word *predict*.

Rather, after the resurrection, New Testament writers read their Scriptures in light of—taking into account—the surprise ending of a crucified and risen Messiah.

The New Testament writers believed that Christ was deeply connected to Israel's story, yet, at the same time, they grappled with this surprise, counterintuitive development of the gospel. This led them (especially Paul and the Gospel writers) to cite the Scriptures well over three hundred times (connecting the gospel to Israel's story), and in doing so to significantly reread, i.e., transpose, Israel's story to account for the surprise ending.

The tendency toward "creative" (i.e., Midrashic) readings of Scripture in Judaism in general at the time is the proper hermeneutical backdrop for understanding this "Christotelic" hermeneutic (another instance of genre-calibration).

This is why—as many Bible readers already know—New Testament writers, when quoting the Scriptures, typically "take it out of context," meaning the context of the original utterance. The gospel *requires* creative reframing of Israel's story.

## INCARNATIONAL

The incarnation is the grand mystery of the Christian faith and an apt and ancient analogy for understanding how the Bible can be embraced as God's word while at the same time unequivocally displaying the mundane properties, cultural infusions, and simple human limitations of any text, ancient or modern.

By using the incarnation as an analogy for the Bible, no claim whatsoever is being made that the Bible is a "hypostatic union" or other language normally reserved to describe the incarnation of Christ. It is an analogy, not an attempt at identification.

An incarnational model of Scripture accounts better for the Bible's own properties than do various inerrantist models, which at some point all need to tame or corral biblical phenomena that do not sit well with certain doctrinal needs.

## ECUMENICAL

I use this term in the broadest sense, meaning that wisdom and insight for interpreting the Bible can and do come from anyone, not limited to Christians alone, or Protestants alone, and most definitely not to particular tribes.

Genuine and deep insight into the nature of the Bible and its interpretation comes from Judaism, the Roman Catholic and Orthodox traditions, agnostics, atheists—even mainline Presbyterians.

Further, insights concerning the Bible come to us from all sorts of unexpected, less cerebral, places, like the world around us—which is God's world.

## PILGRIMAGE

This ancient metaphor for describing the Christian faith as a whole is also apt for describing the interpretation of the Bible. Our understanding always has a provisional dimension to it, and we should expect our views to change over time, as we all change and grow as human beings.

I do not think now as I did half a lifetime ago when I started seminary. I had better not. Nor do I think that my current thoughts are now free from the need for future refinement, change, or abandonment.

Pilgrimage is a metaphor for humility. Pilgrimage encourages us to let go of the need to have final certainty on how we understand the Bible and be less prone to put up walls of division, because we are more willing to discuss, explore, and change than to proclaim, conquer, and defend.

*Thank you, Pete. I love your sense of pilgrimage as it sets the tone for my story. And with that, we're off!*

# DECISIONS, DECISIONS

## HOW AND WHY

*T*he function of a preface is to explain how and why a book came to be. Briefly, *A More Christlike Word* springs from the hundreds of "What about this passage?" Bible questions I've received in the wake of my assertion in *A More Christlike God* that God is Love (period, no buts) or my oddly controversial claim that God is wholly Christlike, without exception. In other words, when we stand firm on Scripture's central revelation—that Jesus Christ, the Word-made-flesh, is what God finally says about himself—biblicism (the notion that the Bible is our final authority) presents a thousand objections in the form of contrary biblical proof texts.

The charge seems to be that (1) Scripture contradicts its own cruciform climax, (2) but an inerrant Bible can't do that, (3) so Jesus is *not* our definitive revelation of God's nature. That is, "God is love, BUT...," "God is Christlike, BUT...." By contrast, I would say (1) the Scriptures *prefigure* their cruciform climax, and (2) the Bible does so through a polyphony of texts in travail, (3) all converging at the crux of God's self-revelation in our Lord Jesus Christ crucified, risen, and ascended.

Christ is the Word, the Lord and point of the Scriptures, and the final revelation of God. Everything said in the Bible about God submits to his revelation of the Father. That this is even in question suggests that a solution is not found in explaining every verse that seems to say otherwise. Rather, it requires unlearning our modernist interpretive assumptions and overcoming our amnesia of how the first Christians read our sacred texts. Those who wrote and gathered the Scriptures taught us to faithfully interpret them as Christ had taught them to on "the Emmaus Way." This book chronicles my long journey there and, with a lot of inspired help, my reflections thus far.

## DECISIONS

I've made two editorial decisions you should know about.

First, on the advice of Fr. John Behr, whose patristic fingerprints are evident everywhere herein, I've chosen to replace the term "Old Testament" with the term the apostles and the early Christians used: "the Scriptures." While I also refer to the whole Bible as Scripture, I want to use the language that Jesus, the Evangelists, and Paul used, and that was retained in every form of the great creeds. "Old Testament" implies an obsolescence when, in fact, "the Scriptures" were the primary texts used to preach the gospel[1] of Jesus Christ. Irenaeus of Lyons (second century), for example, composed a book entitled *On the Apostolic Preaching*[2] that was entirely composed of gospel preaching from the Scriptures without *any* reference to the New Testament. So, as Fr. John says, "If it's good enough for the apostles and the fathers, it should be good enough for us."

Readers will still occasionally see references to the "Old Testament" when necessary or in citations, but take note that "their Scriptures" refers primarily to the sacred texts that Jesus and his disciples were using.

A related issue I address in this book is how the Scriptures were reframed with new and sometimes problematic assumptions when they became "the Bible" through the advent of collected codices and then the

---

1. In this book, *gospel* (lowercase *g*) refers to the message, whereas *Gospel* (uppercase G) refers to each or all of the four New Testament Gospel books.
2. St. Irenaeus of Lyons, *On the Apostolic Preaching*, trans. John Behr (Yonkers, NY: St. Vladimir's Seminary Press, 1997).

printing press. I raise this issue here only to say that "the Scriptures" as read by the church in the context of worship vis-à-vis "the Bible" as a bound book on my bedstand may have the same content, but their different shape and use may render differing interpretations. This is especially true when we read the Bible as a "flat book" (every page having equal authority) versus a collection of Scriptures serving as witnesses to Jesus Christ.[3]

Second, readers will see a variety of genres within this book. I realized quickly that no amount of editing could massage these chapters into a uniform tone or style. And then I thought, "Why should they be uniform? The Bible certainly isn't!" I realized I could model the same diversity found in Scripture. So, you'll see an array of genres that range from memoirs to homilies and epistles (Q & R correspondence), blog articles, semi-scholarly essays, and commentary. Sorry, not sorry. You'll be reminded, by example, that diverse genres require distinct interpretive skills. Think of it as an exercise in nimble reading. Enjoy!

## INVITATION

Finally, as one who has enjoyed a range of church experiences—from Evangelical[4] Baptist to Anabaptist Mennonite, from independent charismatic to high church Orthodox[5]—I discern the body of Christ in its innumerable iterations and want to speak to our common kinship. I invite people of all faith traditions and denominational backgrounds to explore our Scriptures with me. We invoke Jesus Christ our divine Word and his Spirit the holy Illuminator to open the scrolls and reveal the heart of our heavenly Father.

Fiat Lux

---

3. John Behr, "Looking Forward, Reading from the End," *The Oxford Handbook of the Bible in Orthodox Christianity* (Oxford: Oxford University Press, forthcoming).
4. In this book, *Evangelical* and *Evangelicalism* (uppercase E) are used to designate people, concepts, or groups in the modern Evangelical movement.
5. In this book, *orthodox* (lowercase o) is used as an adjective, whereas *Orthodox* (uppercase O) refers to the Eastern church tradition (as in the Greek East vis-à-vis the Latin West).

PART I

# JESUS IS
# THE WORD OF GOD

# INTRODUCTION
# TO PART I

*T*he emphasis of this book, and especially part I, is that Jesus is the Word of God and the Christian Scriptures faithfully testify to him. To speak of the Word of God is to proclaim Jesus Christ as the author, finisher, and final authority of Christian faith.

To speak of the Bible as "inspired" is to affirm its role as a faithful witness to the Word and his gospel. Indeed, the claim of the risen Lord is that Moses, all the Prophets, and the whole Bible speak of him.[6] My dear friend Fr. Kenneth Tanner says,

> If God wants to show humans what he is like, and to make clear in whose image we are made—to show us what it means to be God and what it means to be human—does God send a sacred book or a human who is God?

> The Bible is vital to Christian preaching and central in the life of the church but a book cannot proceed from the Father, a book cannot be one with the Father, a book cannot—as a human person who is God—do what the Father does and say what the Father says.

---

6. See Luke 24:26–27.

I love what God says in the flesh of Jesus Christ. One greater than Moses is now here and is human.

God sends himself.[7]

Readers will perceive in this statement a dual correction, first to those who habitually displace Christ with the Bible as the fullness of divine revelation, and second to those who dismiss the authority and inspiration of Scripture.

Recognizing Jesus Christ as the divine Word and upholding Scripture as an inspired witness is a beginning. Who Christ is and how we describe the Bible gets us into thorny questions and tricky definitions of words such as *infallibility* and *inerrancy*. We'll go there. But we can parse the nature of Scripture *ad nauseam* and still fail to *read* and *interpret* it correctly. Reading the whole Bible as a testimony of Jesus and as the grand narrative of redemption will require us to revisit our patterns of interpretation and layers of reading—attending to the literal, moral, and spiritual sense described by the early church.

All of the above is a journey embedded in my own story as a Jesus-loving Bible reader from my first memories. It's a tale of certitude, unraveling, and rediscovery—of leaving the world of biblical literalism and finding the ancient paths that brought me to *the Emmaus Way*.

---

7. Kenneth Tanner (@kennethtanner), Twitter, July 19, 2019, 5:14 p.m., https://twitter.com/kennethtanner/status/1152325785291776014.

### CHAPTER 1

# HE GREW A BEARD!

"It is Christ himself, not the Bible, who is the true word of God. The Bible, read in the right spirit and with the guidance of good teachers, will bring us to him."[8]
—*C. S. Lewis*

"What John's prologue says of John the Baptist, we can say about the Bible: 'There was a book sent from God that we call the Bible. The Bible came as a witness to testify concerning that light, so that through him all might believe. The Bible itself is not the light; it came only as a witness to the light.' This is not a low view of Scripture but a high view of Christ."[9]
—*Brian Zahnd*

*The Word of God is inspired, inerrant, and infallible. And when he was about eighteen years old, he grew a beard.* That reliable one-liner triggers double takes and snickers whenever I say it. It might even be original to me.

---

8. C. S. Lewis, *The Collected Letters of C. S. Lewis, Volume 3: Narnia, Cambridge, and Joy, 1950–1963*, ed. Walter Hooper (HarperOne, 2007), 246.
9. Brian Zahnd, email message to author, May 10, 2021. Referring to Brian Zahnd, *Sinners in the Hands of a Loving God* (Colorado Springs, CO: Waterbrook Press, 2017), 29–30.

But I'm not just trying to be clever. I'm challenging a cherished assumption—namely, the way my Evangelical heritage habitually and primarily referred to the Bible as "the Word of God."

I adopted this habit very young. As a boy of six, growing up in Manitoba, Canada, I was already listening to *Back to the Bible*, broadcast on CJRB Radio, every night as I settled down to sleep. Their opening song (as best I remember it) exhorted me,

> Back to the Bible, back to the Bible, back to the Word of God.
>
> Strength for today and bright hope for tomorrow,
>
> the everlasting Word of God.

The everlasting Word of God?

See the issue? Yes, there is an eternal Word of God. But in his Gospel, the apostle John teaches us that this eternal Word did not become a collection of stone tablets, papyrus scrolls, or leather-bound books. Rather, the Word who created sandstone, grass reeds, and cowhide *became flesh*. And when he was twelve years old, or thereabouts, the divine Word hit puberty. The Word is a person. The confusion or conflation of inspired texts with the eternal Son of God is deeply problematic, especially when the Bible *displaces* Christ as the "Word of God" and "Scripture alone" becomes our "sole and final authority" instead of him.

The Baptist tradition in which I was raised used to distinguish the living Word of God (Jesus) from the written word of God (the Bible), but in conversation, the default referent for "the Word" was always Scripture. "Brothers and sisters, what does the Word say?" We didn't mean, "What does Christ say?" We meant, "Can you show me a Bible verse?"

That said, the fuzzy identification of the Word of God as both Jesus Christ and my "Holy Bible" was natural for me. That's because the four Gospels—Matthew, Mark, Luke, and John—comprised the main stage on which I "met Jesus" and "heard him speak." Please forgive the proliferation of scare quotes. Trust that they indicate the lingo I was immersed in rather than cynicism about inspired Scripture. I am deeply grateful for, and have no regrets at all about, that early introduction to my favorite book. We

Baptists claimed to have a "high view" of Scripture. I still do. Higher today than ever, I suspect, even if I've demoted it from God's throne in my mind.

But please hear me: I am *not* denying that the Bible is "the word of God" in some real sense. Yes, it is a *witness* to the Word, and it contains the *promises* of God. In John 6, Jesus even suggests that to *chew* on the Scriptures is to *chew* on his flesh and to *eat* him, the living Bread (the manna) who descends from heaven!

Indeed, the Scriptures might even be regarded as an *appearance of Christ the Word*, bearing with the wounds of his passion across its pages:

> ...we read of the rejection and despoiling of the anointed life, a type of crucifixion of the divine Word. It is often done in the name of God in biblical narrative as if by us in our own time. Christ's passion runs like a deep red river through the whole of the Bible, from beginning to end. But the light of Christ is present as well, illuminating human passions and calling us to turn around to self-giving love and the ending of enmity.[10]

Still, in the ultimate sense, I contend that Christ alone is the eternal Word of the triune God and, as such, uniquely reveals his Father and unveils the true meaning of the Scriptures as pointing to him.

## "BACK TO THE BIBLE, BACK TO THE WORD OF GOD"

> Let the first lispings utter Christ, let earliest childhood be formed by the Gospels of Him whom I would wish particularly presented in such a way that children also might love Him.[11]

I have cherished the Scriptures ever since I obtained my first copy, a genuine imitation-leather King James Version (red-letter edition) that I earned by memorizing the books of the Bible in order and reciting my first

10. David J. Goa and Dittmar Mündel, "The Bible and the Land of Shades: Divine Justice and How We Read the Bible," in *Reading the Bible as Life-giving Word*, Occasional Papers of the Chester Ronning Centre II (Camrose: AB: The Chester Ronning Centre for the Study of Religion and Public Life, 2013), 33.
11. Desiderius Erasmus, *Paraclesis, Christian Humanism and the Reformation: Selected Writings of Erasmus*, 3rd ed., ed. John C. Olin (New York: Fordham University Press, 1987), 107.

thirty Bible verses from memory—while still only a second-grade gradu-ate. My dad used to tease me for calling what I did "rememorizing." (These days, that's exactly what I need to do.) I would sing to myself from Psalm 119, "Thy word have I hid in my heart, that I might not sin against Thee."[12] Those prerequisites for Bible ownership were self-imposed. Dad told me he'd get me a copy regardless, but I insisted on crossing some imagined threshold that would reflect the honor of owning a Bible when so many people did not have that opportunity. I sensed a gravity about handling Scripture. I still do.

By the beginning of grade three, I had scoured the entire book of Acts, full of wonder at the apostles' miracles and courage—and wondering why our church didn't look much like what I saw there. Then I went on to read and highlight every verse Dad had marked in his *Pocket New Testament* and *Scofield Study Bible*.

During that time, I also convinced my pastor to baptize me (signifi-cantly underage for that church culture). I recall, immediately after my baptism, receiving a distinct awareness of the Spirit's illumination. The sense of "I get this" surprised me whenever I read. No one suggested this would happen or connected those dots for me. To this day, I'm convinced of the reality of inspiration and illumination because I have experienced it profoundly. At that time, I especially loved the words of Jesus, printed in red letters. I still do, and more than ever.

It must have been during middle school that I first read *The Living Bible* in its entirety (*The Way* edition that the "Jesus people" so loved). It took me a *long* time to read it all, so I was impressed with my Babička, my dad's mom, who used to read the entire Bible every year, even into her nineties. After a couple times through, I found it more helpful for me to stay in one chapter or book for months on end, so I haven't done a complete annual reading for a long time. But I did have that "read your Bible, pray every day" conviction on into high school and, for a while, I practiced read-ing one psalm and one chapter of Proverbs between sets of push-ups and sit-ups each night before bed.

For me, the "Word of God" was not *only* the Bible that I read. It included the words of God I heard from the pulpit and felt compelled to preach. Not

---

12. Verse 11, paraphrase.

long after my baptism, my family moved to Killarney, Manitoba, where, as an elementary student, I composed and preached my first sermon. My key text was Matthew 6:33—the first verse I had memorized in the King James Version: "Seek ye first the kingdom of God, and his righteousness; and all these things shall be added unto you." In that initial homily, I connected this promise of Jesus with the experience of the boy-king Solomon. Having been offered by God anything he wanted—wealth, power, or fame— Solomon chose God's wisdom (literally, "a hearing heart").[13] The sermon went well, I thought. And now, I was not merely a young fundamentalist mimicking his parents' faith. I truly felt called.

On the other hand, with my adolescent insecurities, I confess to an ego element and performance-orientation in my study of Scripture. For example, Nancy MacMillan and I were archrival "sword drill" champs at Bible camp and Sunday school. If you aren't familiar with this competition, a sword drill was a contest where we would all hold our Bibles above our heads, the Bible-master would speak out a reference ("John 3:16"), we would repeat it, and then s/he would say, "Charge!" We'd all pull our Bibles down and furiously race to find the verse. The first to stand up and read the verse out loud would get a point. To be champ usually meant finding the verse in five to seven seconds. It felt satisfying if I could edge out Magnificent MacMillan to win the weekly prize. Heady stuff, that.

## "THE WORD OF OUR GOD SHALL STAND FOREVER"

I entered Bible college with a brand-new *Ryrie Study Bible*, and this too would become a point of pride. I was always towing it along everywhere I went (hey girls, did you notice?) so that, once I'd completed every Bible and theology course available, my copy of the "Good Book" had notations on every page and was MacGyvered together by duct tape.

By the time I'd earned my bachelor's and master's degrees in biblical studies, I'm not sure that I'd ever been further from the actual *Word*. Christ was relegated to the back seat in my academic pursuit of the Book.

Teachers such as Carl Hinderager, my Gospels teacher and mentor, could see through the facade. He did his best to guide me forward, but character comes slow for me. Still does. Happily, the apostle was right:

13. See 1 Kings 3:5–15.

you can't sow in the Spirit and not reap.[14] The six hours a week that Carl gave me through three years as his student marker would later bear fruit in renewing my childhood love for Jesus and in my eventual call to ministry.

For over half a decade, while earning my degrees, every time I drove through the entrance of that Bible college, I was greeted by its motto, which boasted the promise of Isaiah in these words: "...the word of our God shall stand forever."[15]

Although Isaiah was likely referring to the reliability of God's covenant promises, as in "you have my word," we had come to recognize "God's word" as referring to the Bible—*inspired, infallible, and inerrant.* Indeed, these three *I*-words were, for us, the supreme test of orthodoxy. In the faith statements of our "Bible-believing" colleges, in our local "Bible fellowships" and denominations, and at the "Bible camps" where I served, the Evangelical Bible was embedded in official faith statements as *"the Word of God, our final authority for faith and practice."*

I bought in completely. I loved the certitude of "verbal plenary inspiration." I felt secure knowing that "every word of Scripture is true in all that it affirms" (in the alleged "original autographs"). Any contradictions were explained away as transcription errors. But the pristine originals were flawless. I would have proudly signed off on "The Chicago Statement on Biblical Inerrancy."[16] We'll come back to that later.

Sure, we knew that Christ is also the living Word of God as described in the prologue of John's Gospel. But then, when I memorized the book of Hebrews' description of the "word of God," I read that as "the Bible."

> [12]*The word of God* is quick, and powerful, and sharper than any twoedged sword, piercing even to the dividing asunder of soul and spirit, and of joints and marrow, and is a discerner of the thoughts and intents of the heart.                    (Heb 4:12 KJV)

I was taught and believed that this verse referred to sacred Scripture. The Word = the Bible. I didn't notice that the verse following says, "Neither

---

14. See Galatians 6:8.
15. See Isaiah 40:8.
16. "The Chicago Statement on Biblical Inerrancy," International Council on Biblical Inerrancy, https://library.dts.edu/Pages/TL/Special/ICBI-1978-11-07.pdf.

is there any creature that is not manifest in *his* sight" (Heb 4:13 KJV), or that the next says, "Seeing then that we have a *great high priest*" (Heb 4:14 KJV). And really, how could I hope to connect those dots when the translators so often inserted a bold, intrusive subtitle between verse 12 and the rest of the chapter? My edition of the Bible deliberately segmented "the word of God" from the person of Christ, and I failed to notice.

You see my point: I have always LOVED the Bible, and I have always LOVED Jesus. And I still do. But in prioritizing *study* of the Bible ("to show myself approved unto God"[17]) ahead of hearing and following Christ the Word—by making my interpretation of the Good Book my final authority—I learned how to read without intimacy. I could dissect the Bible without illumination. And I most definitely *felt* the absence of the Holy Spirit in my reading as keenly as I had felt the Spirit's presence as a child. I read with a veil over my heart, and in the infrequent pauses between being "wise in my own eyes,"[18] I'm embarrassed to say I absolutely knew it.

## "I WANT TO KNOW YOU"

When I was studying for my first master's degree in the late 1980s, masquerading the poverty of my faith behind Bible studies and theological textbooks was no longer working for me. The dispensational theology I was immersed in while I was growing up, and the Calvinism I had embraced through my first years at seminary, had stifled me spiritually. Now, unable to find satisfactory answers to my growing questions from my advanced studies, I found my faith drifting even further away from Jesus. My mother noticed the dysfunction and repeatedly urged me, "Bradley, you must stay open." It was hard because those theological systems promised certitude while actively denying that Christ speaks today and creating suspicion about anything related to the Holy Spirit. Evangelical rationalism cut me off from the contemplative path, repeatedly labeling those who claimed to hear the voice of God as insane, demonized, or New Agers.

But I had bottomed out. I had to admit to myself that I didn't "know God." I knew for sure that the apostle Peter's description of "joy unspeakable" (1 Pet 1:8) in the Holy Spirit was altogether foreign to me.

---

17. See 2 Timothy 2:15.
18. See 2 Corinthians 3:15; Proverbs 3:7.

In that context, I believe *Abba*, my heavenly Father, slipped me a set of earnest prayers he fully intended to answer. I was studying Exodus 33, jealous of Moses's face-to-face communion with God in the tent of meeting. I longed for God to say he was pleased with me as he had said to Moses, because "I know you by name." I could no longer relate to such a living connection, but the story stirred up a desire for something more, something real.

On the heels of the golden calf incident, Yahweh appears to throw up his hands—even after the Lord had redeemed the Israelites from slavery, they remained incorrigible. God tells Moses he's pretty much done with them. He'll send them on with an angel because Yahweh's own presence would be too dangerous for such a defiant lot. He's ready to pack up with Moses and go start their brand-new nation. Alarmed, Moses boldly makes three urgent demands:

1. *Teach me your ways.*

2. *I won't take one more step without you.*

3. *Show me your glory.*[19]

This is exactly what God was teasing out of Moses—a willing partner and intercessor. More than that, God wanted *a friend.* God responded to all three requests in what turned into a historic breakthrough of God's self-disclosure.

I wanted that kind of encounter—a real and living connection. More than anything. And yet I experienced a deep conviction that Jesus was speaking to me when he castigated his opponents:

[39]You *search the Scriptures because you think that in them you have eternal life*; it is these that testify about Me; [YES, I HAVE DONE THIS!]

[38]*You do not have His word abiding in you,* for you do not believe Him whom He sent.

[37]And the Father who sent Me, He has testified of Me. *You have neither heard His voice at any time* nor seen His form. [NO, I HADN'T!]      (John 5:37–39 NASB, verses in reverse order)

---

19. See Exodus 33:12–18.

By now I had married Eden (1986), finished my MA (1988), and discovered that employment in the academic world was slim pickings. Despite reservations about pastoral ministry, I accepted a call to Bethel Mennonite Church (Eden's home congregation) in southwestern British Columbia, where I quickly fell in love with frontline youth, young adult, and community outreach. My faith was revitalized, and I began praying Moses's prayers religiously and earnestly: "Show me your ways; no further without you; let me see your glory!"

And I began to constantly pray these texts from Psalm 27 and Ephesians 1, personalizing them:

[4]One thing I ask from the LORD,

　　this only do I seek:…

to gaze on the beauty of the LORD….

[8]My heart says of you, "Seek his face!"

　　Your face, LORD, I will seek.

[9]Do not hide your face from me….

[13]I remain confident of this:

　　I will see the goodness of the LORD

　　in the land of the living.

[14]Wait for the LORD;

　　be strong and take heart

　　and wait for the LORD.

(Ps 27:4, 8–9, 13–14 NIV)

I keep asking that the God of our Lord Jesus Christ, the glorious Father, may give ME the Spirit of wisdom and revelation, so that I may know him better. I pray that the eyes of MY heart may be enlightened in order that I may know the hope to which he has called ME. (Eph 1)[20]

---

20. See Ephesians 1:17–18 (NIV).

Selfish prayers. Naïve. Bold. Demanding…even importunate, but a quality in prayer commended by Christ himself! I saw in Abraham, Moses, and David a certain presumption in prayer that God regards as a sign of trust, faith, and friendship. That was my goal.

Did God answer my prayer? Thirty years later, the jury is out. There's some debate about whether I became a heretic or a prophet. Either is too grandiose. I'd just like to become God's friend, since he's always been mine, despite me.

Good news: the verdict doesn't belong to a jury anyway. Christ alone knows what I am. I can't even judge for myself. In the end, he'll decide. And I'm good with that. But I know this: *I've met the Word of God, and he's far more than a book.* I've come to trust in his mercy *absolutely*, and, with the old chorus riffing off Psalm 89:1,

I will sing of the mercies of the LORD forever.

With my mouth, will I make known,

*Great is thy faithfulness!*

### CHAPTER 2

# "LORD,
# TO WHOM SHALL WE GO?"

## SPIRIT OF TRUTH

*W*hen I reoriented from Bible to Christ as the locus of the Word of God, Scripture became my map—or an inspired compass—rather than my destination, its authors, narrators, and events all employed by God's Spirit, directing me to pursue the Person.

I found special help on two fronts during my decade at Bethel Mennonite. First, my friends down the road at the Vineyard church showed me the significance of Christ's own words from John 16.

> [12]"There are many things I still have to say to you," Jesus continued, "but you're not yet strong enough to take them. [13]*When the Spirit of truth comes, though, he will guide you in all the truth.* He won't speak on his own account, you see, but he will speak whatever he hears. He will announce to you what's to come. [14]He will glorify me, because he will take what belongs to me and will announce it to you. [15]Everything that the father has is mine. That's why I said that he would take what is mine and announce it to you."
>
> (John 16:12–15 NTE)

What stunned me was Jesus's twofold claim. First, even after he had spent years together with his disciples, Christ faced a training dilemma. He had *so much more* to say. Second, he had a solution. He would give them the Spirit, who would lead them into *all truth*.

With the completion and canonization of John's Gospel, the words of Christ are now directed to us. He's still speaking and does so by the Spirit. It would have been so easy for him to say, "The Bible will lead you into all truth," but he didn't. Christ, in the Bible no less, says the Spirit will plant the words of God in our hearts—"he will be *with* you and *in you*."[21] The Spirit will be our *counselor* and *guide* on the journey, speaking in a range of voices that includes and aligns with the Scriptures but is not exclusive to them.

Indeed, even to rightly understand the Scriptures will require the illumination of the Spirit. So says Paul:

[10]...as it is written:

> "What no eye has seen,
>     what no ear has heard,
> and what no human mind has conceived"—
>     the things God has prepared for those who love him—

these are the things God has revealed to us *by his Spirit*.

The Spirit searches all things, even the deep things of God. [11]For who knows a person's thoughts except their own spirit within them? In the same way *no one knows the thoughts of God except the Spirit of God.* [12]What we have received is not the spirit of the world, but *the Spirit who is from God*, so that we may understand what God has freely given us. [13]This is what we speak, not in words taught us by human wisdom but in words taught by the Spirit, explaining spiritual realities with Spirit-taught words. [14]The person *without the Spirit* does not accept the things that come from the Spirit of God but considers them foolishness, and cannot understand them because they are *discerned only through the Spirit*. [15]The person with

---

21. See John 14:17.

the Spirit makes judgments about all things, but such a person is not subject to merely human judgments, [16]for,

"Who has known the mind of the Lord
  so as to instruct him?"

But we have the mind of Christ.               (1 Cor 2:9–16 NIV)

## WORD OF LIFE

My second great help came through Rev. Peter Bartel, my beloved senior pastor at Bethel Mennonite Church. He taught me the difference between reading the Bible as a flat text (where every word has equal authority), progressive revelation (where all the words accumulate in a crescendo of consistent truth), and the Christocentric view (where Christ is the pinnacle of revelation and every word must finally submit to him).

Peter opened my eyes to the stubborn fact that *not* every word of Scripture aligns with the living Word of God. It's so plain in the Sermon on the Mount: "You have heard it said, but I say to you...."[22] That's not merely a progression—it's a correction. There, I said it out loud. Yes, *Jesus corrected the Bible*, including words in the Bible formally ascribed to God!

In Mark 10:1–9, the Pharisees cite the law of Moses on divorce certificates, as if this were "God's word." Jesus corrects them: Moses wrote this law as an expression of their hard hearts, not God's heart. That's a correction. Jesus trumps Moses. Jesus trumps the Bible when the Bible reflects our hearts rather than God's.

Rev. Peter's math was simple: Read the Bible. When anything in the rest of the Bible disagrees with Jesus, listen to Jesus. When Moses (the Law) and Elijah (the Prophets) appear with Jesus on the Mount of Transfiguration, what does *Abba* say? "This is my Son. Listen to him."[23] The Law and the Prophets point to Jesus. Never use them to correct him. He's the Word of God. And they are now submissive witnesses to the Word of God, when read by the Spirit.

---

22. See Matthew 5.
23. See, for example, Matthew 17:5.

So, for me, David's reflection "Thy word is a lamp unto my feet, and a light unto my path" (Ps 119:105 KJV) shifted in meaning from "*Thy Bible is my lamp and light*" to John the Revelator's "*Thy Son is my lamp and light.*"[24] Our Bibles bear witness to a living God—Father, Son, and Spirit—and in the Bible's pages, I see and hear the bearded, wounded Word everywhere active, even in—and especially in—our folly.

## DISORIENTATION

On the other hand, when Christ becomes your final revelation of the nature and will of his *Abba*, reading the Bible can trigger various spiritual and emotional responses. When the Scriptures describe God and his acts in ways that look nothing like the *Abba* who Christ revealed, it can throw you into a crisis of faith. If you pay close attention to what the narrators actually claim, you begin to see evidence of a very *un-Christlike* (lowercase) word.

In the early 2000s, I began to ask tough questions:

Could the *Abba* Jesus revealed as all-merciful really instigate death-dealing and say, "Show no mercy!"?

Could the *Abba* Jesus revealed say, "When you come to a city, offer it peace. If they take your offer, enslave them all. If they don't, kill all the men and enslave the women and children. If you see a woman you like, take her for a month. Cut off her hair, fingernails, and toenails. Take away the clothes of her people and dress her up as a Jew. After a month, if you still want her, marry her. If not, don't kill her. Send her away."

Our *Abba* said that? Well, someone said it. In the name of God. It's in the Bible. In Deuteronomy 20–21.

Could the *Abba* Jesus revealed say, "Wipe out the foreigners. Take their women and sort them into virgins and nonvirgins"? (Who checked? How?) "Slaughter the nonvirgins and keep the virgins for yourself. But tithe a tenth of them to the Levites for their use"? (What use?)

*Abba* said so? Or someone said so. In God's name. It's there in Numbers 31.

---

24. Revelation 21:23: "And the city has no need of sun or moon to shine on it, for the glory of God gives it light, and its lamp is the lamb" (NTE).

Could the *Abba* Jesus revealed say, "Go kill all the Amalekites for the sins of their great-great-great-great-grandparents. Why? Because they attacked you when you came out of Egypt four centuries ago.[25] Kill the men, the women, the children, the infants, the animals. Wipe them all out for the sins of their ancestors. No mercy."

Could the *Abba* of Jesus issue these commands? Did he?

First Samuel 15 seems to say so.

Could Christ himself demand merciless death-dealing—the One who commanded us to love, bless, and pray for our enemies? The One the apostles called God, who claimed, "It's the thief who steals, kills, and destroys, but I come that you would have life, and that more abundantly"?[26]

Could *that One*—"the same yesterday, today, and forever"[27]—send out the shock troops and terror raids I read about in my Bible?

I could only conclude that either God is *not* who Jesus revealed him to be *or*, as my friend Anna (seven years old) suggested, the narrators are sometimes confused.

It was at exactly that point of confronting such dissonance that *many* of my Christian friends seemed to set aside their Bibles—some permanently. For them, it was time to cut their losses. Part of the function of the previous chapter was to show you why I didn't do the same. And can't. And so, I *needed* to press the question. When I asked others about it, the range of responses included:

+ **Denials:** *"Where's that in the Bible?"* As if I'm making it up. No, I'm *not*. The problem is that, often, the bibliolaters[28] are ideologues who haven't actually read the hard passages or who skim through those chapters with glazed eyes.

+ **Justifications:** I also heard stunning justifications for why genocide is not genocide and why killing is justified (even holy), and that whatever

---

25. See Exodus 17:8–15, where God promises to war against the Amalekites from generation to generation and to wipe them from the face of the earth.
26. See John 10:10.
27. See Hebrews 13:8.
28. Bibliolaters are those who make an idol of the Bible by exulting it in authority to equality with God. They tend also to excessive literalism.

God wills is good, including the slaughter of innocents (because "no one is innocent" and "God was actually being kind").

I'd hear, "Well, the Amalekites were so wicked, offering child sacrifices and impossible to cure. They were a cancer that needed to be removed." Such claims completely and conveniently ignore the reasons the Bible itself gives in the immediate context, allegedly by God himself.[29] So, now what? We're going to just make stuff up? So much for faithfulness to Scripture!

At least the Swiss Reformers Ulrich Zwingli and John Calvin had the cojones to be honest about the evils ascribed to God in the Bible. But they proposed their own hideous justifications. Both claimed that God could and did command evil without himself being evil and was also completely justified in punishing the evil he commanded his servants to perform. And not just his servants.

In their hyper-sovereignty mindset, Zwingli and Calvin believed that God *ordained* or *governed* every event (including murder and rape) but that only the murderer, the rapist, or even satan[30] was guilty—even if Sovereignty *commanded* that they could not do otherwise. No, that is not merely a caricature or the extremes of later Calvinists. I read it in the *Institutes* again just yesterday. In Calvin's own words,

> But when [the elect] call to mind that the devil, and the whole train of the ungodly, are, in all directions, held in by the hand of God as with a bridle, so that they can neither conceive any mischief, nor plan what they have conceived, nor how much soever they may have planned, move a single finger to perpetrate, *unless in so far as he permits, nay, unless in so far as he commands*; that they are not only bound by his fetters, but are even *forced to do him*

---

29. The reason given for the genocide is that, four hundred years earlier, the Amalekites' ancestors had waylaid the Israelites as they came out of Egypt. (See Exodus 17:8–16; 1 Samuel 15:2.) Talk about holding a grudge!

30. Following N. T. Wright and others, I no longer capitalize *satan*. Brian Zahnd says "the satan" is less than a person, more than a metaphor. It is the real phenomenon of evil, rooted in human sin, and verges on self-awareness. Most importantly, the satan phenomenon is undone by Love. See Brian Zahnd (@BrianZahnd), "@Mikal_Tee. The satan. More than metaphor. Less than a person. A phenomenon. A phenomenon with self-awareness. A phenomenon undone by Love," Twitter, October 28, 2013, 9:45 p.m., https://twitter.com/brianzahnd/status/395003503120097280?lang=en.

*service*,—when the godly think of all these things they have ample sources of consolation.[31]

As I read nearly identical words by Zwingli in a book owned by my colleague, Dr. Peter Fitch, I noticed he had penned his assessment in the margin: *Gobbledygook*. Amen. I might have suggested a more formal term: *blasphemy*.

+ **Warnings:** To my pressing questions, I also received a third response that was just as frustrating to me in my disoriented state: "You should not be asking these questions. You sound like a liberal. A heretic. You're becoming a Marcionite.[32] Serious [unnamed] consequences will follow. Doors to ministry will close. You're on the precipice of hell, and you're leading others there."

For what? For asking why the same God who became flesh looks and sounds, at times in the Bible, more like the satan he came to save us from?

Please hear me. I did *not* find these Bible passages troubling because I *didn't* love and trust the Bible—it was because I DID. Deeply. *Still do*. And now, I had come to love and trust Christ far more, so I couldn't and wouldn't turn a blind eye to texts that appeared to impugn his character. For that very reason, I would *not* opt for the functional Marcionism of *inerrantists* who ignored the "toxic texts" or pretended they don't exist. Nor could I follow the *biblicists*—literalists who were willing to throw the character of God under the bus, painting him as a monster and calling it "good" without blinking. Nor could I follow many *progressives* who had seen the problem but left the Bible behind altogether—and with the Bible, sometimes Jesus too!

I heard Jesus asking, "Do you also want to go away?"

With Peter, I responded, "Lord, to whom shall we go? You have the words of eternal life" (John 6:67–68 NKJV, LXX).

But I was stuck. I needed help.

---

31. John Calvin, *The Institutes of the Christian Religion*, trans. Henry Beveridge (Ingersoll, ON: Devoted Publishing, 2016), 100 (1.17.11).

32. Marcionism (second century AD) was an early Christian heresy founded by Marcion of Sinope. He read the Old Testament literally, concluded that the two Testaments must represent two different gods, and therefore rejected the Old Testament.

### CHAPTER 3

# GANDALF'S PRINTSHOP:
# REORIENTATION

## PSA (NOT "PUBLIC SERVICE ANNOUNCEMENT")

*M*y path out of the quagmire began during my decade with Pastor Peter and the Mennonites, who introduced me to nonviolent ways to read the Bible. This path would include finding alternatives to the premise in penal substitutionary atonement (PSA) theory that the cross was an act of divine violence.[33]

During that time, I experienced my own Damascus Road intervention. God stopped me in my theological tracks with regard to my understanding of the cross. One day, while I was in contemplative prayer, these words—a voice from elsewhere—pierced my heart, loud and clear: *"Stop telling people I was punishing my Son. That is not what was happening."*

I was shocked. I would never abandon any dogma of the faith by attributing to God an alleged personal revelation I had received. Please

---

33. Penal substitutionary atonement is the primary Evangelical view of the cross. In its most popular form, it says that sin cannot simply be forgiven. It must first be punished in order to satisfy the wrath of God. And that Christ willingly endured his Father's punishment in our place. While more nuanced versions of PSA exist today among Reformed and Barthian scholars, the concept of the violence of God dominates Evangelical preaching.

understand, my master's thesis was a 175-page apologetic *defending* PSA entitled "The Nature of Christ's Suffering and Substitution." I zealously wrote, preached, and taught an Evangelical PSA gospel. I was as invested in this belief as anyone you'll ever meet. To me, it was a fundamental doctrine of Christianity. So, this alarming epiphany demanded that, before I took even one more step in a new direction, I undertake a *very* careful assessment from you-know-where: back to the Bible!

I scurried to the Scriptures, disciplining myself to reexamine every passage I had previously used as the bulwark of my soteriology (theology of salvation)—those verses that describe the crucifixion as *wrath appeasement through divine abandonment*. Or so I had assumed. As a young fundamentalist, I had never regarded penal substitution as a *theory* of the atonement. It was my *gospel*—the *only* gospel, plain and simple. Christ died to satisfy the wrath of God as the necessary condition by which he could be both "just and justifier"[34] of those under the fury of his condemnation. Believing Christ suffered his Father's wrath in our place was the confession by which we were saved.

I believed this. It's not a caricature of the Evangelical message, as some have suggested. I know what I believed. If you didn't inherit the same belief, very good. But the "no true Scotsman" fallacy[35] can't negate what I know. I *know* these are the rudiments of my Baptist brethren and Evangelicalism in general. You'll also find these convictions in the bold, founding documents of neo-Reformed movements like the Gospel Coalition and Acts 29 network. More recently, in 2017, the Southern Baptist Convention (SBC) doubled down on these beliefs with a statement, which, after twenty inflammatory "whereas" statements," says,

> ...the messengers to the Southern Baptist Convention...reaffirm the truthfulness, efficacy, and beauty of the biblical doctrine of

---

34. See Romans 3:26.

35. "No true Scotsman" is a purity fallacy that defends a position by excluding counterexamples from it. In this case, some argue that *true* penal substitution does not teach wrath appeasement through divine violence, and they exclude counterclaims as caricatures. In reality, wrath appeasement is by far the dominant view, and those who nuance it do, in fact, depart dramatically from Calvin and default Evangelicalism (usually with a nod to Barth).

penal substitutionary atonement as the *burning core of the Gospel message* and the *only hope* of a fallen race.[36]

For the SBC leadership, PSA is no more a theory than evolution is a theory for Richard Dawkins. They effectively say that unless you believe in PSA and receive it for yourself, you are not saved. I once believed that. And so did my denominational clan. My people deemed all competing views as liberal heresies. Even my raising questions drew accusations that I had become "an enemy of the cross"—the most hurtful label I've ever endured.

But with new eyes and more attentive ears, I waded back into the Scriptures with the Word and the Spirit to weigh alternative interpretations, ancient and modern. What I found was a gospel far more beautiful than I had been taught. The Jericho walls of my old atonement theology began crumbling around me.

Two key passages changed my perception of what Christ did for us on the cross. First, there it was in Isaiah 53:

[4]Yet *we ourselves esteemed Him stricken,*
Smitten of God, and afflicted.
But He was pierced through for our transgressions,
He was crushed for our iniquities.          (Isa 53:4–5 NASB)

WE considered him stricken by God, BUT… Implication: WE were wrong. He was NOT stricken by God. He was stricken by us—by violent human beings. WE did it, just as the Gospels and the book of Acts say over and over.

Then, in Psalm 22:1, I read the "cry of dereliction": "My God, my God, why have You forsaken me?" (NASB). Christ quoted this psalm while on the cross. That was when Jesus bore our sin and the Father turned his face from Christ, right? But wait. Keep reading. If we're going to reinterpret the cross, a proof text without context will not do. I continued down the page of my Bible to verses 22–24, concluding with this:

---

36. "On the Necessity of Penal Substitutionary Atonement," Southern Baptist Convention, June 1, 2017, https://www.sbc.net/resource-library/resolutions/on-the-necessity-of-penal-substitutionary-atonement/.

> <sup>24</sup>For He *has not* despised nor abhorred the affliction of the
> afflicted;
> *Nor has He hidden His face from him;*
> But when he cried to Him for help, He heard.   (Ps 22:24 NASB)

While Christ authentically co-suffered our affliction and bore our despair *with* us, not once did his *Abba* turn his face away, just as the Word of God said:

> <sup>32</sup>Look here: the time is coming (in fact, it's now arrived!) when you will be scattered, each of you to his own place. You will leave me alone—though *I'm not alone, because the father is with me.* <sup>33</sup> I've said these things to you so that you can have peace in me. You'll have trouble in the world. But cheer up! I have defeated the world!
> (John 16:32–33 NTE)

That's Jesus's revelation of *Abba* on Good Friday! *Not* pouring out his wrath on his Son but united with him and with us in his suffering. *Not* turning away. But "God was *in* Christ reconciling the world to himself" (2 Cor 5:19 NASB). You may already know this. I'm just reliving my transformation in the context of a new Word and Spirit hermeneutic (interpretive system).

Nevertheless, I'm fully aware that private, novel interpretations of the Bible do not warrant such a dramatic transformation of one's faith. I began to diligently scour works by James Alison, Tony Bartlett, J. Denny Weaver, Willard Swartley, Gustaf Aulén, René Girard, N. T. Wright, and dozens of other scholars who saw the cross and its corollaries through different perspectives than I had known. They helped me see from Scripture that the violence of the crucifixion was *our* doing—humanity's great murder of God in the flesh—and that the cross represents God's nonviolent response of self-giving love, radical forgiveness, and redemption. It was Christ's opponents who demanded a sacrifice, while God the Father's great love— not his wrath—was revealed *in Christ* on the cross.

One of the best articulations of this reality comes via Brian Zahnd, who recently said:

We see a world formed in violence reaching a hideous apex, and with great violence, the world sinned its sin into the body of Jesus Christ. The wounds on Christ's body—on his hands, his feet, his side—these are entry wounds as sins are violently injected into Jesus. What happens when sin enters the body of Jesus? Sin itself dies. Jesus goes down into death and leaves sin and death there, conquered and defeated. He's raised on the third day; he comes back preaching the first word of the new world: "Peace be with you." The cross is where Christ abolishes war and the myth of redemptive violence and calls us into a new world formed in peace.[37]

Armed with a Damascus Road paradigm shift and a mind filled with new data, I was now ready for the next step: my encounter with Archbishop Lazar Puhalo.

## "YOU WORSHIP MOLECH"

My journey thus far had providentially ripened me for a "cataclysm catechism" at the feet of the old monk, Lazar Puhalo. Today, we might call my transition a *deconstruction*, but I prefer Fr. Richard Rohr's term: *reorientation*. Or to borrow a word from my neighbor David Hickey, *reframing*. Likewise, Brian Zahnd encouraged me toward the language of *art restoration*. When layers of grime overshadow a masterpiece, one does not go to work with the iconoclast's knife. Time and care must be taken to strip away defilement without spoiling what is precious beneath.

Our time with the Mennonites led Eden and me to develop a heart for Christ-centered justice in this world. In 1998, we ventured into a church-planting experience with a group of friends who established Fresh Wind Christian Fellowship, a church for folks on the margins: people who struggled with disabilities, addictions, or poverty. We saw in passages such as Isaiah 58:6–12, Luke 4:18–21, and Matthew 25:34–40 that Jesus's gospel of the kingdom included tangible acts of peace-building and social restoration.

---

37. Brian Zahnd, *Postcards from Babylon: The Church in American Exile* (Global Story Films, 2021).

By 2003, we hoped to establish a magazine featuring the connection between spirituality and justice. I was introduced to another mentor, Ron Dart, who would later become my hiking guide and PhD supervisor. Ron suggested we team up with Abp. Lazar at the All Saints of North America Monastery in Dewdney, BC. Vladika (his Slavic title) was willing to partner with us using his archaic monastery print shop. We launched a three-year run of the *Clarion Journal* before taking it online at clarion-journal.com.

So it was that I met this Gandalf-like monk, complete with floor-length cassock, trailing white beard, and sincere, piercing eyes. Whatever we call my transition, it came to a head in the monastery printshop. Collating, folding, stapling, and trimming hard copy side by side afforded me count-less hours of personal tutelage. In Gandalf's printshop, I was reoriented to Christ, the gospel, and the Scriptures.

I will forever remember Abp. Lazar Puhalo's first words to me. Not *literally* his first words, but the striking statement that launched my final waypoint toward the early church fathers and the Eastern Orthodox church, and their *Emmaus Way* of reading sacred Scripture.

We began by discussing the faith-shift I was experiencing. I remember trying to explain my previous worldview to Vladika. I described my quest to rediscover the apostolic vision of the cross—a gospel more faithful and beautiful than what I had preached.

Abp. Lazar put a question to me straightforwardly: "You mean to tell me you believe God *cannot* freely forgive sin but must first appease his wrath through the violent child sacrifice of his firstborn son on the cross?" He knew the script as well as I did and was not about to pretty it up.

"Well, when you put it that way..." I replied, as if he were being crass, "but yes, that *is* pretty much what I was taught, believed, and preached." More nuanced PSA spins[38] have emerged since the publication of the book *Stricken by God?*[39] (and in part because of it), and the wrath-appeasement

---

38. The best of these are Fleming Rutledge, *The Crucifixion: Understanding the Death of Jesus Christ* (Grand Rapids, MI: Eerdmans, 2015) and N. T. Wright, *The Day the Revolution Began: Reconsidering the Meaning of Jesus's Crucifixion* (New York: HarperOne, 2016).
39. Eventually, the combination of biblical studies, secondary readings, and personal prayer led me to reach out across the body of Christ to gather twenty essays in a volume edited by Michael Hardin and me entitled *Stricken by God? Nonviolent Identification and the Victory of Christ* (Grand Rapids, MI: Eerdmans, 2007).

gospel Vladika had so gruffly described remains the unvarnished and prevailing Evangelical gospel. Again, to challenge it is to risk being condemned as a heretic.

But for me, the sandy foundation of my Calvinist premises had already eroded. Now came the *coup de grâce* (literally, "blow of mercy" or "stroke of grace").

Abp. Lazar replied, *"I see your problem. You worship Molech—not Yahweh."*

Molech was the Canaanite god who demanded wrath appeasement by the fiery sacrifice of firstborn children.[40] "Something," Yahweh says, "that I have never spoken or commanded, and which never even entered my mind."[41]

Abp. Lazar's rather coarse assessment did not offend me. Rather, his words washed through me like a cold flood, awakening me. Something like scales fell off my spiritual eyes. My credible witness was no namby-pamby liberal—this was a hierarch stewarding the same patristic faith that gave us the doctrine of the deity of Christ, the dogma of Trinity, and the Nicene Creed.

"You mean in Eastern Orthodox churches you don't *have* to believe in penal substitution?" I asked, hopeful.

"No, I mean in the Orthodox church you are required *not* to believe in it," he replied firmly, adding, "And there are 350 million of us who have *never* believed it."

That moment confirmed for me, decisively, what I believed God had revealed to my heart directly and in my renewed biblical studies: the Father was not punishing Jesus but forgiving, redeeming, and reconciling us to himself through him. It marked the beginning of a series of falling dominoes that comprised my ten-year-long catechism at Vladika's feet, learning to interpret the Scriptures in the way the church that composed and gathered them had.

---

40. See, for example, Leviticus 18:21; Isaiah 57:5; Jeremiah 19:4–5.
41. See Jeremiah 19:5; 32:35. What? God isn't into burning people? Who knew? It never even entered his mind.

Once PSA fell, every doctrine related to divine retribution began to topple in turn. If God truly is *Love* in his essential nature,[42] the *necessity* of eternal conscious torment, acts of divine genocide, and literalist interpretations of wrath fall too.

And guess what! I did not fall off the outer limbs of the Evangelical tree. Instead, Abp. Lazar drew me down the trunk of the historic church and deep into the roots of apostolic Christianity as taught by the great early mothers and fathers of our faith.

## "NO! *JESUS* IS THE WORD OF GOD!"

Another of our *Clarion* conversations was so pivotal that I memorized Vladika's response verbatim. I was still struggling with the problem of how the Scriptures sanction and command violence.

I could no longer live with "the Bible says it, I believe it, that settles it" when it came to Scriptures in which the narrator declares that God commands merciless slaughters and the enslavement of women and children, and even accommodates the rape of enemy captives.

Yes, that's in there. I read it, and so do the New Atheists who mock Christianity. Those among my Evangelical friends who could still hold an ideology of inerrancy (which we'll discuss later) could only do so by remaining unaware of these texts or reading them in a cartoonish manner that allowed them to praise the Lord without empathy for real human victims. I was done with that.

When I queried Vladika about this, he insisted that the Scriptures are often a revelation not about God but primarily about *us* and our idolatrous images of God. Those who lived the events or wrote about them still awaited the faithful picture that God in Christ would reveal through the incarnation.

One day, I brought his attention to 1 Samuel 15. I was incredibly frustrated with the platitudes of those who affirmed that God commanded Samuel to command Saul to destroy every last Amalekite—man, woman,

---

42. Although John Calvin denied this, saying that God is not love in his nature. He is only love to the elect, and he is "hate" to the reprobate.

infant, and domestic beast—especially when the narrator says that God's justification was the sins of their ancestors many centuries earlier.

I decided to put on my Evangelical hat to interrogate Abp. Lazar about this troubling passage. I assumed a posture toward the text that treated every word as God's inerrant truth, though I had come to see inerrancy as a modernist novelty. Still, I had to be sure.

I read 1 Samuel 15 to Vladika and asked him how the *Abba* whom Jesus Christ revealed as perfect love and unfailing mercy could possibly issue such a command.

Without hesitation, he replied, "He didn't."

I countered, "But the Bible says he did."

He parried with these surprising words: "No, these are the words of Samuel, a cantankerous old bigot who would not let go of his prejudice, projecting his own malice, unforgiveness, and need for vengeance into the mouth of Yahweh."

I was not to be easily deterred. I countered, "But it's not just Samuel saying it. The Bible says *Yahweh* spoke these words to Samuel."

"He didn't!"

"But Vladika," I cried, "it's the Word of God!"

That did it. At this point, the old monk's face grew stern. His long index finger grew toward my face, correcting me with these firm words:

> NO! Jesus is the Word of God. And any Scripture that claims to be a revelation of that God must bow to the living God when he came in the flesh. "No man has seen God at any time, but God the only Son, who was in the bosom of the Father—He has made him known."

I was both duly chastened and filled with joy. The hair on my head stood up, and my entire body tingled with gooseflesh. I'm sure I gasped. I will never forget that lesson. It was not merely a word about reading 1 Samuel 15 or every Old Testament call to religious militarism. What Vladika made crystal clear is the truth that *every* conception of God has always been incomplete and imperfect. Only with the incarnation of Jesus

Christ do we arrive at the final and perfect revelation of God—fulfilling, completing, cleansing, and/or correcting all previous revelations.

All early Christian orthodoxy was founded on that premise. It was the premise of my book *A More Christlike God*, which I dedicated to Vladika. In that book, I say very little beyond what Vladika has taught me since that day: specifically, that if there is a God (forever a faith statement), that God is Love. And God is Love only, for every other attribute of God must ever only be a facet of that one pure diamond.

If we want to know exactly what Perfect Love looks like, we examine the incarnation. "If you have seen me," said Christ, "you have seen the Father."[43] The apostle Paul declares to the Colossians that Christ "is the image of the invisible God" (Col 1:15, numerous translations) and "in Him all the fullness of Deity dwells in bodily form" (Col 2:9 NASB). Hebrews 1 adds that Christ alone is "the radiance of God's glory and the exact representation of His nature" (Heb 1:3 BSB). Most importantly, this revelation of triune love comes to its clearest focus on the cross, where we see Jesus Christ reveal God as self-giving, radically forgiving, co-suffering Love.

"He is a good and merciful God and loves mankind," says the Eastern rite liturgies. Or as Vladika's old friend his eminence Archbishop Irénée of the Archdiocese of Canada says, "God is mercy only." Not "mercy plus...." Not "love, but also...." There is no divine anger, judgment, or wrath as over against God's love.

Such attributes, according to Hebrews 12, are ever only anthropomorphisms[44] of parental love aimed at restoration. That is to say, what the Bible calls "God's wrath" is a metaphor for the self-induced consequences or intrinsic judgment of our own turning from Perfect Love, even though these same "judgments" may become the occasion for God's redemptive acts.

Vladika puts it this way: "The fire of the glory of the love of God extends to all, and our orientation to the fire of love determines whether we experience it as heaven or hell. But we hold to the great hope that love is a cleansing fire, able to purge even the darkest of hearts."

---

43. See John 14:9.

44. Anthropomorphism is the attribution of human characteristics or behavior to a god, animal, or object.

## THE TREK FROM THERE

What then? My path led me back to a deeper study of the early church fathers and mothers ("patristics") who gathered the New Testament and preached the gospel from their Scriptures. Their hermeneutic has largely been ignored or dismissed by both Evangelical and liberal movements, the twin children of modernity. My seminary courses seemed to ignore all of church history between Paul and Luther. But I found that the patristic tradition could help me. The patristics asked the same questions I was asking and actually overcame the Marcionites without preaching an un-Christlike God or losing the Bible. They both explain and model the apostles' Christ-centered interpretation—what I call *the Emmaus Way*.

Those modern commentators who dismiss the first Christians' ancient insights with contempt have not served us well. In fact, they had failed me completely. So, for nearly the past two decades, I've been trying to learn from the early Christians with the help of Orthodox monks, priests, and patristic scholars. Others have also been of enormous help: certain Jewish rabbis, the canonical-contextual folks (Brevard Childs, John Sailhamer, Vern Steiner), some Girardians (René Girard, Michael Hardin, Tony Bartlett), and various Hebrew scholars (Walter Brueggemann, Bob Ekblad, Matt Lynch, and Peter Enns).

I am especially taken with Pete Enns's "Christotelic" interpretation, which is why I asked him to explain it in the foreword to this book. In fact, he's answered one of my most bewildering questions in one sentence:

Why does the Bible contain so many bizarre, offensive, and un-Christlike depictions of God? Pete's answer: "Because God let his children tell the story."

Yet Jesus Christ opens the Scriptures and empowers those who follow him to see beyond our human interpretations to his divine, Christotelic story.

## DISCOVERIES AND PROPOSALS: AN INVITATION

What follows in subsequent chapters is a collection of my discoveries and proposals, gathered since I began my quest. I've tried to organize them logically and theologically, although a number of them were already stand-alone essays that I've been waiting to include in a book such as this. Here is my invitation:

+ I invite you to reorient with me from Bible-centered reading toward Christ-focused seeking—to recognize that Jesus Christ is the Word of God and final authority for faith and practice.

+ I invite you to rediscover with me the Christ-centered riches in Scripture so that, in the Spirit of Emmaus, we'll see the Bible in its entirety gesturing toward the living Lord.

+ I invite you to appreciate with me the complexity, variety, and genius of Scripture as a polyphonic, multi-genred, epic drama of redemption climaxing in the incarnation of the divine Word.

+ I invite you to make an honest inquiry of how the so-called "toxic texts" function as a mirror[45] that reveals the human condition and our habit of projecting our own un-Christlike images onto God, especially in the form of religious violence.

---

45. See Archbishop Lazar Puhalo, *The Mirror of Scripture: The Old Testament Is About You* (Abbotsford, BC: St. Macrina Press, 2018).

### CHAPTER 4

# "WHAT ARE WE?":
## REFRAMING INSPIRATION

*W*hat *are we?*" That awkward question whispers at every bend in a relationship, especially if it moves from the friend zone into romance. In that case, it is doubly awkward when one party wants to keep the relationship casual while the other party is pining for commitment. Hence, "*What are we?*"

When we enter into a serious relationship with the Scriptures, we might well run into that same the awkward question. Our hearts ask, "What are we?" when the Bible begins to confront us with grossly unpalatable images of God and immoral acts committed in his name. Or when we're no longer sure how every word of the Bible is true or how to relate to the God it describes. I previously mentioned my friends who've chosen to "break up" with the Bible—and those who took the further step to divorce Jesus as well. I'm sad about that, and I pray it's a trial separation.

Still, it's understandable when much of Christendom has so seldom delivered on the promise of a "personal relationship" and then issued threats to those who join the exodus. Ghosting that world is justifiable and probably necessary.

But if you've known intimacy with Christ and experienced actual liberation, walking away from his love isn't an option. He's never been unfaithful to me, even when I was unfaithful to him or to myself. He's never once walked out on me, even when I wanted to turn away from him.

> [67]Jesus turned to the Twelve.
> "You don't want to go away too, do you?" he asked.
> [68]Simon Peter spoke up.
> "Master," he said, "who can we go to? You're the one who's got the words of the life of the coming age!"
>
> (John 6:67–68 NTE)

The issue of walking away was settled for me. I bottomed out on plan B until there was no plan B. But I still needed to sort out the "Bible thing." Once you stop drinking the Kool-Aid of biblical literalism, any further connection with Scripture needs to include the answer to that awkward question, *"What are we?"* And it's tough to know *what we are* without also asking of the Bible, *"What are you?"*

As I described in previous chapters, I had been told the Bible is the "Word of God," despite its own insistence that Christ is the Word. How you see the Bible changes your relationship with it. As I keep insisting, Christ gets the final word, and the Scriptures testify to his authority. I relate to Christ as God's Word and to the Bible as one (and not the only) venue where I can hear the living Voice.

I had also been taught that the Bible is God's inspired, infallible, inerrant canon of His self-revelation. Those claims establish a specific kind of relationship with the Bible. If that's not really *what* the Bible is—if the Scriptures are actually a witness to Christ and a revelation of human hearts—then *who we are and how we relate* to the Bible also shifts. When I realized this, it meant I had to *reframe* how I see, read, and interpret Scripture, especially in its all-important role as the Word's witness.

I need not sour on the Bible. Indeed, since I can distinguish it as a "friend of the Bridegroom,"[46] rather than the Bridegroom himself, and am learning to read Scripture as life-giving gospel rather than literalistic law, it is as precious to me as it ever was.

Nevertheless, it gets a little tricky when I say Christ is my final authority while I'm also dependent on a witness that I call *inspired* yet seems

---

46. See John 3:29.

unreliable at times. How does that work? One of my readers put the question this way:

> Some say the Bible is not infallible or inerrant. And while I can see the logic for that view, how then do we know what is written about the life and mission of Jesus is accurate? If the accounts of some of the incidents in the Old Testament are open to question, why not what is written about Jesus?

I think that's a very fair question. Let's begin by addressing the question of *inspiration, infallibility, inerrancy,* and *canon.* Then we'll move on to how our convictions about *what Scripture is* impact our faith in the Gospel narratives about Jesus.

## THE THREE I'S

*Inspiration, infallibility, inerrancy:* these three long *I*-words developed over time, each in their own eras. The early church believed the Scriptures to be "inspired" (*theopneustos*: literally, "God-breathed"), based on this text in 2 Timothy, attributed to Paul:

> *All Scripture is breathed by God* ["inspired," various translations], and it is useful for teaching, for rebuke, for improvement, for training in righteousness, so that people who belong to God may be complete, fitted out and ready for every good work.
> (2 Tim 3:16–17 NTE)

This was among the first verses I memorized as a child—and I'm glad I did. I still believe it. But what does it mean?

As a child, my temperament, my developmental stage, and my faith tradition all leaned to a *literalist* reading of Scripture, except when it was deemed impossible. Our church believed the Bible described a six-day creation (calculated by biblical genealogies to seven thousand years ago). We believed that Noah's flood was actually global and must have covered Mount Everest. We also believed that literally every living species survived on an ark. At the same time, we weren't so naïve as to believe Christ is an actual lamb with seven horns and seven eyes.[47]

---

47. See Revelation 5:6.

In my freshman year at Bible college, my hermeneutics professor taught us that we believed in the "verbal plenary inspiration of Scripture" and that our interpretive method was the "historical-grammatical-literal approach." We learned that the Bible was composed by holy men of God who were "borne along" and "superintended" by the Holy Spirit. Their minds and their quills produced "God-breathed" texts, miraculously without error. Again, at least not in "the original autographs" (hypothetical original manuscripts that no longer exist).

We were told, "The Bible never contradicts itself." Any discrepancies could be written off as either a copyist's transmission error, insufficient scientific data, or the reader's misinterpretation.

Our first tier of proof texts included Isaiah 40:8, John 10:35, 2 Timothy 2:8–9, and 2 Peter 1:21. Solid. That is, we felt those texts (in isolation) made for a coherent and airtight theology of Scripture. To say, "the Bible says" was to say, "God says." That made the Bible "God's Word." The upside was that we spent a lot of time attending to the Scriptures. The downside was that we couldn't question what we saw there. To question whether "God had really said" was to echo the talking serpent (also literal) from Genesis 3—evidence that, like Eve, we were being tempted to question God and therefore being deceived.

We defended ourselves against the charge of "dictation theory" by saying, "We don't believe in dictation theory." But, of course, we did. Did the authors hear a voice saying, "Write this" and then write what they heard? No, we said, they wrote as the Holy Spirit guided their hearts, minds, and pens—infallibly—never swerving from the precise words or meaning that God was communicating.

Um...yeah, that's dictation. Or possession.

I was so convinced of our circular argument ("The whole Bible is always true because it says it is always true") that seeing through it, for me, could not involve setting the Bible aside. Nor should we. Rather, it meant delving much deeper into the Bible, taking it far more seriously and perceiving its inspired genius beyond what inerrancy can allow.

## INSPIRED: THAT WORD AGAIN

*Inspiration*—that's my point here. At an Open Table Conference in Oregon hosted by John MacMurray, author of *A Spiritual Evolution*, I questioned whether God's commands in the Old Testament to carry out acts of genocide without mercy truly came from the *Abba* whom Jesus revealed. A very bright and sincere young man challenged me. He was troubled that I had rejected the "written Word of God" as the exact words of God. And he was doubly worried when my Hebrew-scholar friend Caleb Miller questioned the historicity of some biblical events (as opposed to their being rabbinic storytelling). With gravity and respect, the young man echoed the arguments I outlined above, reciting the familiar verses. I knew there was no way to walk him through my decades-long transition in the space of a Q & R session.

But as I fumbled along, MacMurray noted what 2 Timothy 3 *doesn't* say:

+ It doesn't say, "All Scripture is inspired and therefore *inerrant*."

+ It doesn't say, "All Scripture is inspired and therefore *infallible*."

+ It doesn't say, "All Scripture is inspired and therefore *historically accurate*."

+ It doesn't say, "All Scripture is inspired and therefore *theologically true*."

+ It doesn't say, "All Scripture is inspired and therefore to be *read literally*."

For those who hold a very high view of the Bible, as I do—that the Bible is a sacred and inspired text pointing to Christ—we can actually claim too much for the Bible. Scripture never purported to do or be all that. MacMurray suggested that we not place an impossible burden on 2 Timothy 3:16–17 with words and terms that are not there.

What does the passage say? That all Scripture is "God-breathed," or "inspired," and therefore *"useful."*

Note: "inspired" here is an adjective. The verse isn't a theology of what the Bible is but rather of what it's for or how it functions. Neither Jesus nor apostles such as Paul focused on *what* the Bible is but instead about *why* it is and *how* to use it.

The function of the Bible, according to Jesus—who is the WORD of God—is, first of all, to witness to him.[48] The Bible itself testifies that Christ alone is the perfect and final Word of God[49] to whom it points. Scripture is inspired, first of all, for that testimony. Second, the Timothy passage, interpreted through a Christ-focused lens, tells us that Scripture functions to develop a community trained in righteousness, equipped to do good—that is, to become like Christ in this world.

In 1 Corinthians 10:1–13, Paul explains that our training in Christlikeness often takes the form of learning cautionary stories from Scripture—tales illustrating what "un-Christlikeness" looks like and showing us how not to be. Here is a portion of that passage:

> [6]*Now these things were patterns for us, so that we should not* start to crave for wicked things as they did. [7]*Nor should we* commit idolatry, as some of them did—as the Bible says, "The people sat down to eat and drink, and got up to play." [8]*Nor should we* become immoral, like some of them became immoral, and twenty-three thousand fell on a single day. [9]*Nor should we* put the Messiah to the test, as some of them put him to the test, and were destroyed by serpents. [10]*Nor should we* grumble, as some of them grumbled and were destroyed by the destroyer.
>
> [11]*Now these things happened to them as a pattern, and they were written for our instruction*, since it's upon us that the ends of the ages have now come. [12]As a result, anyone who reckons they are standing upright should watch out in case they fall over.
>
> (1 Cor 10:6–12 NTE)

Do you see how Paul draws from negative stories to discern a positive lesson? "These things happened as a pattern, for our instruction. Therefore, watch out!" We don't read the ugly parts of the Bible as bygone histories or dismiss them for their bad theology. Rather, we enter these stories and experience them as floodlights revealing our own issues. Here is David Goa's take on this:

---

48. See John 5:39; Luke 24:27; 1 Corinthians 15:3–4.
49. See John 1:18; Hebrews 1:1–3.

[I invite] the faithful to a particular spiritual discipline when they read the hard texts in the First (Old) Testament that speak of the anger, wrath, and judgement of the divine, including those that seem to be the wrathful words of God spoken directly, but are instead *revelations of human passions, of the appetite for divine justice, assigned to God*. This discipline invites us to put on "the mind of Christ" in all our hearing of the scriptures. We are invited to listen to and for the Lover of creation speaking to us an illuminating word in the unfolding of all the narratives in the Bible. Each of us is encouraged to grow in the spiritual life so that Christ's way of being—his teaching, his heart and mind, the fullest expression of the human nature—comes to be the prism through which we see creation and minister to the world, and the mind through which we read both Testaments....

...All biblical revelation, along with the revelation of the Holy Spirit, is *a light shone on our passions* and thus on our way of seeking and knowing the world and our presumptions about God's ways and God's will. Revelation illuminates God's love for us, but we need it also to *shine light on our personal and collective darkness*, the shadows in our life, our relationships, our moment in history, our place in culture.[50]

These two points comprise a central key for interpreting Scripture:

+ How does any given passage point to Christ?
+ How does any given passage form Christlike people?

Today, I see *inspiration* in this way: the authors of Scripture were carried along[51] by the Holy Spirit so that, through their words, by the Spirit, God breathes (present tense) a testimony to us that reveals our redemption and destiny in God through Christ. Scripture is the witness (and not the only one), and Christ is the revelation. When we read the Bible in that s/Spirit, we see the grand narrative and where it's all pointing: to Christ

---

50. Goa, "The Bible and the Land of Shades," *Reading the Bible as Life-giving Word*, (Chester Ronning Centre, 2013), 45–47. Author's emphasis.
51. See 2 Peter 1:21. "Carried along" / *pheromenoi* (φερόμενοι) is literally "borne along" as the wind bears along a sailing ship (as in Acts 27:15).

and his gospel. To miss this is to miss everything, just as most of the religious leaders of Jesus's day had—just as I had.

Let's review Jesus's indictment of these leaders:

> [36]But I have a *testimony greater than that from John.* For the deeds that the Father has assigned me to complete—*the deeds I am now doing*—*testify about me* that the Father has sent me. [37]And the *Father who sent me has himself testified about me.* You people have never heard his voice nor seen his form at any time, [38]nor do you have his word residing in you, because you do not believe the one whom he sent. [39]You study the Scriptures thoroughly because you think in them you possess eternal life, and it is these same *scriptures that testify about me,* [40]but you are not willing to come to me so that you may have life.          (John 5:36–40 NET)

What do you notice in this passage? Jesus cites four interdependent witnesses pointing to him: John the prophet, God the Father, the deeds of Jesus, and the Jewish Scriptures. What else does Jesus say? That seeing Scripture, instead of Jesus, as the point ensures that they will *not* hear the voice of God in the Scriptures or in their hearts. It's possible to spend a lifetime studying the Bible without once hearing the Father or knowing the Word.

Apparently, the inspiration of Scripture is only real and relevant to us insofar as we fix our gaze on the One to whom it points. Otherwise, we're like Jack, a dog I used to own, who would fixate on the end of my finger when I'd point to his hidden treasures.

While debates rage about what "inspired" signifies, this biblical term and historic conviction assure us that the breath of the Spirit does blow through the Bible's sometimes bewildering words. It teases us with problems of divine and human authorship, of covenantal continuity and discontinuity. But if you can hold the tension, the complexity of the Scriptures only confirms their inspiration. The Bible is a unique, sacred library unlike any other—and with the caveats of John 5 in mind, you can meet God there. I still hold this conviction because the more I read, study, and pray the Bible's words, the more taken I am with the supernatural genius that transcends its distinctly human qualities.

Amid the polyphony of conflicting worldviews that I see among its authors, I'm always *inspired* to see God's fingerprints everywhere across its pages.

## INSPIRATION AND EXHALATION

Let's try this distinction: *inspiration* is not the same as *exhalation*. When we read that a biblical author is *inspired*, could it mean that God's Spirit breathed *into* them and then, through their own creativity, worldviews, faith practices, religious beliefs, political biases, personal temperaments, and so forth, they *exhaled* a range of beautiful, unique, divine-human hybrid texts? A careful reading shows that God indeed inspired (breathed into) these men and women, who then exhaled a text that bears the aroma of both the Spirit's divine genius and the authors' truly human agency.

How about this: the author of Genesis, inspired by the Holy Spirit, exhaled a prophecy of salvation, fulfilled in Jesus Christ.[52] The Spirit disclosed this revelation to that author inside the language and genre appropriate to that time and place while supernaturally sharing a truth for all time. We take that message to be gospel truth, literally. And we take it to be the point. The epic saga of redemption is heading somewhere, to Someone—this is the grand narrative of our sacred text, inspired by the Spirit, that we trace through the ages of human stumbling. But as we shall see, this inspiration does not end with the initial composition of the biblical text. It is also contingent on that text's *unveiling* through Christ and *illumination* by the Spirit.

## INSPIRATION: FOUR ASSUMPTIONS

In recent years, rediscovering "inspiration" has been a happy surprise for me. Inspiration is not quite what I had been taught and certainly not *less* than I was taught. In a lecture entitled "The Passion of Jesus as the Key to Reading Scripture,"[53] Fr. John Behr describes four ancient assumptions that characterize the reading of Scripture and refocuses how we come to see inspiration:[54]

---

52. See Genesis 3:15.

53. John Behr, "The Passion of Jesus as the Key to Reading Scripture," YouTube video, 34:55, April 2, 2017, https://www.youtube.com/watch?v=D8zIng6pB8E.

54. The four assumptions are drawn from Hebrew scholar James L. Kugel in works such as *How to Read the Bible: A Guide to Scripture, Then and Now* (New York: Simon & Schuster, 2008). While Kugel establishes the categories, Behr transposes them in the unique way I describe.

1. **The Scriptures**[55] **are cryptic:** That is, the meaning of the Scriptures often needs to be opened to us. There is a veil that needs to be lifted. Before the passion of Christ, many people read the Scriptures, but nobody could actually see how the relevant passages pointed to this event. As the Scriptures are opened up to us, so Christ is opened to us.

2. **The Scriptures are contemporary:** The narrative of Scripture is not merely recorded history. According to Christ, what was written has implications for us today. Jesus said, "If you believed Moses, you would believe me, because *he wrote about me*" (John 5:46 NET). Not, "Moses wrote about things that happened ten thousand years ago, and now we're in the next stage of the master narrative." No, says Behr. No, says Jesus. *"He wrote about ME."* The apostle Paul would add, "These things are written for *our benefit* upon whom the end of the ages has come" (1 Cor 10:11, my paraphrase). About Christ. For us.

3. **The Scriptures are harmonious.** Can we find contradictions across the Bible? Of course. But the Emmaus claim—Jesus's claim—is that *all* the Scriptures speak about the One who opens to us their meaning. Moses, the prophets, and other biblical authors all wrote about how the Son of Man had to die to enter into his glory.[56]

4. **Finally, the Scriptures are inspired.** This fourth point—*inspiration*—flows out of the other three. I had been taught to believe that inspiration was something that happened as an episode in history. For example, I would think, "Isaiah beheld the Lord in his temple many centuries before Christ. He was inspired by the Holy Spirit, and then he wrote down his oracles." Behr challenges this perspective: "We have no idea what was in Isaiah's mind while he was writing. But we do know for a fact that no one was reading Isaiah as speaking about a crucified Messiah born of a virgin until after the event." Therefore, we *cannot* separate the inspiration of the Scriptures from their opening/unveiling by Christ. Likewise,

---

55. In the lecture, when Father John refers to "the Scriptures," this is biblical and creedal language for what we call the Old Testament.
56. See Luke 24:27.

we can't separate inspired writing from the inspired reading (illumination) of Scripture.

So, *the* **act of inspiration** *brings together the* **writer** *and the* **reader,** *and both turn upon* **Christ,** *who opens the book to the reader to show how the writer spoke about him.*

## BEYOND AUTHORIAL INTENT

The way that Fr. John Behr sees the reader as part of the inspiration process led me to ask him, "How much of any Scripture's 'meaning' is derived from the author's conscious decisions, how much is being infused after the fact, and how much is coincidental?"

For example, in John 21:11, it seems obvious that John is being purposeful when he describes the disciples counting their catch of 153 fish. But why 153? Some interpreters see a numerical connection (gematria) to Ezekiel 47:10, symbolizing the gathering of all nations into the kingdom of God.[57]

Others point in an entirely different direction: that John is referencing the Greek mathematician Archimedes, whose "Measurement of a Circle, Proposition 3"[58] is a method for calculating the value of $\pi$ (pi), where the formulas repeatedly end with the denominator 153.[59] At the end of his Gospel, might John be tying universal geometry to the *logos* of his preface for the sake of an Ephesian audience?

Are these explanations plausible? Or are the interpreters seeing everything "redly" because they are wearing red lenses? Are we seeing what John intended? Or are we seeing something important regardless of John's intent? I'd love some criteria that measure the scale from "definitely" to "nice try."

---

57. These interpretations range from as far back as St. Jerome (*Comm. Ezech.* [PL 25:474C]; available at https://books.google.ca/books?id=jHzYAAAAMAAJ) to modern times (Richard Bauckham, "The 153 Fish and the Unity of the Fourth Gospel," *Neotestamentica: Word, Sacrament, and Community: Festschrift for Professor J. N. Suggit* [36:1/2, 2002]: 77–88. See https://www.jstor.org/stable/43049111).

58. Mike Bertrand, "Archimedes and Pi," *Ex Libris*, May 16, 2014, http://nonagon.org/ExLibris/archimedes-pi.

59. See Wm. Paul Young, "'Fish Pi': Gospel of John (21) and Archimedes (153)," in *The Gospel According to Hermes: Intimations of Christianity in Greek Myth, Philosophy, and Poetry*, ed. Ron Dart and Bradley Jersak (Abbotsford, BC: St. Macrina Press, 2021), 75–81.

Father John responded to my question about how we derive meaning from Scripture by saying:

> In understanding any historical work, it is of course necessary to read them within their historical context, bearing in mind the possible range of meanings for words in a given epoch.
>
> But, as with any great work of art, its meaning goes beyond that of the original artist. Indeed, sometimes one comes across an interpretation of a piece of art (literature, art, music, etc.) that is so good that you can never see the piece of art in the same way again.
>
> In this case [John 21:11], whose work of art are you now looking at? It is both that of the original artist and the interpreter. The best interpretations are never merely repetition, but creative. The meaning of Scripture is not (simply) found in its original setting, but in the reading of that text throughout all time (including the future) by the community that it creates/forms: it is eschatological, and we are still on the way.
>
> Now, of course, that raises questions about whether a reading is "right" or not, but the lively engaged discussion about this, always in process, helps sort out those interpretations that abide, that are accepted by the whole community throughout time, or in a sense, become one with the original text.[60]

## INFALLIBILITY

The word *infallible* literally means "incapable of making a mistake." The word's origin goes back through French to fifteenth-century Latin, but sometimes it's also used to translate older words from other languages. For example, if we travel back through the centuries to the most thorough and authoritative book written by the early church on how to read the Bible, we arrive at the *Philocalia of Origen*.[61] The book is a compilation of Origen's principles of interpretation, compiled by Saint Basil the Great and Saint Gregory the Theologian in the mid-fourth century. But the original

---

60. John Behr, email message to author, March 15, 2021.
61. See Origen, *The Philocalia of Origen*, trans. Rev. George Lewis (Edinburgh: T&T Clark, 1911), http://www.tertullian.org/fathers/origen_philocalia_02_text.htm.

documents date back to the early 200s AD, when Origen was the church's leading theologian and most prolific exegete.

Origen will come up again later, but for now, here's what I notice: from chapter one onward, he repeatedly affirms the *inspiration* of Scripture, but the word *infallible* only comes up once and is reserved for God alone. Only God is infallible—by which Origen means all-knowing.

Gregory of Nyssa also affirms the *inspiration* of Scripture, but for him, infallibility refers to "the Infallible Being,"[62] and his focus there is on how God *created* all things through Christ by the Spirit.

In Gregory the Theologian's funeral oration of his friend Basil, he uses *infallible* more as a moral designation:

> ...it belongs to God *alone* to be completely infallible [ἄπταιστον, *aptaiston*—"without stumbling/morally faultless"] and uninfluenced by the passions.[63]

Again, the term makes more sense applied to God and particularly to Jesus as a sinless human. Jesus's infallibility is not about his grades in elementary school. It's a reference to the truth that he alone was without sin, unlike anyone we might eulogize at a memorial. It's not really a word you'd apply to a book.

Later, the fathers' use of *infallibility* is extended to the *Holy Spirit's* guidance of the church as it preserved the true gospel (the "canon of faith" or "faith once delivered," as it's called in Jude 3). You've probably heard disputes about *papal infallibility* or the *infallibility of the church* in non-Protestant traditions.[64] Church history realists will roll their eyes, but the following claim seems pretty reasonable by New Testament standards: Christ established his church and then gave it the Spirit of Truth so that, by grace, Christ's infallible gospel would be preserved.

---

62. Gregory of Nyssa, "On the Holy Spirit, Against the Macedonians," New Advent, https://www.newadvent.org/fathers/2903.htm.

63. Saint Gregory Nazianzen, "On Saint Basil the Great, Bishop of Caesarea," in *Fathers of the Church*, Vol. 22, *Funeral Orations by Saint Gregory Nazianzen and Saint Ambrose*, ed. Roy J. Deferrari (New York: Fathers of the Church, Inc., 1953), §28, 51.

64. For the Catholic view, see Fr. William Saunders, "Explaining the Idea of Infallibility," EWTN Global Catholic Network, 1999, https://www.ewtn.com/catholicism/library/explaining-the-idea-of-infallibility-1011. Originally published in the *Arlington* (VA) *Catholic Herald*, January 5, 1995.

But have we preserved it? The great ecumenical councils hoped to preserve the gospel when they composed the Nicene Creed. They regarded the creed as an "infallible testimony" of our faith. But given all the disputes over the creed and the revisions to it, as much as I love both the Bible and the great creeds, I think I'll retreat to Gregory's position: God alone is infallible.

With regard to the Bible, we can say that the infallible Holy Spirit partnered with fallible people to coauthor a text that features divine truth and obvious human mistakes. Those who deny the mistakes or attribute them to later scribal errors aren't paying attention. Knowing that *Scripture is inspired* but *only the Spirit is infallible* does not induce the same level of faith crisis as believing the Bible itself is infallible and then being confronted with a long list of blatant errors and contradictions. Admitting where the text gets it wrong does not undermine Scripture. But insisting on infallibility inevitably does.

If you need evidence of the problems, see Bob Seidensticker's *Patheos* article entitled "Top 20 Most Damning Bible Contradictions."[65] I've found similar lists composed of over four hundred fact-check discrepancies.[66] *Not typos*—I'm referring to self-evident errors. And when the biblicists spin them, they do *more* violence to the text they claim to defend. I know this by experience because I did it, too, until my conscience could no longer live as a pundit in the spin room.

This would trouble me if I thought my faith rested on an *infallible* Bible. But I see no such claim in its pages. Rather, as I expressed earlier, I hear within Scripture a polyphony of voices in conversation throughout centuries of spiritual development in a typically dysfunctional religion—all pointing upward and forward to the only *infallible* Word of God, *Abba's* Messiah, Jesus Christ.

Some biblicists seem to define infallibility more modestly: they say the Bible is "reliable and trustworthy." Okay, but if you read more carefully,

65. Bob Seidensticker, "Top 20 Most Damning Bible Contradictions," *Patheos*, October 20, 2018, https://www.patheos.com/blogs/crossexamined/2018/10/top-20-most-damning-bible-contradictions.

66. See Hemant Mehta, "An Incredible Interactive Chart of Bible Contradictions," *Patheos*, August 19, 2013, https://friendlyatheist.patheos.com/2013/08/19/an-incredible-interactive-chart-of-biblical-contradictions.

they claim this on the *a priori* premise that it *must* have no defect whatsoever and that if you trust its *infallible* teachings, you'll never be led astray. Lucky for us, that's never happened. (Oops!)

## INERRANCY

The term *inerrancy* was coined more recently and has a great breadth of definitions, depending on who you ask. The most recognized definition—the one I had adopted—was standardized in "The Chicago Statement on Biblical Inerrancy." That statement asserts that "Holy Scripture, being God's own Word, written by men prepared and superintended by His Spirit, is of infallible divine authority in all matters upon which it touches."[67]

What does it "touch on"? The committee claimed that,

> Being wholly and verbally God-given, Scripture is *without error or fault in all its teaching* [but not only that!], no less in what it states about God's acts in creation, about the events of world history, and about its own literary origins under God, than in its witness to God's saving grace in individual lives.[68]

Then, they corner themselves into this ideology by saying that "the authority of Scripture is *inescapably impaired if this total divine inerrancy is in any way limited or disregarded…*." Come on, guys.

Do you see what they did there? They've made their definition of inerrancy the standard of authority and conceded that any demonstration to the contrary (all too easy for people who read it) destroys the authority of Scripture! Talk about giving away the farm!

That's why so many first-semester university students lose their faith. Any skeptic that demolishes their faith in inerrancy also destroys their confidence in the Bible and their faith in Christ *by this definition*.

"Hit me, go ahead. I dare ya!"

"*Okay!*"

---

67. "The Chicago Statement on Biblical Inerrancy," A Short Statement, number 2, https://library.dts.edu/Pages/TL/Special/ICBI-1978-11-07.pdf
68. "Chicago Statement," number 4.

*Bloody nose ensues.*

What a horrible deal to make with oneself and to impose on the next generation. Inerrancy effectively became a world-class evangelist for the New Atheists. And the Bible was their most potent weapon.

What if, instead, we admitted what is there without apology or worry? Namely, that across the entire Bible, there is a range and mixture of factual accuracy (from vague/dubious to detailed/precise) and inspired revelation (filtered through shifting religious biases). What if we account for the variance based on the worldviews and vantage points of real people who experienced or recorded the events?

What if we considered these differences in view of real-life circumstances?

1. *Developing worldviews*: A tribal warrior (David), circa 1000 BC, complains that God isn't smiting his enemies and asks him for help. When the warrior defeats these enemies in bloody battle, he's happy and sings a song of praise that God is on his side.[69]

2. *Historical distance*: An unknown Jewish rabbi[70] exiled in Babylon (587 BC) records oral traditions about the world's origins dating back five thousand years. That is, the *stories* have been repeated and distilled for five millennia. The *truths* conveyed through the stories are timeless.

3. *Genres*: That same rabbi recognizes he's recording ancient mythology through his own cosmology, but many modernist Christians think they need to read it "literally" or else the Bible is not true, or Jesus isn't alive.

4. *Overt disagreement*: The author of 2 Samuel says *God tempted David*, but the author of 1 Chronicles disagrees: *Satan tempted David*.[71] The apostle James sides with the Chronicler. *God tempts no one.*[72]

---

69. See Psalm 69 or 109.
70. Scholars and theologians differ in opinion regarding the attribution of authorship for various biblical books. In the case of the Torah, while some regard Moses to be the actual author, others cite internal evidence in the book (content, language, locations, and so on) of later dating so that the attribution to Moses reflects the Moses tradition and legacy.
71. See 2 Samuel 24:1; 1 Chronicles 21:1.
72. See James 1:13.

OR "The Law [of Moses] says \_\_\_\_\_," yet Jesus (God's Word) says, "You've heard this. But I say to you _____."[73]

## AUTHORITY

When I'm honest about the human element (yes, discrepancies) in the text, the question arises, "Do you or don't you believe in the authority of Scripture?" Let's start with a definition of the adjective *authoritative* from Merriam-Webster:

**Definition of *authoritative***

1. : having, marked by, or proceeding from authority
   // *authoritative* church doctrines
   // an *authoritative* decision
   // an *authoritative* manner
2. : possessing recognized or evident authority: clearly accurate or knowledgeable
   // an *authoritative* critique
   // an *authoritative* source of information[74]

Here we have two different senses of *authoritative*. Applied to the Bible, the first sense would describe how the Bible's authority is derived from its *source*. In other words, is it *authorized*, and if so, by whom? The second definition includes a subjective side—is it *recognized* as having authority, and if so, by whom? Let's take each in turn.

First, is the Bible authoritative according to its source or sources? Do we understand God as the ultimate source? Or was it authored by the people of God? Or some combination of the Holy Spirit and human scribes? And since we know for sure that people wrote it down, to what degree are their limited perspectives and temporal worldviews in play?

While that is an interesting set of mysteries open to debate, I come at it differently. I start with the authority of Jesus. I recognize his authority as ultimate. Does he authorize the Scriptures, written before him or after him? And to what degree?

---

73 See, for example, Matthew 19:7–8.
74. Merriam-Webster.com Dictionary, s.v. "authoritative," https://www.merriam-webster.com/dictionary/authoritative.

Jesus affirmed the authority of Scripture by how he used it, and he also demonstrated the limits of its authority relative to himself. For Jesus, both the extent and the limits of biblical authority are defined by what I'm calling *the Emmaus Way.* That is, to the degree that the whole Bible testifies to Jesus and points to his authority, he (and we) read it as authoritative.

In John 5, when Jesus rebukes the religious leaders, he makes it clear that you could spend your whole life studying the Scriptures and never once hear the Father's voice through them *if* you don't understand they are a testimony of his life, teachings, passion, and mission. In fact, the first Christians would not have asked whether the Bible was authoritative. Instead, they would have said that Jesus was their authority, and then they would have asked, "Which books testify to this?" Those that did were chosen for inclusion in their written canon, which I discuss in more detail in the next section.

Second, is the Bible authoritative according to the *recipients?* That depends on our orientation to it. Does it operate as an authority in our lives in practice? Does what it says matter to us? Do we read it as skeptics, looking for reasons to dismiss it? Do we read it as radical fundamentalists, looking to weaponize it? Do we read it as literalists, oblivious to much of its spiritual meaning? Only you can decide whether you recognize its authority in your life. And if so, how so?

I personally receive the Scriptures as authoritative insofar as they testify to Jesus. But I don't see them making authoritative claims on matters of history, science, or even religion (e.g., I don't submit myself to the purity laws of Leviticus). Rather, I ask, "How are the Law and Prophets not abolished but *fulfilled* in Jesus?"[75] I let the authors say what they say on their own terms and then ask what the message is saying to me about Christ, his gospel, and his call for me to grow in love, by grace, toward God and my neighbors.

The technical term for this is the "tropological" sense of Scripture. That's a fancy word that asks, "When you read the Bible, do you allow its message (Jesus) to transform your will?" If you do, then you'll experience its inspiration firsthand. You'll sense the Spirit breathing life into you and changing you from the inside as you reciprocate in obedience to the voice of Christ.

---

75. See Matthew 5:17.

If we're not reading Scripture with open hearts willing to be changed, then it seems it actually withholds its meaning from us. In this situation, all we're doing is playing chess with the Bible in our heads. Practically and subjectively, it has no authority for us.

My conclusion is that the Bible's authority, both objective and subjective, derives from Jesus's authorization of Scripture and our willingness to live under his lordship. Apart from reading it for its point, it becomes an impenetrable mystery and probably an offense.

## CANONICITY

Speaking of the Bible's authority, you'll often hear the term *canon* to describe the collection of authorized, inspired Scriptures. The word *canon* combines two definitions: a *criterion* (an authoritative ruler used to judge authenticity) and a *collection* (especially of sacred books regarded as authentic).

I was taught that the *canon* of Scripture is our inerrant plumb line and final authority. Why? Because the books in the *canon* are inerrant and authoritative. Again, this way of thinking verged on circular reasoning, but we meant that the church ultimately canonized the books it recognized as inspired. Used in this way, the canon of Scripture naturally and subtly replaced Jesus Christ as the Word of God and our final authority for faith and practice.

This is how people in the Sikh religion see their holy book, the *Guru Granth Sahib*, which they treat as their last and perpetual living guru. They symbolically seat it on a throne in the temple and put it to bed at night. The message is that their book is the current guru that succeeded the ten previous human gurus.

Is that what Christianity has done in practice? I see two problems with this sense of *canon*:

+ The Christian "canon" did *not* originally refer to the authorized collections of Scripture. It referred to the gospel message itself, that is, "*the canon of faith.*"[76]

76. For a thorough exposé on this topic, see John Behr, "The Tradition and Canon of the Gospel According to the Scriptures," *The Way to Nicaea*, The Formation of Christian Theology, vol. 1 (Yonkers, NY: St. Vladimir's Press, 2001), 17–48.

✦ Recognition of inspiration was *not* the criterion for a book's inclusion in Scripture. A text's alignment to the *canon of faith* determined where it was inspired and included. Let's discuss each point.

**1. Originally, the *canon* did *not* refer to authorized collections of inspired Scripture.** Rather, from at least the second century, the church spoke of *"the canon of faith"* or *"rule of truth,"* which is to say, "the faith… once delivered" (Jude 1:3 KJV), by which they meant *the apostolic gospel* they had received, which centered on Jesus Christ.

A beautiful, early example of "the canon of faith" is found in Paul's first letter to Corinth:

> ³For what I *received* I passed on to you as of first importance: that Christ died for our sins according to the Scriptures, ⁴that he was buried, that he was raised on the third day according to the Scriptures.                    (1 Cor 15:3–4 NIV)

Irenaeus of Lyon (second century) asserts that it was to establish this *rule(r)* that John wrote his Gospel:

> …to establish the rule of truth in the Church, that there is one God, the Almighty, who made all things by his Word, both visible and invisible, showing at the same time that by the Word, through whom God made the creation, he also bestowed salvation on the human beings within creation, thus commenced his teaching in the Gospel: "In the beginning was the Word."[77]

Notice that the *canon of faith* is not a library of bound books. It is a *message*. Further, it is not something composed. It is received and passed down—from Christ to the apostles to the church. And notice, too, that in Paul's time, the message is "according to the [Jewish] Scriptures" that prophesied these events.

By *this* canon—this ruler, this standard, this gospel—the early church measured what should or should not be included in the New Testament. Books that measured up to the canon of faith—to the gospel—were favored for inclusion; books that did not were excluded. Others were

---

77. Irenaeus, *Against Heresies*, 3.11.1, in John Behr, *John the Theologian & His Paschal Gospel: A Prologue to Theology* (Oxford: Oxford University Press, 2019), 66–67.

debated, right until the end of the fourth century. That is, the *canon of faith* was established by Christ and his apostles from the beginning, but the *canon of Scripture* has always been hotly contested. In fact, the canon of Scripture differs from Protestant to Catholic to Eastern Orthodox to Coptic Orthodox to Ethiopian Orthodox and beyond...to this day![78]

The canon of faith, representing a summary of the gospel story, was preserved and then standardized and dogmatized in the creeds. Interestingly, the councils believed that the Holy Spirit *infallibly* guided them, not to *compose* prescriptive doctrines enshrined in the creeds but, rather, to *remember* the gospel they had received—that is, the truth-claims of Christ.

They were conscious and dependent on Jesus's promise that the Spirit of truth would guide them into all truth.[79] All truth about what? The truth of who Jesus is and what he has done. The ecumenical councils felt it essential to be led by the *infallible* Holy Spirit to remember the gospel and articulate it *infallibly* in the first creeds—even before they finalized what books were *canonical*.

**2. "Canonical" = aligns with the *canon of faith* (*the gospel*).** Based on this confidence, let's review a little more church history: Saint Athanasius became a living legend and defender of Christian orthodoxy in the aftermath of the Nicene council, where the canon or symbol of faith was first formalized (AD 325). We can imagine him using that canon standard as he compiles, for the very first time, the list of New Testament books we recognize today. After that, debate continued over which books made the cut. In fact, even after the completion of the creed at the second council (381), the chairman, Gregory the Theologian, still openly opposed the inclusion of Revelation. And Saint John Chrysostom excludes it altogether from use in worship in his Divine Liturgy, which is still used today in the East. Only in the 390s was Revelation finally and formally included.

---

78. Even as a young Protestant, it troubled me that Reformers such as Martin Luther, who promoted the principle of *sola scriptura* (Scripture alone!), were, ironically, willing to cull whole books out of the Bible fifteen hundred years after the fact. They claimed the Bible was *infallible* but were willing to shrink it down to fit their new theological systems and political agendas. This kind of mastery over the text betrayed the Reformers' alleged commitment to the text. Sixty-six books? Since when? Those removed: 1–2 Esdras, Tobit, Judith, Esther 10:4–16:24, Wisdom, Ecclesiasticus (Sirach), Baruch, Daniel 3:24–90, Daniel 13–14, and 1–2 Maccabees. Luther also called into question Hebrews, James, Jude, and Revelation.
79. See John 16:12–15.

This process was hugely significant because it means that when we say the New Testament books are *canonical*, we mean they were judged to measure up to the *canon* (the gospel itself as summarized in the creeds). Do you see? Again, *canonical* doesn't mean "in the Bible" so much as it means "those books that align with the gospel message." So, which had more or final authority? The apostolic gospel or the biblical books? What was being measured, and by what rule? In practice, what did the compilers of the Bible treat as the object and measure of the Spirit's infallible guidance? It was the person and gospel of Jesus Christ. You know: the Word of God!

## WHY THE CANON OF FAITH MATTERS

Why did the canon of faith matter so much to the first Christians? Why did the apostles and their protégés work to develop a gospel framework through which to read Scripture? What's wrong with a "Scripture alone" approach to interpretation?

Teachers like Irenaeus arrived at the answers to such questions through hard experience with the false teachers of their day. Irenaeus describes the problem in four stages and with a vivid illustration. First, the four stages:

1. The false teachers would begin by gathering ideas from sources other than the Scriptures.

2. From these ideas, they would weave what he called "ropes of sand," anchored to nothing but fantasies.

3. To make their ideas seem more probable, they would adapt scattered sayings from the prophets, Christ's parables, and the apostles to affirm their opinions.

4. And thus, they would dismember the Scriptures and reassemble them according to their deception.

Irenaeus illustrated this process by describing a statue made of gems, first in the image of a king and then remade into a fox or dog.[80] He relates how a beautiful image of a king is constructed by a skillful artist out of precious jewels. But then someone else dismantles the statue, reducing it to

80. See Irenaeus, *Against Heresies*, 1.8.1, in *Ante-Nicene Fathers*, vol. 1, eds. Alexander Roberts, James Donaldson, and A. Cleveland Coxe, trans. Alexander Roberts and William Rambaut (Buffalo, NY: Christian Literature Publishing Co., 1885). Revised and edited for New Advent by Kevin Knight, http://www.newadvent.org/fathers/0103108.htm.

pieces, and begins to rearrange them. He refashions them into the form of a dog or a fox—and, even then, does a poor job of it. After this, with great audacity, he announces that the distorted image *is* the king that the skilled artist had created in the first place. When this fraud is challenged, the false artist points to the jewels themselves, obviously genuine, to persuade onlookers that the gems themselves prove that the dog is in fact a king. And those who had no initial conception of the king are persuaded that this miserable likeness of a dog is in fact the image of the beautiful king.

Irenaeus laments at how the jewels that compose our Scriptures have been violently disconnected and then patched together into something ugly rather than beautiful, doggish rather than kingly. His point is that the same stately gems can be repurposed into any number of false images of the King to serve "baseless fictions." And so, we need the gospel image of Christ the King (summarized in the canon of faith) to regulate our interpretation and use of the individual gems.

In modern Christianity, the need is no less urgent, as we are accustomed to seeing how the treasury of Scripture can be reconstituted to serve hideous images in the name of the King that, in fact, do not resemble Christ at all.

## UNVEILED: PROGRESSIVE ILLUMINATION

When I was attending Bible school, the theory of inerrancy taught me that every word of Scripture was true in all that it affirmed. As I previously mentioned, we used the phrase "verbal plenary inspiration" to describe the supernatural veracity of the original manuscripts down to the last letter (admitting transmission errors). In hindsight, ex-inerrantists call this a *flat Bible* because inerrancy sets every verse on the same level of "objective truth."

"It's either true or it ain't. You callin' God a liar?"

But let's not construct a straw man. At the time, we would respond, "No, we're not saying it's a *flat Bible*. We believe in *progressive revelation*." We meant that while every word is true, we don't get the complete truth all in one package. Through the centuries, the Holy Spirit built one brick of truth upon another until the whole house was assembled and complete when John the Revelator wrote his final "Amen" and the canon of Scripture was closed. No single brick could tell the whole story, but neither could any one brick (not "one jot or one tittle"[81]) be untrue or mistaken. In our minds, admitting that possibility would degrade the brick house into a house of cards. When one card falls, they all do. And if that's your model, those who point out the problem texts are big bad wolves trying to blow the house down. Pardon the mixed metaphor.

Paul offers the Corinthians a different model. He sees the truth of God's message breathing through the inspired text. But, he explains, we have a problem. We read through veils. These veils cover our eyes and our hearts so that we may read what the Bible *says* but can't perceive what it *teaches*. The words are all there, but when read by the letter (literalism) rather than the Spirit (the gospel sense), the message becomes a source of *death* and *condemnation*.

Yet, when we behold Christ in the Bible by the Spirit, the Spirit removes the veil from our hearts so we can see how the entire message has always been pointing to *life* and *reconciliation*. Instead of progressive revelation (stacking bricks), we have progressive illumination (removing veils). It's best if you see this for yourself in Paul's words:

> [5]...our sufficiency is from God, [6]who also made us sufficient as ministers of the new covenant, *not of the letter but of the Spirit*; for *the letter kills, but the Spirit gives life.*
>
> [7]But if the *ministry of death*, written and engraved on stones, was glorious, so that the children of Israel could not look steadily at the face of Moses because of the glory of his countenance, which glory was passing away, [8]how will the *ministry of the Spirit* not be more glorious? [9]For if the *ministry of condemnation* had glory, the *ministry of righteousness* exceeds much more in glory. [10]For even what was made glorious had no glory in this respect, because of the glory that excels. [11]For if *what is passing away* was glorious, *what remains* is much more glorious.
>
> [12]Therefore, since we have such hope, we use great boldness of speech—[13]unlike Moses, who put a veil over his face so that the children of Israel could not look steadily at the end of what was

---

81. See Mathew 5:18 KJV, NKJV.

passing away. [14]But *their minds were blinded.* For until this day *the same veil remains unlifted in the reading of the Old Testament,* because *the veil is taken away in Christ.*[15]But even to this day, *when Moses is read, a veil lies on their heart.*[16]Nevertheless when one turns to the Lord, *the veil is taken away.*[17]Now the Lord is the Spirit; and where the Spirit of the Lord is, there is liberty. [18]But we all, *with unveiled face, beholding as in a mirror the glory of the Lord, are being transformed into the same image from glory to glory, just as by the Spirit of the Lord.*                    (2 Cor 3:5–18 NKJV)

Here we see Paul drawing multiple contrasts:

- The glory of Moses (representing the law) versus the glory of Christ (unveiled in the gospel)
- That which is passing away (the old covenant) versus that which remains (the new covenant)
- Reading by the letter (literalism) versus reading by the Spirit (gospel)
- The ministry of condemnation versus the ministry of life
- The fruit of death versus the fruit of life

Paul's use of these metaphors is complex—he is simultaneously saying "Moses" (the law) is fading away before the glory of Christ (the gospel) while also telling us how to read "Moses" *as gospel* (by the Spirit).

Further, the veils are not only being removed from our own hearts as we read Scripture. Over the millennia, veil upon veil has been progressively removed *within the Bible itself.* That is, the authors who produced the Scriptures by the Spirit were themselves subject to temporal veils. Their veils glorified tribalism and nativism, militarism and violence, racism and misogyny, imperial and colonial ambition, and so on. Just like us! The chroniclers who recorded the Israelites' sacred history with Yahweh often misapprehended their God. They recounted their experiences *through these veils,* embedding Israel's patently narrow, shallow, and ugly projections onto God within their writings—sometimes *affirming* them, at other times *critiquing* them.

And that's an important point. These authors were not unbiased, arm's length observers. They had agendas in how they selected and told their stories. A wise reader asks, "Why are you telling me this?" Sometimes the authors are propagandists for the king or temple, and at other times scathing critics of Israel's policies. Sometimes they justify national violence as a divine mandate. Elsewhere, they represent violence as a reprehensible problem.[82]

An Emmaus reading of their accounts sees these agendas. When the authors rationalize bloodshed, we ask, "How do they prefigure the Sanhedrin's rationale for Jesus's crucifixion?" And when they problematize violence, we ask, "How do their critiques anticipate Christ's denunciation of violence?" As I read any given text through Christ, I need to consider whether the author's perspective reveals a veil that Christ has since removed or an *unveiling* that foreshadows his revelation of God.

Boiling it down, Paul says that "we," including the biblical authors, "see through a glass, darkly" (1 Cor 13:12 KJV). The Greek word for "darkly" is *en ainigmati*, which literally means "in an enigma"! They saw the truth through veils that are evident in the text.

But we also see the Holy Spirit at work within that process, not adding truth upon brittle truth (as if all their primitive notions of God had been correct) but, rather, progressively removing veils for the people of God even as their story moved forward. We see divine illumination transforming their image of God all along, preparing them to see what God had revealed to Abraham from the beginning: that God's heart was to bless the whole world through his Seed (Jesus Christ). Thus:

+ God is not a bigoted national deity—God wills to bless the world.

+ God is not a violent militarist—God's agenda is peace for all.

+ God is not a maniacal death-dealer—God is a redeeming Lover.

So, throughout the Bible, we see the veils, and we see them being removed, layer after layer, uncovering a clearer image that comes into sharpest focus in the Gospels.

---

82. Matthew Lynch's landmark study, *Portraying Violence in the Hebrew Bible* (Cambridge, UK: Cambridge University Press, 2020) shows how Old Testament authors use four "grammars" to describe and problematize violent acts in Israel's story.

## THE RELIABILITY OF THE GOSPELS

...these writings [the four Gospels] bring you the living image of [Christ's] holy mind and the speaking, healing, dying, rising Christ himself, and thus they render him so fully present that you would see less if you gazed upon him with your very eyes.[83]

Paul's claim regarding the God-breathed nature of Scripture is not the self-authenticating ideology I was raised on. Contra the apologist Josh McDowell, Paul did not count on "evidence that demands a verdict." Rather, the apostle posits *inspiration* as an *experience* of Christ if we will search the Scriptures for their witness to him—and if we are trained by the Scriptures to become like him. As we incorporate the Bible into our faith practice through study, prayer, and obedience, we will indeed conclude that it is not only useful but also wonderfully and uniquely inspired.

For Paul and the Christians many centuries afterward, Christ—not a rickety theology of the Bible—is the Word of God and final Authority. They saw in the Gospels an unparalleled testimony of human witnesses to the truth that Christ had been and continued to be in their midst. The New Testament narratives form a reliable record of their experiences from their perspectives. And they long for us to share in that experience:

> [1-2]From the very first day, we were there, taking it all in—we heard it with our own ears, *saw it with our own eyes, verified it with our own hands. The Word of Life appeared right before our eyes; we saw it happen!* And now we're telling you in most sober prose that what we witnessed was, incredibly, this: The infinite Life of God himself took shape before us.
>
> [3-4]We saw it, we heard it, and now we're telling you *so you can experience it along with us, this experience of communion with the Father and his Son, Jesus Christ.* Our motive for writing is simply this: *We want you to enjoy this, too.* Your joy will double our joy!
>
> (1 John 1:1–4 MSG)

---

83. Desiderius Erasmus, *The Paraclesis* [preface to the 1516 edition of Erasmus's Greek and Latin New Testament], in *Christian Humanism and the Reformation: Selected Writings of Erasmus*, ed. and trans. by John C. Olin (New York: Fordham University Press, 1987), http://www.people.virginia.edu/~jdk3t/ParaclesisErasmus.pdf.

The apostle John was convinced that their Gospels are venues for encounter. They are the stage on which Christ appears to us—a doorway through which he comes to us. They broker the apostles' experience of Jesus to the open-hearted reader.

But what about the discrepancies across accounts? Don't these undermine our confidence in their testimony?

When the four Gospels offer differing versions of the same events, we needn't be crushed by that. I'm amazed that they didn't collude to get their stories straight. To me, the differences don't undermine the central truths they absolutely agree on—instead, they verify the eyewitness accounts by negating charges of collusion (that existed from the beginning).

Here's an easy example: take some time to read only the resurrection-morning accounts in all four Gospels. Really do it. Carefully. Factual questions arise:

1.  Which women came to the tomb? The lists vary.

2.  Who greeted the women at the tomb? A young man, one angel, or two angels? Where were they situated? Inside the tomb? Outside the tomb?

3.  Who met the risen Christ first? Mary or several women? Do they touch him or not? The facts seem to vary.

4.  Where did the resurrected Jesus first appear to the eleven disciples? Jerusalem (Luke 24:33–36; John 20:18–29) or Galilee (Matt 28:10, 16; Mark 16:7)? Depends on which Gospel you're reading.

That's just one of many examples where the four Gospels *cannot* be harmonized to the standards required by inerrancy. Not if you let the Bible say what it says without twisting it into a pretzel. Sadly, some people are so committed to their ideology of Scripture that they feel compelled to force nonmatching puzzle pieces to fit. Now *that's* a real violation of the authority of Scripture.

Next, let's go back to the same text. Watch for the points of interdependent convergence—watch for the revelation.

1.  Was Christ truly and fully dead? How do the Gospels witness to this?

2. Was Christ truly buried (by Sanhedrin members!) in a tomb, sealed with a large stone and guarded by Roman soldiers?

3. Was the stone rolled away, the tomb empty, and the body gone? Were there supernatural encounters at the tomb experienced by multiple witnesses?

4. Were there eyewitnesses of the risen Christ that morning, that evening, and a week later? If you wanted verification from those who were initially skeptical, who could you ask? What changed their minds?

The witnesses don't give us an uncomplicated unison account of all the facts. And yet they agree on the inspired truth without any question. What's the inspired truth? That the Bible is inerrant? No! That Christ is risen! That Jesus is alive! And their apparent inability to agree precisely about all the details, while fascinating, confirms my own experience—that Christ is risen and alive, and, in fact, we've met him too.

## LEARNING TO READ AGAIN

There you have my journey of *reframing inspiration*—how I've had to rethink infallibility, inerrancy, canonicity, and authority. In good faith, I've taken seriously the veiling and unveiling at work across the Bible's divinely inspired and truly human testimonies. Losing literalism has *not* undermined my faith in Christ or caused me to set aside my Bible. I love Christ more than ever, and I experience joy and wonder in the Scripture more than ever. I read the Bible far more carefully than I ever have, and I try to help those who are repulsed by it because they were told they *must* believe God literally smites his children, commands genocide, or tortures people in a fiery furnace forever.

Of course he didn't. How do we know? Because Christ is the final and only perfect Word of God…just as the Scriptures claim. But it also means we'll need to learn how to read it again—from scratch.

### CHAPTER 5

# BEFORE WE OPEN THE SCROLLS: PRECONDITIONS FOR READING

"In regard to figurative expressions, a rule such as the following will be observed, to carefully turn over in our minds and meditate upon what we read till an interpretation be found that tends to establish the reign of love."[84]
—Augustine of Hippo

## WHAT IS WORTHY OF GOD

*I* noted earlier that we all come to the Bible with preconceived notions. You may come with the assumption that Scripture is God's inerrant word and cannot contain any errors or contradictions. Others may come with a fundamental prejudice against the Bible as being fantastical, misogynistic, and violent. We all have assumptions, conscious or not, before we "open the scrolls." It can't be helped. Therefore, beginning with the right predisposition can be of great help. What would that look like?

---

84. Augustine of Hippo, *On Christian Doctrine, in Four Books*, 15.23, https://www.ccel.org/ccel/augustine/doctrine.xvi_2.html.

We might say *the proper orientation for entering Scripture is love for God, humility before God, and openness to God*. Reading well also requires some fundamental theological presuppositions—commitments we hold prior to our reading. In this section, we will see how a faith commitment to the goodness and love of God are required for a reading of Scripture "worthy" of God's character.

What follows is a summary that you can explore more deeply in Mark Sheridan's must-read study *Language for God in Patristic Tradition: Wrestling with Biblical Anthropomorphism*.[85] I had previously seen these basic ideas during my PhD studies, but Sheridan's fine book has taken the research much further down that path and is loaded with primary sources. I'm grateful to him for giving me more boldness to relate the basics as follows.

## PLATO

About ten years ago, I happened to read Homer's epic poem *The Iliad* (c. 850 BC) and Plato's *The Republic* (c. 375 BC) at the same time. *The Iliad* is a dramatic and tragic story of the Trojan War in which military heroes and the Greek pantheon of gods engage in contemporary ideas of glory, wrath, nobility, and fate. The poem conceives of these gods as conniving, fickle, violent, and vengeful. French philosopher Simone Weil called it "a poem of force" and read it as a critique of how opting for violent force ultimately dooms us to become victims of it.

In *The Republic*, Plato's great work on political philosophy and justice, his mentor Socrates is very critical of Homer's poems, primarily because of how the gods are portrayed. He argues that if you want children to develop into just people who create a just society, why would you indoctrinate them with literature that models the gods as such horrid characters?

Socrates posited that our conceptions of the divine need to be *worthy* of God or *the Good* in the ultimate sense. For Socrates, God is One, and that God is goodness itself. The Good (God) subsists of Beauty, Truth, and Justice as ideas or forms that emanate from the Good and are mediated into the world by Love. In a dialogue between Socrates and Glaucon

85. Mark Sheridan, *Language for God in Patristic Tradition: Wrestling with Biblical Anthropomorphism* (Downers Grove, IL: IVP Academic, 2014).

(Plato's brother), Glaucon goes so far as to say that if the Good were to become particular in this world, it would be as a perfectly just (righteous) man, and that the world would ultimately reject, beat, and crucify him.[86] You can imagine how this statement got the attention of the early church fathers who had studied Greek philosophy! Anyway, the bottom line for Plato is that the divine is infinitely good and only does good. God is not like those pseudo-divine rotters on Mount Olympus.

Later, other philosophers, such as Heraclitus and Plutarch (or authors using their names) wanted to retrieve Homer's works by arguing that they should be read as poetry, as metaphor or allegory, not describing actual gods at all. We see how these lowercase gods are expressions of the fallen human passions, driving temperaments, and the like. They aren't actual entities that possess Homer's characters but the internal and external forces that drive us—akin to what the Bible describes as the desires of the flesh and the lusts of the world. If we read Homer's poetry that way, it can provide us with useful cautionary tales of the human condition.

## PHILO

Now fast-forward a few centuries and travel to Alexandria, Egypt, in the time leading up to the events and composition of the New Testament. Alexandria was a thriving center of Greek philosophy and home to Jewish rabbis who had already translated their Hebrew Scriptures into Greek and integrated the best of Jewish and Greek thought into their theology. Among the great rabbis of Alexandria was Philo, who lived during the time of Christ. He had picked up on these debates about Homer's gods. Similar to Plato, he observed that the God described in the Hebrew Scriptures sometimes seemed to be as reactive, wrathful, and violent as Homer's gods. Like Plato, he believed that these character traits were deep flaws unworthy to be attributed to Yahweh. For Philo, Yahweh must not be reduced to a Jewish version of Jupiter/Zeus. Like Plato, he believed that God is the Good (pure and infinite goodness), the source of all beauty, truth, and justice. When we read in the Old Testament that God is gracious and

---

86. Plato, *The Republic*, Book II.360–61. From *Plato in Twelve Volumes*, vols. 5 and 6, trans. Paul Shorey (Cambridge, MA: Harvard University Press; London: William Heinemann Ltd., 1969), http://data.perseus.org/citations/urn:cts:greekLit:tlg0059.tlg030.perseus-eng1:2.362.

compassionate, that his mercy kisses justice, and that his lovingkindness endures forever, this is language "fitting" or "worthy" or appropriate of God.

But when God is *not* that way—when God appears cruel or vindictive, consumed by wrath—how can that be? Philo believes that such descriptions are *not worthy* of God. But there they are in the Scriptures. And he's not about to ban his Bible as Plato sought to ban Homer's works. So, across his works,[87] Philo asks, in effect, "Then how shall we read them? How *must* we read them?" Philo reasons that if Yahweh is truly God—the ultimate Good—then brutal descriptions of Yahweh must be anthropomorphic projections, that is, attributing human attributes and actions to God. We *must*, therefore, read those passages allegorically, because to read them literally would be *unworthy* of God.[88]

That is, prior even to opening the scrolls, the famous rabbi Philo understood that God is all-good and all-merciful. That understanding became his first interpretive principle. It predetermined how Scripture was to be understood and applied. Where God is portrayed as good, Philo instructs us to read that as a revelation of the good God. Where God is *not* portrayed as good, he instructs us to read allegorically, because we must never allow a literalist interpretation to negate our understanding of God's goodness. Rather, we search the Scriptures for what is worthy of God and useful for us. That way, every story (even the disturbing ones) can show us something of how to become righteous people who do justice, love mercy, and walk humbly with our God,[89] without impugning God's character.

## ORIGEN

We skip ahead to the early church teachers, whose interpretations follow this pattern but now also include the gospel revelation of God through Jesus Christ. Beginning especially with Origen (notably also of Alexandria), he and many others (e.g., Gregory of Nyssa, Basil the Great,

87. See, for example, David Winston and John Dillon, *Two Treatises of Philo of Alexandria: A Commentary on De Gigantibus and Quod Deus Sit Immutabilis* (Chico, CA: Scholars Press, 1983) and *The Works of Philo Judaeus*, trans. Charles Duke Yonge (London: H. G. Bohn, 1854–1890), http://www.earlychristianwritings.com/yonge/index.html.
88. See Pieter Willem van der Horst, "Philo and the Problem of God's Emotions," Études platoniciennes 7 (2010): 171–178, https://journals.openedition.org/etudesplatoniciennes/636.
89. See Micah 6:8.

John Cassian, John Chrysostom, and Augustine) transpose Plato's and Philo's assumptions about God into their reading of the Bible. Like Plato and Philo, they were committed to reading the Scriptures under the assumption that God is good, and all God does is goodness.

And now, in Christ, they are also informed by the apostolic revelation that God is infinite Love in God's very nature. They know that God is Light, and in God there is no darkness at all. They believe that God is Life, and in him there is no death at all. They preach that God is Mercy, and in him is no retribution at all. The revelation that God is immutable Christlike love, light, and life precedes their reading of the Bible and guides their interpretation of every line.

Knowing this up front, the great fathers and mothers of the church could then read the Scriptures and watch for Christ to be revealed. And where God appears to be un-Christlike—the author of hatred, darkness, death—they are preconditioned to read those portions as allegory, just as they had been trained to read Homer. Again, they resist literalism wherever it would paint God as *not good* or redefine *good* as something that is actually *evil*. Instead, they insist that God is light (Christlike), and in God is *no* darkness (un-Christlikeness) at all.

Said another way, the first Christians committed themselves fully to the gospel of Jesus Christ and his revelation of triune Love. *Then* they would open the Scriptures. This theological precommitment dramatically impacted how they read and translated the Bible. And so it can for us today.

## SUPERCESSIONISM?

An Emmaus hermeneutic, in which one reads the Hebrew Scriptures through the gospel lens of Christ, is our primary precondition for reading Scripture. Yet this approach can sometimes lead people to claim that such a reading is "supercessionist." How might we best respond to those who have this concern?

First, what is a *supercessionist*? It depends on who you ask. Generally, the term is pejorative for those who believe (1) that Christ's new covenant supersedes the Mosaic covenant and (2) that the Christian church has displaced Israel as God's chosen people. The worry is that these convictions stoke the flames of anti-Semitism.

Before anything else, we need to address this final point directly. I condemn anti-Semitism. Full stop. I reject anti-Semitism as anti-Christ. Nothing in the way the Rabbi from Nazareth read his Scriptures, practiced Judaism, or claimed to be Israel's Messiah should ever be misused to persecute or harm his own people. And yet that has been one of the ugliest and most violent aspects of Christianity's historical record.

Then what do we make of Jesus's claim to be the *fulfillment* of Hebrew prophecy? When he claims to be the Seed of Abraham, the heir to David's throne, the Suffering Servant of Isaiah, the "new covenant" of Jeremiah, or the Son of Man of Daniel, is his *fulfillment* of the Hebrew Scriptures *supercessionist?*

The common error shared by both supersessionists and their opponents is their failure to recall that the New Testament writings are a Jewish proclamation by Jewish Christians to follow a Jewish Messiah into a renewed Jewish covenant prophesied by the Jewish Scriptures. Christianity was, from its foundations, a stream within the Jewish tradition that recognized Jesus as both Messiah of Israel and Savior of the world, according to the Jewish Scriptures.

In other words, both sides presume wrongly that the New Testament is "the Christian Scripture" and that Christians are appropriating the Hebrew Scriptures ("the Old Testament") as their own. They forget that Christians and Jews are siblings, reading the same Scriptures but in very different ways. In the first century, there were *many* Jewish readings (Pharisee, Sadducee, Essene, Zealot, and so forth). Somehow the rabbi Gamaliel's tolerant interpretation of the early Christians[90] had been warped into Saul of Tarsus's violent actions against them. But when Saul met Christ on the road to Damascus, he did *not* convert from Judaism to Christianity. He converted from violence to peace, in submission to the Prince of Peace, without ceasing to identify as a Jew. The inability of some supercessionists to see this—or their own failure to repent of violence—should in no way negate the rabbi Jesus's particular Jewish hermeneutic. The fact that rabbinic Judaism and Christian Judaism (with their Gentile

---

90. See Acts 5.

converts) would part company and become hostile toward one another only played into this fallacy. As a Christian who worships the God of Abraham and identifies Jesus as both Messiah and Savior, I know that reading Scripture the Emmaus Way continually nurtures my love for Jesus's kinsmen in the flesh, sends me to their rabbis for help, and deepens my opposition to anti-Semitism.

## THE "BIBLIFICATION" OF SCRIPTURE

A final consideration regarding preconditions for reading Scripture is the medium through which we read it.

### THE MEDIUM IS THE MESSAGE

Marshall McLuhan is most popularly known for the slogan "The medium is the message," which was his call to be mindful of the implicit impacts that come with the adoption of any new technology. He suggested four questions (labeled "the tetrad of media effects") that will help us see the ups and downs of any new medium:

1. What does the medium enhance?

2. What does the medium make obsolete?

3. What does the medium retrieve that had been obsolesced earlier?

4. What does the medium reverse or flip into when pushed to extremes?

Today, technology advances so rapidly that whatever you can imagine is likely already in development or patented somewhere. The pace of our lives and social obligations to "keep up" puts mindfulness in the back seat. Speed-of-light communication has drawn us into our smartphones and the universe of social media without sufficient attentiveness to McLuhan's questions. *The Social Dilemma* (2020)[91] was a documentary wake-up call to the alarming levels of algorithmic manipulation and privacy invasion to which we've assented—but it had little to no effect on our practices. The world system simply does not allow us to be Luddites.

---

91. Jeff Orlowski, dir., *The Social Dilemma* (Exposure Labs, The Space Program, Agent Pictures, 2020).

Prior to the digital age of computers and the Internet, the greatest technological breakthrough was surely Gutenberg's printing press. With the printing press, in concert with the impulse for Scripture translation, came the mass production and distribution of the Bible in the language of the people. It's easy enough to see how Gutenberg's gift could variously enhance, make obsolete, retrieve, and subvert the practice of Bible reading (and even literacy) wherever the Good Book became available. I suppose much ink has been spilled on that question.

## THE BIBLE AS TECHNOLOGY

What fascinates me is how *the Bible itself became a technology* that repackaged and reframed the Scriptures, with real effects on the message itself. Scripture has always come to us through delivery systems: oral and written, scrolls and codices, liturgies, and lectionaries. These delivery systems are, in themselves, technologies. How might the medium—the way we package and deliver Scripture—affect or become the message itself?

## "BIBLIFICATION"

Using McLuhan's tetrad, consider the following:

1. *How does the Bible medium enhance Scripture reading?*

We could say that the Bible gathers together the Scriptures into a single collection that clarifies which books our Christian tradition considers inspired by the Spirit. We give that collection priority in terms of authority in our individual lives and churches. The Bible, seen as a holy book, is set apart from other sacred literature and communicates the uniqueness of our Scriptures. We come to see that we are not only in possession of a library of independent and disconnected booklets but that the many booklets have converged into a coherent, grand saga.

2. *What does the Bible medium retrieve that had been obsolesced earlier?*

I've moved McLuhan's third question up to number 2 in order to point out a corollary. Having the Bible in one affordable book and accessible in our own language retrieves the Scriptures for us because we can read them in our own vernacular. The authors who produced the Scriptures in Hebrew, Aramaic, and Koine Greek meant for those who heard them to understand what was written. But through great stretches of Christian history, lay people could only hear Scripture read in foreign languages (e.g., Latin) through priests who might not understand it any better than they did. That someone can now hear and read John 3:16 in their own tongue is a grand retrieval.

3. *What does the Bible medium make obsolete in Scripture reading?*

The increase in accessibility to Scripture is to be celebrated, but there is also a downside. As a bound collection of books available to the masses in hardcopy, on a smartphone app, or online, what gets lost? What previous medium might become obsolete that compromises the message?

I would suggest that the liturgical reading of the Scriptures in the context of community worship and the lectionary cycles, with its connections of linked texts, provided an essential medium for understanding the message that preceded the Bible—an understanding that is not as obvious in the printed version. In other words, the "divine liturgy" of the church is a medium that functions to frame the Scriptures within the canon of faith— the message of the gospel—showing how they work together within the drama of redemption that inexorably points to Christ crucified and risen. So, too, the lectionary cycles: these frame the Scriptures within the church calendar precisely in order to lead us to Christ and his gospel.

Fr. John Behr suggests that reading the Bible apart from its gospel framework, preserved in the liturgical tradition, may not even be reading it *as Scripture*. If I sit down with my Bible and flip it open to any page in the book, I've potentially removed that page from its specific role in its gospel context. One could study the Bible their whole lives and yet miss the essential reality of who *all the Scriptures* point to. Certainly, Jesus's opponents had.

4. *What does the Bible medium reverse or flip into when pushed to extremes?*

This, then, suggests the potential for a terrible reversal if a Bible medium combines with the extremes of bibliolatry. We see this subversion when the Bible is elevated to the right hand of the Father and honored with the title "Word of God"—the name that belongs to Jesus Christ alone.

I have often seen people, through a flat reading of the Bible, use particular Scriptures to argue against the very teachings of Jesus Christ, justifying from the idolized text that which the Word himself forbade. When the

Bible becomes our final authority, Jesus is demoted to a mere episode in the Good Book. Ironically, the message of the Scriptures becomes lost to the medium we call the Bible when its Emmaus-Way framework is subverted by new technology.

I recognize that some of these concepts may be entirely new to readers unfamiliar with liturgical calendars or liturgical services, but consider that our Jewish forbearers observed an annual cycle of feasts and fasts, that the Gospel of John is organized according to these events, and that Jesus consciously framed those festivals as prefigurements of his story.

## WHAT THEN?

No, I haven't thrown out my iPhone or canceled my online accounts. Neither will I discard my excessive collection of Bibles or cease all private study of its wonderful pages. But what I can commit to is submitting my reading of the Scriptures to their gospel context. I can read them in the way prescribed by the church, as the message concerning Jesus, the One who is the I Am, whose day Abraham foresaw; the One of whom, Jesus says, Moses wrote; the One to whom all the Prophets and Scriptures bear witness. And I will see the Scriptures within the canon of faith before I read them within Morocco-leather bindings. And I will read and hear the Scriptures as a product and function of the church, ancient and modern, that faithfully stewards them.

I'm seeing ever more clearly how the annual calendar of feasts and fasts, and the weekly divine liturgy, are the framework through which we see the Scriptures come together to tell our story of redemption both yearly and weekly. By stripping Christianity of the liturgical framework in which all Scripture has its role and place in the great story—in the name of breaking free from tradition and religion—we're left with a Bible organized only by genre, with no clue how Moses, the Prophets, and the rest of the Scriptures prefigure the passion of Jesus, and a randomized sequence of sermons contrived by independent preachers.

The annual calendar is like an auger that cycles deeper and deeper through the clay to access the pure springs of a deep faith. Too often, we've opted instead to dig random holes throughout the yard, so that, when the rain comes, we're drinking from a selection of shallow, muddy puddles.

## IT'S NOT ABOUT THE CALENDAR

Having explained the framing function of the church calendar and lectionary, let me say that it's not about the calendar! What I'm talking about is framing the Scriptures *within the gospel*. Even if you're unfamiliar or uncomfortable with liturgical life, I'm sure you know Jesus's parable of the prodigal son(s)[92]—and that's his gospel in a nutshell.

If all Scripture is meant to be read in the context of the gospel, and since the gospel is summarized so beautifully in that parable, why not try the following experiment?

Imagine that the whole Bible is simply an incredibly *long* version of the parable of the prodigals. And conversely, imagine that the parable is Jesus's ingeniously brief summary of the whole Bible, distilled into short-story format. We can do this because both offer us the same gospel narrative... one in an expansive library and the other in a tight paragraph. So, here's what we can do: turn the parable into an imaginary walk-in closet organizer for every section, every book, and every chapter of the Bible.

That means any passage where you see rebellion, disobedience, or lostness—any story where you see the trials of Israel's wandering, exile, slavery, or destruction—can be slotted into the younger son's descent into the pigpen. And all of those Jewish tales of judgment, condemnation, legalism, or "bad laws"[93] might be assigned somewhere within the older brother's part of the tale. The former exposes humanity's addiction to rebellion, the latter to humanity's demand for retribution. These are two sides of the same coin: *alienation*, where both boys "slaved away in the fields."

But don't stop there. Continue to every biblical passage where we see repentance, grace, flourishing, and celebration. All of these find their spot in the gospel of the son's return, the father's welcome, and the homecoming banquet in the kingdom of God. You might ask, as I did, where Jesus's incarnation, passion, and resurrection fit into the story.

As with the Scriptures, so in the parable: look for him *everywhere!* Christ *is* that moment of clarity when the son asks himself, "*What am I doing out here in this pigpen?*" Christ *is* the impulse to return, and he *is* the road home. Christ *is* the Father's embrace. Christ *is* the open door into the

---

92. See Luke 15:11–32.
93. See Ezekiel 20:25–26.

Father's house. Christ *is* the ring, the robe, and the banquet table. And, surely, if Christ can be the Lamb of Passover, he can also be the delicious, fattened Calf offered at the great feast of God. Christ *is* even there in the Father's plea to the elder son: *"Please, son: come inside! Join the party!"*

If we were compelled to structure *all* of our Scripture reading into that brief narrative, we could see how the whole Bible leads us to Christ. We could see how every brick in the Bible finds its important space in the gospel road. Even the ugly bits. Further, we might see why Jesus says he did not come to abolish the Law or the Prophets but to *fulfill* them, so that "every jot and tittle" reveals an important waypoint in our own experience as sons and daughters on our way home. This is why I referred to a *walk-in* closet. The approach becomes personal when we actually enter the story ourselves and remind ourselves of where we have been, where we are, and where we're heading. The story draws us in and welcomes us to receive everything the Father has for us. It becomes our personal invitation to experience the gospel.

### CHAPTER 6

# GOSPEL, INSPIRATION, AND TRANSLATION

"However surprising this might be to a modern reader, it was a commonly acknowledged point to early Christians,…evident in the Gospel of John and the writings of Paul: 'the fundamental arrow in the link joining Scripture and gospel points *from the gospel story to the Scripture and not from the Scripture to the gospel story*. In a word, with Jesus's glorification, belief in Scripture comes into being by acquiring an indelible link to belief in Jesus's words and deeds.'"
—John Behr[94]

## TRANSLATIONS

*I*'m frequently asked which Bible translations I prefer. I certainly use many within this book. With all the English Bible translations available

---

94. John Behr, "Introduction," in *Origen: On First Principles, A Readers Edition*, Oxford Early Christian Texts, trans. John Behr (Oxford: Oxford University Press, 2019), xlviii–xlix. In this paragraph, Fr. John is citing J. Louis Martyn, "John and Paul on the Subject of Gospel and Scripture," *Theological Issues in the Letters of Paul* (London, UK: Bloomsbury Academic, 1997), 209–30.

today, like most readers, I tend to pick favorites based on *readability, accuracy,* and/or *beauty.*

For example, when going for readability, I enjoy the *New Living Translation* and N. T. Wright's *Kingdom New Testament,* also known as *The New Testament for Everyone* (NTE). When I want accuracy, I use the *New American Standard Bible* and David Bentley Hart's *The New Testament.* For beauty, I most love the *New King James Version,* the Orthodox *Psalter,*[95] and Robert Alter's translation entitled *The Hebrew Bible* (both beautiful and accurate). But when reading the Old Testament Scriptures, I also use *The Orthodox Study Bible* because its Old Testament section is based on the Septuagint (LXX), the Greek version of the Hebrew Scriptures, which was translated before Christ and is the most popular source for New Testament authors who cite the Old Testament.

As for the primary biblical languages, I'm useless with Hebrew and know nothing of Aramaic, so I stick close to a few experts who are intimate with the Old Testament languages. My five semesters of New Testament Greek taught me for certain that I can follow along and do close lexical work, but I don't kid myself into thinking I *know* Greek.

So, I read my favorite translations side by side with gratitude, and I check an array of others to discern where they best express the gospel sense of Scripture. See what I did there? *Before* I choose a translation, I already have in mind the gospel. Readability, accuracy, and beauty are secondary to the testimony of Jesus when selecting translations.

## GOSPEL BEFORE TRANSLATION

If that idea seems risky, I'm merely following the first Christian interpreters. *Before* trying to translate the Bible, they established in their hearts the gospel revelation they had received through Jesus Christ and his apostles. They didn't feign objectivity, as if that were completely possible. They believed the Scriptures could not be understood, much less translated, unless the gospel unveils their spiritual meaning.[96] They could not conceive of "rightly dividing the word of truth" (2 Timothy 2:15 KJV, NKJV) apart

95. *The Psalter: According to the Seventy* (Boston, MA: Holy Transfiguration Monastery, 1974).
96. See 2 Corinthians 3.

from the gospel lens. Indeed, Christians could only regard the Hebrew Scriptures as inspired in the illuminating light of who Christ was and what he taught. This means that the gospel formed and affected their translation work. The best modern translators know this and don't pretend to be unbiased by their theology (because of course they are).

In this chapter, I will offer three examples of how Bible translations both form and are formed by the gospel we preach.

## GOD'S HEART: TO CRUSH OR TO CURE?

I begin with Exhibit A, from Isaiah 53, that famous chapter that prefigures the crucifixion of Jesus Christ. Let's look at Isaiah 53:10 in the KJV, the NIV, and the LXX (Septuagint):

KJV: "It *pleased* the LORD to *bruise* him; he hath put him to grief."

NIV: "It was the LORD's *will* to *crush* him and cause him to suffer."

LXX: "The Lord *wishes* to *cleanse* Him of His wound."

The first two versions depict God fulfilling his will and apparently even being pleased by *crushing* or *bruising* the suffering servant. This may serve the vision of penal substitutionary atonement, but it's a galaxy away from the nature of God revealed in Jesus. Indeed, the New Testament authors *never* use any part of Isaiah 53 to teach or imply that God the Father was punishing his Son.

The LXX reads and translates the Hebrew text differently—dramatically so. In translating the word rendered "bruise" or "crush" in the other translations, they use the Greek word *katharisai* (from καθαρίζω), which the New Testament uses many times for Jesus's ministry of healing. Its literal meaning is to "cleanse" or "purify," with healing connotations, as when Jesus *cleansed* the leper in Matthew 8:3.

As a pre-Christian translation, the LXX predates but also beautifully prefigures New Testament revelation of God's self-disclosure as the Great Physician in and through Jesus Christ.

How is it that God is seen to cleanse the wound of the suffering servant, especially if this figure refers to Jesus? And what is the wound? Aside from the obvious (raising Christ from the dead), we can see an atonement theology at work here that has nothing to do with a retributive transaction. Rather, in his humanity, Christ takes on the wound of Adam (all the effects of the fall), and the Father cleanses the human race in the body of his Son. Not through punishment but through the healing touch of divine love. This perspective matters because a gospel-informed translation into English perceives God as a divine healer rather than a cruel punisher.

In other words, inspiration is about more than the Hebrew, Greek, or translated texts. The inspiration of Scripture by the Spirit necessarily includes our understanding of the gospel, and how this impacts our view of God. The same dynamic also affects our view of humanity and vice versa.

## YOUR HEART: DECEITFUL OR DEEP?

Exhibit B comes from Jeremiah the prophet. The verse is Jeremiah 17:9, which I memorized as a young Evangelical. Once again, we'll compare the KJV and NIV translations with the ancient LXX.

KJV: "The heart is *deceitful* above all things, and *desperately wicked:* who can know it?"

NIV: "The heart is *deceitful* above all things and *beyond cure*. Who can understand it?

LXX (v. 5): "The heart is *deep* beyond all things, and *it is the man.*

Even so, who can know him?

The first two translations perfectly matched and formed the low view of humanity of my Reformation heritage—debauched, debased, and totally depraved. We came by our "worm theology" honestly, assured even in early Sunday school that our hearts (and everyone else's) were deceitful, *desperately wicked*, and *beyond cure*. (One Christian elementary school in my area currently teaches its kindergarten students—five-year-old children—"*You have a dark heart.*")

You could never really trust your heart, even if you "prayed the prayer" and Jesus exchanged your "heart of stone" for a new "heart of flesh."[97]

---

97. See, for example, Ezekiel 36:26.

This view imparted to us an early sense of cynicism and sowed distrust, especially of outsiders, with a thousand anecdotes to prove the point. By dehumanizing humanity, we felt we had a better gospel to sell.

But now compare this picture to the LXX: "The heart is *deep* beyond all things, and it *is* the man." The human heart is indeed deep, complex, and truly wonderful. While we are complicated beings, a mysterious blend of nature, nurture, and coping mechanisms, the apostolic gospel was never what some call "worm theology." Christ's mission embodied the message that the heart of every person on this planet is a priceless gift—think of a diamond or pearl. No matter how tarnished by life experiences and poor choices, at heart, we remain valuable beyond all measure. Who can know such depths? Who can retrieve and restore the priceless treasure of our true selves? This treasure is calculated by Christ's costly sacrifice of love:

> [44]"The kingdom of heaven", Jesus continued, "is like treasure hidden in a field. Someone found it and hid it, and in great delight went off and sold everything he possessed, and bought that field.
>
> [45]"Again, the kingdom of heaven is like a trader who was looking for fine pearls, [46]and who found one that was spectacularly valuable. He went off and sold everything he possessed, and bought it."
>
> (Matt 13:44–46 NTE)

The next time you make eye contact with another human being, look through their eyes to the depths of their heart, to the treasure that is their true self, and then look to the deep joy of Christ's adoring gaze. Leave behind the worm theology that judges another person's deepest heart as deceitful and desperately wicked. Value them as you would a priceless gem—because Jesus did.

Before proceeding to our final exhibit, let's review. The first Christian interpreters established in their hearts the "canon of faith"—the gospel of Jesus Christ—*before* reading, interpreting, or translating the Scriptures. They believed that, apart from that gospel, the Bible could not be understood, much less translated, as inspired Scripture. The gospel formed and affected their translations.

Our first two examples came from Isaiah 53:10, which affects our view of God, and Jeremiah 17:9, which informs our view of humanity. We saw how, while modern translations feature God as taking pleasure in crushing his servant and describe the human heart as incurably wicked, the New Testament authors' favorite translation of the Old Testament (the Septuagint or LXX) rendered these verses much differently. What pleased God? To *cleanse/heal* his servant. How does God view the human heart? Not as impossibly *deceitful* but as wonderfully *deep*.

## WHOSE WRATH?

For Exhibit C, we return to the nature of God and God's relationship with "wrath." We'll compare various versions of Romans 5:9 (as I have done in detail in *A More Christlike God*).

These first three versions translate verse 9 as if the Greek text were saying Jesus's death saves us from God's wrath:

NIV: "Since we have now been justified by his blood, how much more shall we be saved from God's wrath through him!"

ESV: "Since, therefore, we have now been justified by his blood, much more shall we be saved by him from the wrath of God."

NTE: "How much more, in that case—since we have been declared to be in the right by his blood—are we going to be saved by him from God's coming anger! [Oh, even an exclamation mark!]

Clear enough. But wait—is that what the Greek New Testament actually says? In fact, no. The phrase "of God" is not in a single Greek manuscript. Not once.

Here are two other versions that include "the wrath of God" but at least have the decency to admit "of God" is *not* in the Greek manuscripts:

NASB: "Much more then, having now been justified by His blood, we shall be saved from the wrath *of God* [translators' addition] through Him."

NET: "Much more then, because we have now been declared righteous by his blood, we will be saved through him from God's wrath.

[The footnote after the word "wrath" reads, "*Grk* 'the wrath,' referring to God's wrath as v. 10 shows."]

Do you see how the NASB italicized *"of God"*? When a translation
does that, it means the translators have inserted words because they feel it's
implied in the passage. It's *understood*. Understood by whom? In this case,
it reflects the translators' bias.

The NET doesn't italicize "of God," but it does include a footnote
claiming that "of God" is "referring to God's wrath *as v. 10 shows*." Does
verse 10 show that? What does this verse actually say? In this case, despite
their mistaken assumption in verse 9, a careful reading of verse 10 in the
NET reveals the enmity as one-sided:

> For if while we were enemies we were reconciled to God through
> the death of his Son, how much more, since we have been recon-
> ciled, will we be saved by his life?          (Romans 5:10 NET)

It is *we* who were enemies of God, *not* God who was our enemy. It
was *we* who needed to be reconciled to God, *not* God who was reconciled
to us. And it was *our* wrath that God in Christ endured, *not* God's wrath
that was waiting to crush us. Yes, this too is an interpretation, one based
on a closer reading of the text informed by the apostolic and early church
gospel.

Idea! When in doubt, what if we just translate the words Paul actually
used? Thankfully, a few translations are faithful to those parameters in
this verse:

> KJV: "Much more then, being now justified by his blood, we shall
> be saved *from wrath* through him." [My emphasis.]

> YLT: "Much more, then, having been declared righteous now in
> his blood, we shall be saved through him from *the wrath*.

What does God send Christ to save us from? Does God (Jesus) save
us from God (Father)? Think about it, and you'll realize that makes little
sense apart from some naughty indoctrination. Imagine:

+ My neighbor's child offends me somehow.

+ I am so enraged that I cannot forgive him.

+ I send my child over to his house to confront him.

+ My neighbor's child responds by beating up my child.

+ I cannot freely forgive my neighbor's child.

+ Justice demands satisfaction.

+ How are the demands of justice satisfied? Through wrath (literally, violent anger, causing suffering).

+ To what extent? Death. Because all sin warrants death.

+ But I love my neighbor. So does my child. Can't we just forgive him? No. Justice requires his punishment.

+ Solution: My child consents to serve as a substitute who will appease my wrath in his place. I kill him instead. Justice is served.

+ Now I am able to forgive my neighbor's child. Why? Because I punished my child in his/her place.

+ Thus, my son saves my neighbor's child from me.

A caricature? Which line exactly? If it is a distortion of the gospel, then preachers and evangelists should stop preaching this theory of atonement as if it were the gospel. Never mind. Let's return to reality. What's really going on in Romans 5?

"The wrath" we're saved from is not "the wrath of God." Paul knew his Scriptures and the Jewish tradition. That helps. He used the Septuagint in his letters. In that translation, we find a book called "Wisdom of Solomon"—a book in *all* Christian Bibles until the 1500s, when the *sola scriptura* people removed it. Paul engages the Wisdom of Solomon throughout his epistle to the Romans. In Wisdom of Solomon 18, we find a key text for understanding "the wrath":

> [22]So he overcame *the destroyer*, not with strength of body, nor force of arms, but with a word *subdued he him that punished*, alleging the oaths and covenants made with the fathers.
> [23]For when the dead were now fallen down by heaps one upon another, standing between, he *stayed the wrath* and parted the way to the living.                    (Wis 18:22–23 KJV)

What is "the wrath" that Yahweh's servant overcomes? "The wrath" is another name for "the destroyer," who, by the time Wisdom was written, Jews no longer associated with God but with satan. Jesus saves us, but not from his loving Father; he is sent by his Father to save us from *the wrath, the destroyer, satan.*[98]

This translation is more in line with the gospel of Jesus Christ. Wisdom of Solomon predates and prefigures the gospel that Paul preached. And it's more in line with the themes and actual words of Romans 5. Maybe adding words isn't always a great idea after all. Maybe our intrusions into the Bible actually expose theological agendas more than they reveal Paul's meaning.

## THEN WHAT?

When I point out such differences, it can frustrate people because they don't know the original languages and are concerned about which translation to trust. They don't want to be dependent on scholars (we are, anyway, if we're holding an English Bible), but they don't know which versions are most accurate.

Here's the good news! You don't need to know Greek or Hebrew, and you don't need to figure out which translation is most accurate. *What you most need to know is the gospel!* The gospel of Jesus Christ *is* the best way to judge any given translation of any given verse. When you compare translations side by side, *the question is NOT necessarily which one best represents the first manuscripts, but which one best represents the gospel.*

In this chapter, I've compared key verses in various translations. Some renderings felt better to us than others. Why? Because we want the translation that feels best? Perhaps some versions felt better because they resonated with the gospel we've come to know through Jesus by the Spirit. That doesn't matter to all modern translators, but it mattered to the first Christians, and it can matter to you, regardless of the word of supposedly unbiased translators (an oxymoron). Again, what I'm saying is that, for most Bible readers, the best standard for judging a translation is not your linguistic ability or your academic credentials. It is your personal

---

98. See Richard Murray, "'Wrath of God' or 'Works of Satan'?" *Clarion Journal for Religion, Peace & Justice*, August 3, 2016, www.clarion-journal.com/clarion_journal_of_spirit/2016/08/wrath-of-god-or-works-of-satan-richard-murray.html.

knowledge of who Jesus is, the nature of God as he revealed it, and the gospel he preached.

Go with that.

## TOO CLOSE TO EISEGESIS?

A reader asked me, "Brad...is that not getting a little close to *eisegesis?* My personal growth is so dependent on my openness to God revealing things to me about himself and myself that the Bible needs to challenge my well-formed, dysfunctional personal theology."

What a good question. Aren't we in danger of reading our whims and dysfunctions (rather than the gospel) into the text?

So...yes and no, depending on what you mean by *eisegesis. Eisegesis* wrongly defined is "making the Bible say whatever you want it to say." If that were what *eisegesis* actually meant, then I think it's an obvious error.

But to be technical, *eisegesis* is defined as "the process of interpreting a text in such a way as to introduce one's own presuppositions, agendas, or biases. It is commonly referred to as *reading into the text.*"[99]

Even that definition exposes the problem of reading one's own bias into the text. In modernist hermeneutics, we were taught never to do that, as if we could come to the text with no theological presuppositions or assumptions. As if we could interpret it "according to the letter," through the science of hermeneutics, and without the illumination of the Spirit or the lens of the Emmaus Road. As I previously mentioned, I am very skeptical that such a path to interpretation is even possible, much less biblical or spiritual.

We all wear the interpretive lenses of our family of origin, our educational system and training, our race and gender, our national culture or regional subculture, our religious heritage, and our personal temperament and history, including our wounds. These factors color everything we read—perhaps the Bible most of all. And while that presents a challenge, it's not really a "*bad thing*" as long as you are mindful of it. Typically, the

---

99. *Webster's New Collegiate Dictionary*, 8th ed. (1976), s.v. "eisegesis."

critics of *eisegesis* are modernists who deceive themselves with their imaginary objectivity.

The more I read how New Testament authors interpreted the Hebrew Scriptures and how the early Christians instructed disciples how to understand the Bible, the more I regard warnings about subjective reading as a modernist invention that Paul rejects in passages such as 1 Corinthians 2 and 2 Corinthians 3. In these passages, he denies that one can interpret Scripture apart from the Spirit and says that to do so is to read the Bible as the "letter that kills"—that is, as "biblical literalists" in the tradition of Jesus's opponents.

Of course, we should not just read *our own* personal biases back into the text as a way to avoid undergoing its transforming challenges. That's where the reader's question hits the nail on the head.

And yet the New Testament makes it very clear that we *must* make a pre-commitment to *the gospel* if we're to interpret Scripture correctly. The authors (and Christ himself) show us that we have no business interpreting any part of the Bible without reference to Christ and the gospel because the Lamb slain and risen is our hermeneutical key. On the Emmaus Road, Christ said,

> ²⁵"How foolish you are, and how slow to believe all that the prophets have spoken! ²⁶Did not the Messiah have to suffer these things and then enter his glory?" ²⁷And beginning with Moses and all the Prophets, he explained to them what was said in all the Scriptures concerning himself.                        (Luke 24:25–27 NIV)

How does a Christ-follower interpret "Moses, the Prophets, and all the Scriptures"? By asking how they prefigure Christ and his gospel. The point of this chapter, "Gospel, Inspiration, and Translation," is to show how even translation is an *interpretive* process, and to translate without the gospel lens may lead to mistranslation. Translators who pretend they are reading with sterile objectivity are more likely to impose personal biases on the text, as I think the verses we sampled made obvious.

The solution is to admit we have preconceptions, identify them as best we can, and then choose the *Jesus Way* or *Emmaus Way* as our path into the text. Do we read our own biases into the text? YES. Should we? NO.

But we should and must read the gospel *into* the text AND *from* the text, or we risk reducing our Bible to the same dead letter the Pharisees read so fruitlessly.

With these historic Christian premises in mind, we're ready to tackle the problem of "biblical literalism."

### CHAPTER 7

# MUCH ADO ABOUT LITERALISM

"The reason…for the false beliefs and impious or ignorant
assertions about God appears to be nothing else than Scripture
not being understood according to its spiritual sense,
but taken as regarding the bare letter."[100]
—Origen of Alexandria

## "THE BIBLE CLEARLY SAYS…"

*T*he Bible clearly says…." How many times have I heard that phrase
in past years, regularly in polemical tones and aimed against my proclamation that God is Love and that God is revealed perfectly in Jesus Christ?

"The Bible clearly says." Literalism in a nutshell.

Used in that way, "The Bible clearly says" degrades Scripture to blocks
of words stripped of historical and canonical context.

Used in that way, "The Bible clearly says" reads the Bible *literalistically*,
instead of according to its various genres, idioms, and rhetorical devices,

---

100. Origen, *On First Principles: A Reader's Edition*, trans. John Behr (Oxford, UK: Oxford
University Press, 2020), 4.2.2.

and apart from divine or authorial intent. So-called "plain readings" fail to "accurately handle the word of truth."[101]

Worse, "the Bible clearly says" generally strips our reading of the illumination of the Spirit, the gospel of Jesus Christ, and the heart of our heavenly *Abba*. Thus, our life-giving message is reduced to a dead letter.

To be sure, the Bible *does* say some things *very* clearly. Oddly, those very clear statements are frequently negated by the paper cuts of a thousand caveats from, of all people, "the Bible clearly says" camp.

Did that sound grumpy? Now, Jesus doesn't need me to be his next self-assigned defender, but I confess to finding the pastoral and evangelistic damage literalism causes upsetting. The edge comes from seeing Christ thrown under the bus again and again through an agenda-laden, simplistic misuse of our sacred texts...with the ironic claim that this constitutes faithfulness.

David Bentley Hart weighs in,

> ...Fundamentalist literalism is a modern heresy, one that breaks from Christian practice with such violence as to call into question whether those who practice it are still truly obedient to the apostolic faith at all. That is not an accusation, but it is a lament....
>
> ...Not to read the Bible in the proper manner is not to read it as the *Bible* at all; scripture is in-spired, that is, only when read "spiritually."[102]

Hart is no stranger to throwing down the gauntlet. Perhaps "shock value" is an oxymoron, but read on if you're as concerned for biblical faithfulness as I am.

## LITERAL VERSUS LITERALIST

First, let's define our terms: the *literal sense* reads Scripture carefully to discover the author's intent from the words they use and how they use them (including the use of genre, rhetoric, figures of speech, symbols, poetics

---

101. See 2 Timothy 2:15 NASB, BSB.
102. David Bentley Hart in Peter Leithart, "Good God? A Response," *Theopolis Institute*, October 7, 2019, https://theopolisinstitute.com/leithart_post/good-god-a-response. Hart's emphasis.

excess, hyperbole). But *literalism* is generally tied to believing that truth is reduced to actuality, factuality, and historicity, whether or not the human or the divine author intended any such thing. The *literal sense* asks the text what it is doing. Literalism, on the other hand, presupposes, assumes, and presumes to tell you what the text must do and cannot do. The *literal sense* is our launching pad on to the moral (tropological) and spiritual (gospel, typological) reading of the Bible. *Literalism* is often the terminus for what the text has to say and derides further spiritual exploration as "spiritualizing."

## INERRANCY VERSUS AUTHORITY

If you haven't picked up on it yet, the *literal sense* is essential to my reading of the Bible. But I believe that *literalism* and its handmaid, *inerrancy*, sprout from modernist ideology. Claiming a high view of Scripture, literalism actually undermines biblical authority by pre-imposing on the text a standard of sterile uniformity at the expense of:

+ authorial worldview
+ the narrator's role
+ authorial intent (or not)
+ immediate or canonical context
+ verifiable historical truth
+ verifiable scientific truth
+ the polyphony of voices in harmony, dialogue, debate, and travail
+ the authority of Christ as the Word of God over the Scriptures

In short, *biblical literalism* and *inerrancy* predetermine limits on what the Bible cannot do or say before even reading the text or allowing it to speak for itself. The result is an unwitting assault on the authority of Scripture, which itself is subordinate to Christ the Word. Inerrancy, then, is a modernist ideal that stands *over* Scripture (and *over* Christ!), attempting to master the text—to dissect it with the scalpel of *literalism*.

## PERILS OF BIBLICAL DISSECTION

In my mind's eye, I see the vivid image of a young man in a white lab coat, his eyes locked on mine, leaning forward, and sputtering loudly,

"What about the spleen?! What about the spleen?!" Only a small laboratory table creates breathing space between us…not enough to spare me the wayward moisture of his insistence. I really wish he were wearing a mask.

On the table lies a frog in a petri dish, pinned back and spread-eagle, its guts exposed in glorious detail. My nostrils cringe at the assault of wafting formaldehyde vapors. Our amateur biologist wields the scalpel—poking, poking, poking at the mince that had recently been a recognizable and attached organ—and continues to press, "What do you do with the spleen?!"

And I'm puzzled about what to say. Pinning down, slicing open, and dismembering this fascinating creature seemed a grotesque way to understand its essence. Its breath evacuated, the glistening skin now dull, the frog-song silenced forever. Never again to catch a fly, to hop away, or to reproduce tadpoles. That's one mutilated amphibian! And now, the spleen removed and mashed, I'm being interrogated on the meaning of a maimed fragment of rotting tissue. As if a dogma could be derived and developed from death and dismemberment.

I snap out of the unpleasant vision into an equally sour surreality. Before me, with Bible flayed and splayed wide, a young theologue is barking at me—his index finger jabbing testily at the page. "What do you do with this verse?! How do you explain this?!" He wants me to see how terrifically *biblical* he's being. How so thoroughly he's refuting me with his holy surgical blade. Yet, somehow, the smell of Moroccan leather bears the death-taint of formalin, and the verse he's dissected looks like mangled pâté. Previously, I'd have drowned under such waves of certitude, exegesis having devolved into an ugly execution. Now, I pray, "Lord Jesus Christ, have mercy on me. I thought your words bring life. Can these bones yet live?"

Then, suddenly, gloriously, a sign and a wonder! Like Christ from the tomb, conquering death…a loud croak resounds. There in the hands of our young firebrand, the Scripture transmogrifies before my eyes—and with a broad, wry grin, springs from his grasp and escapes free…spleen and all! Happy day!

These are the perils of biblicist dissection. We become too dull to perceive the Spirit of God breathing through the text. We lose our sense of what the book is doing, and we can't hear what Christ is saying. Inerrancy attempts to pin Scripture down to a flattened univocality (uniform voice), deadening its polyphonic contours. Biblicism of this sort reduces a living voice into a lifeless corpse—the very indictment Christ brought against the scribes of his day.

## PREDETERMINED SYSTEMS

This kind of scribal biblicism is also invariably fused to our preloaded theological systems. To be fair, as I wrote earlier, we all bring assumptions to the text, but when our doctrinal biases are reified into a system that the text must *inerrantly* affirm, our pet theology becomes our real final authority. Thus, any Scripture that does not agree with my system must either be ignored, twisted, or subordinated while other texts are privileged.

Let's face it, we all read the Bible that way. Indeed, reading Scripture *as Scripture* actually requires a predisposition, rooted not in our personal temperament or our theological structures, but in Christ and his gospel. But the stubborn fact is that inherited doctrinal traditions function as powerful lenses that may clarify or distort our Bible reading. And pretending we read the "plain text" without them is a fool's errand.

For example, I inherited an eschatology (end-times system) that presupposed an end to history when Christ would divide all people into two groups—the sheep (the elect of God) and the goats (the damned)—and send them to their respective eternal destinies: heavenly paradise or everlasting torment (the lake of fire). We established a set of proof texts that affirmed our theology and claimed they were *inerrant, infallible,* and to be read *literally.* The passages that affirmed our eschatology were, in our minds, *literally* true beyond question, and therefore authoritative. But the truth is that our real authority—our own assumptions—were carved in stone before we cracked open the leather cover. I know this for a fact by the way we treated passages that didn't fit: we willfully ignored or spun them, or found ways to demote them.

So, with our literalist reading of Revelation's "lake of fire" already embedded as dogma, how could we authentically hear Paul when he says, "As in Adam, *all people* die; so in Christ, *all people* shall be made alive,"[103]

---

103. See 1 Corinthians 15:22.

or "God consigned *all people* to disobedience so he could have mercy on *all people*"?[104]

Overlooking Paul's understanding, intent, and argument, we began with what he *can't* mean. Namely, he *can't* possibly mean what he actually said. So, here we have Revelation's apparently *infernal exclusion* head-to-head against two obviously *universal inclusion* verses...but because we believed the Bible is *inerrant*, we knew the two authors could not possibly be in conflict or contradiction. We must force them to agree. How? With our own eschatology, of course.

So, Paul's straightforward and all-inclusive statements were violently retrofitted to undergird our infernalist[105] system. Ideologically, Paul's words *must* be true. Theologically, they simply *can't* mean what they say. When Paul says "all," he must really mean "all of the elect" or "all believers." There. That works. "It's understood." Is it?

This example is especially remarkable given that it's hard to imagine Paul making a stronger case for inclusion than he does. What more could he have possibly said? Yet his rhetorical argument was all but swept away by my *literalist* interpretation of Revelation's figurative genre. At this point, the claim of *inerrancy* was employed to violate the Bible's authority in the service of my end-times dogmatism. And maybe that's *all* inerrancy ever really meant in practice.

Of course, one's theological bias may also simply reverse these texts, using Paul as the *inerrant* standard while ignoring John's dire visions, rendering the warnings vacuous. The problem is *not* the Bible's diversity of genres, doctrines, or points of view. The issue is the way *inerrancy* subsumes these and is used to squeeze the Bible into our narrow theological models.

My takeaway is that theological *inerrancy* comes at a very high price: at the expense of inspiration and authority. Ultimately, the problem was exacerbated by biblicism's modernist method of reading, the scalpel we call *literalism*—the same crass, letter-of-the law, puddle-shallow approach that Christ and Paul confronted in their opponents. We just didn't realize they were correcting us.

---

104. See Romans 11:32.
105. "Infernalism" is the dogmatic declaration that eternal conscious torment is an essential of the gospel.

## INERRANTIST LITERALISM

As a modern *inerrantist*, I used the word "literal" obsessively and sloppily. But I used it *a lot*. I distorted its meaning and mistook what the early church meant by "literal."

Remember, I had been taught directly and repeatedly that a *literal* interpretation of the Bible meant that we *must* interpret the words, phrases, and figures of Scripture *literally* except when to do so was impossible—even in genres laden with figurative language. We confused the words "literal" (the *way* words refer to things) with "actual" (the *things* the words refer to). N. T. Wright says,

> The word *literal*, like the word *metaphorical*,…refers to the way that words refer to things, whereas what we often *mean* is the distinction between concrete and abstract—concrete being something definite, physical, substantial, abstract being like an idea.

> Now you can refer metaphorically to something concrete. If I call my car "the old tin can," that's a metaphorical reference…. Or you can refer *literally* to something abstract….

> So, when we say, "Is Genesis to be taken literally?"…that doesn't settle ahead of time the question of what it actually refers to. And when we are reading any text, it ought to be an open question: What does this text intend to refer to, and *how* does it intend to refer to it?

Wright contrasts the difference between parables, which we read as metaphors (we don't ask, "Where is this farm? How do I go there?" of the prodigal son), and actual events such as the resurrection (which the Gospel authors meant as more than a subtle metaphor). He continues,

> When Jesus himself tells a parable, the point is not that this actually happened somewhere and we're drawing lessons from it. The point is this is a cheerfully fictitious story, but often, the real meaning remains concrete…. "If *you've* got a poor man covered in sores by *your* gate, you ought to be looking after him."[106]

---

106. N. T. Wright, "A Conversation with N. T. Wright: What Do You Mean by 'Literal'?" interview by Dr. Peter Enns, The BioLogos Foundation, September 8, 2010, video, 4:29, https://youtu.be/fxQpFosrTUk.

As a young *literalist*, I confused these categories all the time. Worse, my practice was also arbitrary. I knew the Psalms are poetic and Revelation is apocalyptic, but I only read their words poetically or figuratively when I couldn't do otherwise. Again, I knew that trees don't actually "clap their hands" and that Christ doesn't actually have seven horns.[107]

At the same time, I regarded *Sheol* as an *actual* place where the dead were in *actual* torment, but *not actually* "under the earth." I regarded the "lake of fire" as an *actual place* with *actual flames* that would *actually* torment its inhabitants forever and ever, but I guessed it wasn't an *actual* lake I could find on a map under the earth.

My brand of literalism *did* attend quite carefully to the words and grammar of Scripture; we nodded to historical context and even allowed for a very constricted attention to genres. But when we created our own straitjacket that claimed, "If you can take it literally, you must...," then even the visions and dreams of mythic and apocalyptic literature had to be literalized. Actual lions would "literally" become vegetarians. Demonic locusts from the pit were concretized into Apache helicopters. And the lake of fire was envisioned as eternal conscious torment.

Similarly, when I read Genesis, I reasoned that if the Bible says the universe was created in six days, well, days means *actual* twenty-four-hour periods, right?

And if Adam and Eve were our historical proto-parents, then Cain and his surviving brother were made to be the incestuous fathers of all people (with imaginary sisters and inexplicable already-populated cities).

And if the Bible says Noah's floodwaters "covered the face of the earth," it meant the entire globe, immersing Mount Everest, right? *Literally.* Er—*actually.*

And if the Bible said God commanded the genocide of every last Amalekite, then he did, right? *Literally. Actually?*

For me, these couldn't be "*just stories.*" My biblicism demanded these stories were *literal* in the sense that you'd need to be able to record them on your smartphone. *If* they didn't happen *that way*, then the Bible's not true, and if you say they didn't happen *that way*, you're attacking the Bible.

---

107. See Isaiah 55:12; Revelation 5:6.

That's *inerrant literalism* as it stands today. And any Scriptures that challenge these theological commitments are an inconvenience we overlook. When the authors or characters go off-script—when Jesus frequently colors outside the lines—we could no longer even see it.

Like its modernist liberal counterpart, biblical literalism often ignores or negates the necessity of illumination by the Spirit, prayerful discernment, and obedient action as conditions for understanding Scripture. It replaces moral or spiritual readings with a scientific formula every bit as secular as the world it tries to escape. But, worst of all, a literalist reading of Scripture depicts God as a moral monster, capable of constructing, committing, and commanding evils that violate any healthy human conscience. But it hasn't always been this way. There was a richer, deeper, *literal* sense in the early church—one that didn't lead to crass caricatures of our loving God.

## PATRISTIC LITERAL SENSE

Please notice that I am not slagging a "literal" reading of the text. I'm resisting the modern "literal-*ism*" that misdefines the term and then crowns it king of hermeneutical faithfulness. On the other hand, the early church did teach us the initial and essential layer of reading what they called the "literal sense." I affirm it wholeheartedly. What they meant was the following:

+ We so honor the words of Scripture that our *first* order of business is to determine what the text meant to the human author when he wrote it. We might also call this the historical sense.

+ We so honor the words of Scripture that we rely on scholars to gather the very best manuscripts and do the hard work of textual criticism to ensure that we are reading the most accurate sources.

+ We so honor the words of Scripture that we rely on translators to do their very best at transposing ancient and foreign words and expressions to cross great linguistic, cultural, and temporal distances into our languages and cultures so that we can hear what they said and meant.

- ✦ We so honor the words and phrases of Scripture that we pay careful attention to their shifting historical meanings, and we examine their grammar and syntax carefully to see how the words are put together.

- ✦ We so honor the words of Scripture that we work hard to read them in their literary context (i.e., the genres, rhetorical devices, and idioms in which the words are embedded).

This kind of literal reading, practiced by the early church, is dependent on teachers who know foreign terms, grammatical rules, and stylistic idiosyncrasies, and how to translate these while losing as little in verbal and cultural translation as possible. These experts (or teams of experts) depend upon linguists and grammarians in Hebrew, Aramaic, Greek, and the target language (e.g., English), as well as competent historians and sociologists. Without them, you don't have an English Bible. Or Hebrew or Greek editions, either, for that matter. And that's just at the first and literal/literary stage. We're not done yet.

Further readings will require much more than that, since the Scriptures claim the necessity of illumination by the Spirit and the gospel of Jesus to remove veils over our hearts and eyes that would otherwise obscure God's message.

The best and most influential Bible commentators among the early church fathers believed their Scriptures needed to be interpreted *literally*, *morally*, and *spiritually*. But the literal sense they described breathed far more deeply and demanded much more than the literal-*ists* of modern-*ist* Evangelical-*ism*. The three-fold stack of -isms in that last phrase is no accident. As I've said, literalism today is an ideology that frequently trumps any truly moral or spiritual reading and, indeed, exerts a formulaic mastery over the text that is observably little more than an autopsy—its exegesis a coroner's report.

The literal sense of the ancient church was wiser and more careful than the literalism I see today. When opened out into its moral and spiritual senses, the message of Scripture was consistently more *beautiful*—more poetic, the stuff and source of hymns.

Specifically, the literal sense of Origen, Gregory the Theologian, and Basil the Great expands on the following features:

+ Textual criticism
+ Genre analysis
+ Lexical exegesis

Briefly, **textual criticism** involved gathering every manuscript available, then compiling and comparing them in order to determine and engage the most accurate source material possible. Today, textual critics continue to update this important work, continually discovering new manuscripts and distilling them into the Hebrew and Greek collections from which commentators and translators work.

Second, **genre analysis** meant taking seriously the genres of Scripture, including myth, poetry, history, prophetic visions, apocalyptic dreams, Gospels, parables, epistles, and so forth. For the church fathers, the literal sense of myth or poetry or apocalyptic literature was decidedly *not* to "take it literally," but rather to read myth as myth, poetry as poetry, symbols as symbols, and fiction as fiction.

That's right: the true literal sense even included distinguishing which texts were non-fiction and which were fiction. And to read fiction literally (not literalistically) is to identify and read it *as fiction* to discern its intended meaning and affirm that meaning as *true*.

Modernist literalism cannot seem to grasp this idea. It constantly stumbles into thinking that if a text (such as Genesis 2, Job, or Jonah) is not accepted as factual history, then it isn't true. But consider this: is the parable of the prodigal son not profoundly true? Is Christ's story of the good Samaritan not supremely true? Or must it pass the literalist "camera" test? Do we really believe that if you couldn't take a photograph of a seven-day creation, global flood, or man-eating fish, then the stories mean nothing, and God is not our Creator? And worse, if we were to discover that these stories were mythical, poetic, or fictional, need we leap to the counterfactual corollary that Jesus never existed or that his resurrection itself is doubtful? Seriously?

Well, it wasn't so for the fathers, and it isn't for me anymore. They could read genres for what they were. They were able to say, "No, serpents don't actually talk, trees won't actually clap their hands, rocks won't actually sing, the sun doesn't actually rise, and God doesn't actually have temper tantrums."

BUT, of course Christ rose from the dead! The resurrection is not presented as Homeric myth or poetic embellishment. The resurrection accounts present four theological perspectives reflecting on the eyewitness testimonies of first-century people. That's the genre we call the Gospels.

## RESTORING THE LITERAL SENSE TODAY

Finally, the fathers considered *lexical exegesis* to be an important aspect of the literal sense. In other words, they took very seriously the layered meaning of words and the grammatical shape of the Hebrew, Aramaic, and Greek sentences they worked with. They believed the meaning of the Scriptures was found within the actual words in its pages. The textual key is found *in* the text, not in the ever-shifting sands of speculative reconstruction contrived by biblical historians.

Today, we continue to upgrade our understanding of the literal sense, rightly understood. We've relearned how the four Gospels are more than objective historical biographies. They are theologically shaped and faith-biased reflections on the meaning of this very real life of Jesus of Nazareth.

We've learned that the Epistles are more than propositional teachings and ethical letters. Ben Witherington III and David deSilva have helped us to see these New Testament Epistles as sermons, written to be preached and crafted by masters of first-century rhetoric.[108]

We've learned to pay close attention to every stage of the Bible's composition and development. Scholars across disciplines examine:

+ The events described

+ Theological reflections about those events

+ The distillation of the tradition through oral tradition

+ The development of manuscripts (through human authors, scribes, and narrators)

---

108. I talk further about their approaches in chapter 16, "No Empty Rhetoric: Parental Love and Frightening Warnings," and chapter 17, "The Diatribe Dilemma."

+ The redaction of texts through editorial geniuses
+ The collection of the texts for use in the worshipping community
+ The canonization of texts in alignment with the canon of faith

We've learned the complexity of a many-layered biblical context. We study:

+ Originating events and first hearers
+ Developing documents and their first readers (often much later than the events)
+ The big picture: where and how each part fits into the drama of redemption
+ Canonical context: how a passage fits within a particular book and in the larger collection of books
+ Liturgical context: how and when the text is used liturgically
+ Contemporary culture: how canonical authority speaks to every generation
+ Contemporary devotion: how the Spirit speaks to contexts

All of this and more speaks to the revival of the ancient *literal* sense—the "first reading"—as over against modern "clearly says" literal-*ism*. Yes, there's much ado about literalism, but we just can't ignore how dramatically modernists have departed from the ancient literal sense, and the havoc they've created for Bible readers trying to faithfully interpret the sacred text.

For the past two decades, I've been playing catch-up, and I am still just scratching the surface. I've been immersing myself in those fathers who taught us how to read the Bible as Scripture and as gospel—perceiving Christ in Moses and the Prophets by the illumination of the Spirit and the example of the apostles and their successors. Said another way, I'm rediscovering the *Road to Emmaus*. Let's head there now.

### CHAPTER 8

# EMMAUS FOUND:
# A MORE CHRISTLIKE BIBLE

"If I find in Moses and the prophets the sense of Christ, then I do not
speak according to my own heart but according to the Holy Spirit."
—Origen of Alexandria[109]

*M*y childhood was filled with many wonders. From the time I was
in elementary school, I was enthralled by the beauty of scientific discovery
in the fields of astronomy, biology, geology, paleontology, and archaeology,
to name a few. Ten years before Indiana Jones burst onto the big screen, I
was digging up the corner of my parents' backyard with a spade, sifting the
soil for fragments of bone and unusual stones. That my parents let me do
that was pretty cool.

I still love that stuff and scan my news apps for science articles each
morning. I still thrill in new finds by archaeologists sorting through the
ancient rubble of the Bible lands.

---

109. Origen, "Homilies on Ezekiel," 2.2, in *Ezekiel, Daniel*, Ancient Christian Commentary
on Scripture, Old Testament, vol. 13, ed. Thomas C. Oden (Downers Grove, IL: IVP,
2008), 45.

Imagine, then, my sense of joy and unearned cleverness when, just as I was discovering metaphorical Emmaus, I learned that scientists might have unearthed the historical town of Emmaus! (Metaphorical Emmaus? More about that shortly.) The article began:

> Archaeologists have uncovered the massive walls of a 2,200-year-old Hellenistic fortification [at Kiriath Yearim] that may have been built by the Seleucid general who defeated Judah the Maccabee, the famed Jewish leader at the center of the Hanukkah story. In an unexpected twist, the discovery could also help identify the location of the biblical town of Emmaus, where the Gospels say Jesus made his first appearance after being crucified and resurrected.[110]

This archeological discovery has exciting possibilities, but what of metaphorical Emmaus? Let me tell you! We'll start with the gospel story—Jesus's *second* resurrection appearance. (The article is wrong: remember that Mary Magdalene met Christ first. Sorry, I couldn't let that slide.)

In Luke 24, we find two disciples on the seven-mile trek from Jerusalem to Emmaus. It's Resurrection Sunday, and the risen Christ appears to them, but, for whatever reason, they don't recognize him. Despite the eyewitness reports of the myrrh-bearing women, these guys are still rattled by grief and bewilderment over Jesus's death. Hear their disillusionment: "But we were hoping that he was going to redeem Israel!" (Luke 24:21 NTE). They don't get it.

Jesus teases out details of the weekend before dropping this stinger:

> [25] "You are so senseless!" he said to them. "So slow in your hearts to believe all the things the prophets said to you! Don't you see? [26]This is what had to happen: the Messiah had to suffer, and then come into his glory!"
> [27]So he began with Moses, and with all the prophets, and explained to them the things about himself throughout the whole Bible. (Luke 24:25–27 NTE)

110. Ariel David, "Israeli Archaeologists May Have Found Emmaus, Where Jesus Appeared After Crucifixion," *Haaretz*, September 3, 2019, https://www.haaretz.com/israel-news/.premium.MAGAZINE-israeli-archaeologists-may-have-found-emmaus-where-jesus-appeared-after-crucifixion-1.7774167.

This passage used to frustrate me, not because Jesus seems a bit gruff, but because, although he shows the two disciples how to find Christ throughout the whole of Scripture, what he says isn't recorded for us, the readers. These disciples were treated to a lesson in hermeneutics that I had never been taught.

Sure, I could see Christ in a bunch of obvious messianic prophecies, maybe even dozens. But, in my religious background and training, I had been dissuaded from looking for "types and antitypes" unless the New Testament specifically named them. It was obvious to me that we were nowhere near seeing Christ in "Moses" and "*all* the prophets" throughout "*the whole* Bible." I was also aware that whatever unrecorded words Jesus relayed on the road to Emmaus, they did not fit into the historical-grammatical-literal approach (i.e., literalism) of my education. Frankly, I felt ripped off.

Even when others ventured into the "types and antitypes" territory, my dispensationalist teachers cautioned against accepting their method of "spiritualizing" the text or "allegorizing" the stories. Yet, for all the grief I think my former Calvinism deserves, I must say that John Calvin and his Christian Reformed progeny had no such fears. Somehow, they felt free to preach the Old Testament stories as allegories of the gospel. Scholar Ben Myers has proposed that John Calvin did it best! So, what was the difference that gave them that freedom but repelled my fellow Evangelicals? I suspect we were looking to tether our interpretation to literalist dispensationalism, while they anchored theirs in their famous "covenant theology." In other words, for us, each dispensation of salvation history was self-contained. For them, *all the covenants pointed to Christ.*

I would have paid lip service to that idea, but it was not until I dove into commentaries and homilies of the early church fathers that I started to see how it works. Somehow, their bold, Christ-centered interpretations convinced me to go to the source himself. Why not follow our Master Rabbi's example—if not on the way to Emmaus, where else? Our Lord's use of the book of Jonah provides a perfect test case.

## THE SIGN OF JONAH

Earlier, I explained that Origen's first layer of reading was a profound commitment to the *literal sense* of Scripture—the words, sentences, grammar, and genres of the manuscripts before him. I tried to show how the first Christians' literal sense was decidedly not *literalism*. Origen included within his literal sense the need to discern and distinguish (1) *actual history* from (2) *fictitious history* (when we can) composed by the Spirit to communicate *more-than-literal* truth. In either case, the message the story conveys is *true*.

A literal reading of Jonah, for example, does not depend on finding a fish big enough to swallow a man, or discovering when in history Nineveh actually repented, if ever. Rather, the literal reading of Jonah asks what truth the author of this strange story meant to convey. The scandalous prophetic message of the book is that God's mercy extends to all, even the tyrannical Ninevites, the same evildoers who are condemned in the book of Nahum! The punchline in Jonah's book comes from the mouth of God:

> And should I not have concern for the great city of Nineveh, in which there are more than a hundred and twenty thousand people who cannot tell their right hand from their left—and also many animals?                                     (Jonah 4:11 NIV)

That covers the *literal* meaning of the story. The message of Jonah is *true* whether the story of Jonah is historical fact or moral fiction. But we're not done at this point. Really, we've hardly begun! We now proceed through two more senses of the text: the *moral* and the *spiritual*.

For simplicity's sake, I will follow the Cappadocian fathers who adopted Origen's threefold model of a literal, moral, and spiritual sense, as described in his *Philocalia*. In the Latin West, from Augustine's *On Christian Doctrine* through Thomas Aquinas's *Summa Theologica* and into the *Catechism of the Catholic Church* (CCC, 115–118), scholastic minds developed a fourfold hermeneutic.

> 115. According to an ancient tradition, one can distinguish between two senses of Scripture: the literal and the spiritual, the latter being subdivided into the allegorical, moral, and anagogical senses. The profound concordance of the four senses guarantees all its richness to the living reading of Scripture in the church.

116. The literal sense is the meaning conveyed by the words of Scripture and discovered by exegesis, following the rules of sound interpretation: "All other senses of Sacred Scripture are based on the literal." [St. Thomas Aquinas, S Th I, 1, 10, ad I.]

117. The spiritual sense. Thanks to the unity of God's plan, not only the text of Scripture but also the realities and events about which it speaks can be signs.

1. The allegorical sense. We can acquire a more profound understanding of events by recognizing their significance in Christ; thus, the crossing of the Red Sea is a sign or type of Christ's victory and also of Christian Baptism.

2. The moral sense. The events reported in Scripture ought to lead us to act justly. As St. Paul says, they were written "for our instruction."

3. The anagogical sense (Greek: anagoge, "leading"). We can view realities and events in terms of their eternal significance, leading us toward our true homeland: thus the Church on earth is a sign of the heavenly Jerusalem.

118. A medieval couplet summarizes the significance of the four senses:

The Letter speaks of deeds; Allegory to faith;
The Moral how to act; Anagogy our destiny.
[Lettera gesta docet, quid credas allegoria, moralis quid agas, quo tendas anagogia.][111]

Origen used the analogy of a body, soul, and spirit. If the body of Scripture is its *literal* sense, then the soul is the *moral* sense and the spirit is the *spiritual* or mystical sense.

---

111. "III. The Holy Spirit, Interpreter of Scripture," Catechism of the Catholic Church, Latin text (c) Libreria Editrice Vaticana, Citta del Vaticano 1993, http://www.vatican.va/archive/ENG0015/__PQ.HTM.

## MORAL READING (DISCIPLESHIP SENSE)

The truly *literal* work provides a foundation for its moral and spiritual reading. By *moral reading*, I'm not merely speaking of "the moral of the story" or, worse, to the toxic purity codes of fundamentalism. Rather, a *moral* reading of the text asks this question of any given Scripture: *"How will this passage nourish my growth as a follower of Jesus Christ?* That is, *"How will it transform me so that the truth of my being (the image of Christ) becomes the way of my being (the likeness of Christ)?"* The *moral* meaning, then, is also *tropological* (it transforms the will) and *existential* (it addresses my real-life dilemmas).

Using the book of Jonah as an example, the moral meaning is overt: don't be like Jonah, whose xenophobia blinded him to *the other*.[112] We're called to humanize those whom we have previously demonized, to see God's heart of compassion for them, and to invite them to reorient their lives toward the Light.

And talk about relevance for today! For example, the Veggie Tales animated movie about Jonah delivered the moral meaning of that ancient book to our culture just when we needed it most. The 9/11 attacks had just occurred, and the neoconservative administration was clamoring for a misdirected invasion of Iraq (where Nineveh was once situated). The Jonah movie was released in 2002, calling us to rethink our us/them hostility and to humanize those we'd labeled "enemy." Of all people, you would hope Christians would remember Jonah's moral message and show restraint. Alas, through contrived evidence of nonexistent weapons of mass destruction (WMDs), a coalition of Western nations entered and shattered that nation, demonstrating that we not only failed to perceive Jonah's moral point but had also so hardened our hearts as to become the new Nineveh.

The *moral* sense follows 2 Timothy 3:16–17, affirming that since the Old Testament is regarded and received as Christian Scripture, then it must be useful to Christians. This isn't merely about using the message of Jonah to moralize. Rather, sound interpretation demands that we discern how to *preach it* as the gospel (good news) message to modern Ninevites

---

112. "The other" is a sociological term that refers to people, groups, or cultures who have been marginalized, excluded, or demonized. "Othering" describes ways that the in-group does this. "De-othering" is essentially including *the other* as Jesus did.

and how *to use* it to develop (instruct, correct, equip) would-be Jonahs into growing Christian disciples.

While the story of Jonah is easy pickings for a moral message, early Christians scoured *all* of Scripture for the inspired message that would profit believers with encouragement, correction, and instruction in Christian righteousness (i.e., loving God and neighbor). As I wrote previously, in 1 Corinthians 10:1–10, Paul explains how, more often than not, the lessons we find in Scripture are cautionary tales of what *not* to do and how paths *other* than the *Jesus Way* harm others and ourselves. The traumatic training offered in the Bible's R-rated material should not be read as the threats of a violent deity but as the loving (and dramatically memorable) warnings of a good Father in good faith. The people of God made countless missteps that become vivid moral lessons for avoiding landmines. God wastes nothing.

This limits our use of Old Testament "toxic texts" to what can be applied to Christ-centered gospel preaching and Christlike exhortation. For example, because of Jesus's instructions on loving, forgiving, blessing, and praying for our enemies, and his explicit rejection of retaliation, vengeance, and violence, we must never use a text where the Philistines are slaughtered to call for the slaughter of "infidels." Rather, we might see how they foreshadow Christ's victory over the nonhuman enemies of satan, sin, and death, and our personal battles with the spirit of pride, malice, and other un-Christlike attitudes within ourselves. Clear?

And yet we're still not done reading. We have not yet gotten to the heart of the matter. On to the *spiritual* reading that renders the *gospel* sense of the Scriptures.

## THE SPIRITUAL READING (GOSPEL SENSE)

The *spiritual*[113] reading follows Jesus's promise and example that the whole of "Moses and the Prophets and all the Scriptures" anticipate Christ, his gospel, his suffering and death, and his resurrection and reign. The *literal* sense invoked the *spiritual* sense, meaning that a careful literary

---

113. The spiritual reading is also sometimes referred to as the mystical reading (when focused on our inner transformation) or the typological reading (when focused on the incarnation).

reading of the words in the context of their genres would bear the good and necessary fruit of seeing Jesus there.

In Galatians, Paul models this type of reading and calls it *allegory*—a virtual swear word to the literalists. I feel embarrassed when I remember the disdain with which I used to describe those who "spiritualized" and "allegorized" the Bible. Not just because I chose an anemic interpretive system, but also because I closed my heart to the way Christ and his apostles read the whole Scriptures *as gospel*.

Fr. John Behr, whom I have quoted previously in this book, is one of our foremost patristic scholars, and he says, "If you aren't reading the Old Testament allegorically, you're not reading it as Scripture!" This comment is shorthand for what we have just been discussing:

- The whole of the Old Testament points to Christ and his gospel, according to Jesus on the road to Emmaus.
- To read the Old Testament *as Scripture* is to read it as a revelation of the gospel.
- To read the Old Testament Scriptures as a revelation of Christ requires reading them allegorically. To not do so is to not read them as Christian Scripture.

Strong words, but also liberating and hope-filled, because they could just lead us back to an *apostolic reading* that retrieves and amplifies the Emmaus-Road experience.

To advance from the literal sense to the spiritual sense of Scripture is not actually "spiritualizing," if that means making concrete stories ethereal or reducing historical facts to theological analogies. Neither is it "lifting the veil" to see something else. Rather, apostolic preaching regarded the Law, the Prophets, and salvation history as shadows cast by and unveiled in the incarnation of Jesus Christ—ultimate Reality—moving from the shifting sands of history to the solid Rock or, better, to the living flesh of Christ crucified, risen, and ascended.[114] Thus, to read Scripture in its spiritual sense is, in fact, to read it as the cruciform gospel.

---

114. Yet...as my friend Fr. Kenneth Tanner says, this is no escape from the material world of history, but rather its transfiguration and exaltation by a cross that brings resurrection.

Again, this *spiritual* or *allegorical* sense ultimately argues that all Scripture points to Jesus Christ and his gospel, or we are misinterpreting and misusing it. How might any given Old Testament text point to Christ and his gospel? Let's consider Jesus's use of Jonah! In Jesus's view, the story is a *sign* (σημεῖον) pointing to his resurrection. There, the Emmaus principle is already at work:

> ³⁸ Then some of the Pharisees and teachers of the law said to [Jesus], "Teacher, we want to *see a sign* from you."
> ³⁹ He answered, "A wicked and adulterous generation asks for a sign! But none will be given it except *the sign of the prophet Jonah*.
> ⁴⁰ For as Jonah was three days and three nights in the belly of a huge fish, so the Son of Man will be three days and three nights in the heart of the earth. ⁴¹ The men of Nineveh will stand up at the judgment with this generation and condemn it; for they repented at the preaching of Jonah, and now something greater than Jonah is here."                                    (Matt 12:38–41 NIV)

Jesus's *Emmaus Way* of reading Jonah looked beyond the literal and moral sense to the gospel sense, where Jonah's time in the belly of the fish and his escape from it would prefigure Christ's death and resurrection. Remarkable! Isn't that a bit of a stretch? Not if you read the Jonah passage carefully. And the ironic thing is that Jesus makes his case by reading literally the poetic prayer of Jonah from the fish! Behold (from the Septuagint):

> ¹Now the Lord commanded a huge sea creature to swallow Jonah, and Jonah was in the belly of the sea creature three days and three nights.
> ²And from the belly of the sea creature Jonah prayed to the Lord his God,
> ³and said:
>> "I cried out in my affliction to the Lord, my God,
>> And He heard my voice;
>> *Out of the belly of Hades*, You heard the cry of my voice.
>> ⁴You cast me into the depths of the heart of the sea,
>> And rivers encompassed me;
>> All Your surging waters and Your waves passed over me.

⁵And I said, 'I have been driven away from Your sight;
Shall I again look with favor toward Your holy temple?'
⁶Water is poured over me to my soul;
The lowest depth encircled me;
*My head plunged into the clefts of the mountains.*
⁷*I descended into the earth,*
*The bars of which are everlasting barriers;*
*Yet let my life ascend from corruption, O Lord, my God.*
⁸When my soul was failing from me, I remembered the Lord.
May my prayer be brought to You, into Your holy temple.
⁹Those who follow vanity and lies forsake their own mercy.
¹⁰But with a voice of thanksgiving and praise,
I will sacrifice to You.
As much as I vowed, I shall offer up to You,
To You, *the Lord of Deliverance.*"
¹¹*Then the Lord commanded the sea creature, and it cast up Jonah onto the dry land.*                                         (Jonah 2:1–11 LXX)

Do you see what Jesus did there? He allegorized the story to prefigure his death and resurrection by a careful, literal reading of the words in the scroll. You can see how the message was embedded there from the beginning but could not be perceived until Jesus unveiled it.

What I'm saying is that the early masters of Scripture such as Origen in the East and Jerome in the West were simply following Jesus's own hermeneutic and training us to emulate our Master-Teacher. And while literalists are skittish of allegory, Jesus makes it necessary for an *Emmaus-Way* interpretation. Contrary to my training, early church fathers didn't come up with allegorical interpretation—Jesus and his apostolic successors were already adept at using and modeling it to unveil the gospel.

## PAUL AND ALLEGORY

While the authors of the New Testament frequently speak allegorically, "allegory" is explicitly named by Paul only in Galatians 4:

²¹Tell me, you who want to be under Law, do you not listen to the Law? ²²For it has been written that Abraham had two sons, one

from the maidservant and one from the freewoman. [23]But [indeed] the one from the maidservant was born according to the flesh, and the one from the freewoman through the promise. [24]*These things are told allegorically*; for these are two covenants—the one from Mount Sinai, giving birth for slavery, is Hagar. [25]And this Hagar is Mount Sinai in Arabia, and corresponds to present-day Jerusalem, for she slaves along with her children. [26]But the Jerusalem above, who is our mother, is free.... (Gal 4:21–31 DBH)

In a striking irony, Paul appears to be "trolling" the Judaizers who think Gentiles aren't full Christians by identifying them with the slave woman Hagar and associating the Gentiles who have been freed through the gospel with Sarah. The key phrase for our purposes is in verse 24.

Some translations treat Paul's words subjectively—as if we're to *read* it allegorically (which is allowed):

+ "These things are being *taken* figuratively" (NIV).

+ "*Treat* this as picture-language" (NTE).

But the passage actually may go further, claiming that these accounts were *told* or *spoken* allegorically:

+ "These things are *told* allegorically" (DBH).

+ "This is allegorically *speaking*" (NASB).

David Bentley Hart, whose translation (DBH) you see above, explains,

...one should not assume that Paul does not mean precisely what he says and does not take the tale to be essentially (not merely secondarily) allegorical. His interpretive habits are rarely literalist.[115]

That is, Hart does not see Paul's *Emmaus Way* of reading the story as *eisegesis*. Paul is not merely reading the gospel back into the text or overlaying the gospel onto the history. Rather, Paul's use of ἀλληγορούμενα (allegorizing) implies that the text itself *is written* as allegory and that a gospel reading unveils a truth already there!

Origen saw this and wanted to train his students to see it too. His heart was to faithfully use the Bible to proclaim Christ. But he was also

---

115. David Bentley Hart, *The New Testament: A Translation* (Yale University Press), 376n1.

engaged in a battle to preserve the Scriptures from the Marcionite heresy, which employed literalism to justify dumping much of the Bible altogether.

The same thing happens today. Many disillusioned Christians, embittered ex-Evangelicals, and haughty New Atheists denigrate the Bible in the easiest possible way: they continue to read it as fundamentalist literalists—then use their misinterpretation of the sacred Scriptures against it as ammunition. Well, at least they're reading it. But are they?

If we want to move past that shallow discourse, we must remember that, for Christ and in Christ, the entire Bible is a Christian book. In Christ it lives and moves and has its being.[116] Therefore, our task is to always pursue and determine a Christ-centered reading of it.

> *Did not the Messiah have to suffer these things and then enter his glory?... Everything must be fulfilled that is written about me in the Law of Moses, the Prophets, and the Psalms.* (Luke 24:26, 44 NIV)

---

116. See Acts 17:28.

### CHAPTER 9

# "UNTO THE END": CHRISTOTELIC READING

## HESITATIONS

*N*ow, it's one thing to discover a holistic reading that is literal, moral, and mystical. It's quite another to take the leap of trying it on for size. I had to face and overcome my personal hesitations because I definitely wanted to learn the *Emmaus Way* of reading the Bible—especially since those who don't do so are rapidly setting their Bibles aside or doubling down on an ugly and un-Christlike vision of God. So, why hesitate?

First, for me, searching the Old Testament for Christ used to mean looking for overt prophecies explicitly fulfilled and cited in the New Testament. Anything I did beyond that felt untethered and entrepreneurial. Let's face it: novelty has often been an enemy of sound interpretation. I feel the scary responsibility of freedom when it's not clear that I'm interpreting Old Testament passages in ways that depart from the authors' intended message in their immediate context. Some of my first Bible teachers frowned on deriving or assigning a "fuller meaning" (*sensus plenior*) that was intended by God but not the human author. While some giants of Evangelicalism such as J. I. Packer endorsed the practice[117] (in a

---

117. See J .I. Packer, "Infallible Scripture and the Role of Hermeneutics," in *Scripture and Truth*, ed. D. A. Carson and John D. Woodbridge (Grand Rapids, MI: Baker Book House, 1992), 350.

limited sense), other scholarly voices cautioned against it.[118] All in all, it felt presumptuous and sketchy to give it a go ourselves.

I remember how, as a young modernist, I objected that such creative play makes the Bible mean anything you want until it means nothing at all. My crowd virtually demanded that exegesis scientifically reveal the "objective truth" deposited in any given Scripture. Or at least it should require a bounded set of criteria—a mechanical process that submits exegetical control to a set of rules and yields a list of propositions. So much safer than allowing the notoriously unreliable reader to read "subjectively."

All this was, admittedly, rooted in fear of open spaces and what Old Testament scholar Peter Enns aptly calls "the sin of certitude."

Something else worried me. In theory, I was all for a Christ-centered reading of the Bible. But it appeared to me that we had an existing Jewish sacred text that should be read on its own terms. Weren't we in danger of superimposing our gospel *over* that text and imposing an anachronistic Christian lens on the Jews' sacred scrolls? Talk about cultural appropriation. I think that objection needs to be taken very seriously. Imagine a Hindu picking up our New Testament and telling us what it *really meant* through the filter of one of their gurus! So, a little empathy is in order for the Jewish rabbi who hears a Gentile Christian pastor try to tell them what Moses *really meant*.

As I've puzzled over that problem, two responses have proven most helpful. First, a *"Christian reading"* of the Old Testament isn't a *non-Jewish interpretation*. Every Jewish reader is informed and influenced by some rabbi or rabbinical tradition that helps them work with the Torah. For Christians, Jewish or not, Jesus of Nazareth is the Jewish rabbi who serves as our sponsor into the Scriptures. His Jewish students (or disciples) and other Jewish rabbis (e.g., Paul) used their Scriptures to make sense of the life of Christ. Gentiles like me were welcomed to the table by Jews like them. I'm doing my best to follow that particular Jewish Rabbi and his *Emmaus Way* of unveiling the books he revered as Scripture.

---

118. Douglas Moo and Andrew David Naselli, "The Problem of the New Testament's Use of the Old Testament," in *The Gospels and the Scriptures of Israel*, ed. Craig A. Evans and W. Richard Stegner (Sheffield, UK: Sheffield Academic, 1994), 732ff.

I will say this to all Christians, Jewish or Gentile: we have no business in the Jewish sacred writings without reference to our Rabbi and his
*Emmaus Way* of reading them. And that way of reading always points to
and prostrates before him.

Second, as Christ-centered methods of interpretation are happily
emerging, it is a mistake to imagine the Old Testament, as such, waiting
for us to lay a Christ-lens over it, as if the Christ-directed focus were not
already there. The *Emmaus Way* was never about changing what the Bible
meant after the fact. Rather, it's an unveiling by the Spirit of God, who was
already breathing through the words in anticipation of the incarnation.

As I mentioned previously, Peter Enns coined a beautiful word for this
*Emmaus Way* type of reading: a *Christotelic* reading.[119] Again, that word
comes from *Christ* and *telos*. *Telos* refers to the "end" or fulfillment or completion of something. On the cross, when Jesus prayed, "It is finished" (John
19:30, various translations), he used that word. He said, "Father, forgive
them" (Luke 23:34, various translations), and the Father, through Jesus's own
mouth, replied, "It is *accomplished!*" The cross represents the fulfillment of
Christ's messianic mission, the capstone in the construction of the kingdom
of God he was erecting throughout his life and ministry. It's the flowering
of the first gospel seed planted in Genesis 3:15. It's the completion of God's
creation and re-creation of humanity begun in Genesis 2. It's the fulfillment
in Christ of God's purposes for the cosmos from eternity. That's *telos*.

When the Greeks spoke of *telos*, they used analogies like the acorn and
the oak tree. The oak tree is the *telos* of the acorn—its fullness and fulfillment. And conversely, all that the oak tree becomes in maturity was there
present in that tiny acorn.

As we apply this concept to Rabbi Jesus's way of handling Scripture, his
Emmaus claim is that his person, his suffering, and his glory are the *telos*
of the acorn found in Moses, the Prophets, and the rest of the Scriptures.
The acorn was already there as the Spirit breathed the Jewish Scriptures
into life. From the outset, Christ and his gospel were embedded in the soil
of the Old Testament by the Spirit. Now, behold its *telos* in Jesus Christ!

---

119. I first encountered the term *Christotelic* in Peter Enns, "Apostolic Hermeneutics and
an Evangelical Doctrine of Scripture: Moving Beyond a Modernist Impasse," *Westminster
Theological Journal* 65 (2003): 263–87.

Imagine Jesus saying, in all humility, "I hate to make this all about me...BUT, yeah, it really is." Even without recognizing that it was Jesus speaking to them, the two disciples on the road to Emmaus witnessed, "Did not our hearts burn within us at what he showed us!"[120] That burning was the resonance of the Spirit—both through the Scriptures and within their hearts.

## "UNTO THE END"

By way of confirmation, have a look at Psalm 22. Don't skip the super-scription in tiny letters at the top. Such notations before particular psalms are not part of the psalm proper, but they are 100 percent part of our Bibles. Do you see the opening note there? It is variously translated as "For/To the choirmaster" (BSB, RSV), "For the choir director" (NASB), "For the music director" (NET, NIV), and "To the chief musician" (NKJV). If you check the best commentaries, they usually admit that their translation of that phrase is a guess. That's because they're dealing with an ancient Hebrew word they don't actually understand. Oh, well.

But wait. What if we ask the Jewish rabbis who translated those words from Hebrew to Greek *before* the time of Christ and gave us the Septuagint (LXX), that favorite version used by New Testament authors? How would these rabbis, experts in both ancient Hebrew and Greek, translate the phrase? (And how arrogant not to ask them!). Here's what they say: *Eis to telos.* "Unto the end."

Recognizing this meaning is a dramatic discovery, as it was for Saint Gregory of Nyssa, who wrote a whole book on the superscriptions.[121] He observes that "Unto the end" is like a dedication to *the Telos* (Christ). A psalm with this notation will always end up either pointing to a messianic *telos* (Origen's spiritual sense) and/or describing the process of a disciple's maturation in Christ (Origen's moral sense).

Far from a throwaway line directed only for the conductor, the psalm-ists or redactors outright tell us they have planted the acorn in their song. That's too important not to mention. Which psalms include these hints? In

---

120. See Luke 24:32.
121. Gregory of Nyssa, *Gregory of Nyssa's Treatise on the Inscriptions of the Psalms*, trans. Ronald E. Heine (New York: Oxford University Press, 1995).

Protestant Bibles, you'll see the phrase in Psalms 4–6, 8–9, 11–14, 18–22, 31, 36, 39–42, 44–47, 49, 51–62, 64–70, 75–77, 80–81, 84–85, 88, 109, and 139–140. That's a *lot* of hints for disciples on the *Emmaus Way!* "You looking for Christ? Right this way, folks!"

But I wanted to be sure because, you know, my English Bible and I have a better track record than seventy pre-New Testament rabbis and Saint Gregory. My hubris was pretty amazing. Then Vern Steiner, my Old Testament professor during my MDiv program, clinched it. He pointed to the last verse of the prophet Habakkuk. How do most standard Hebrew-to-English Bibles render verse 19? Let's look at the NIV:

> The Sovereign LORD is my strength;
>> he makes my feet like the feet of a deer,
>> he enables me to tread on the heights.
>
> For the director of music. On my stringed instruments.
>
> (Hab 3:19)

*"For the director of music"?* Now THAT is odd. Yes, the last chapter of Habakkuk is written in verse, but, seriously? "For the director of music" is a huge stretch considering modern Hebrew scholars usually admit they aren't sure how to translate this phrase.

Idea! Ask the LXX! Here's how the last line is translated from Hebrew to Greek (*knowing* what it meant):

> του νικήσαι με, εν τη ωδή αυτού. / *Tou nikēsai me en tē ōdē outou.*
>
> ("*so that I might conquer with his song,*"[122] or "*so to conquer by His song*" [LXX])

Could it be that these Jewish translators, if not Habakkuk, end his book with a final victory song—not with a choral notation but with a shout of triumph? Could it be that the Holy Spirit is embedding messianic hope in a historic victory, anticipating ultimate victory? Could it be that the New Testament apostles who used this book also saw this notation as prefiguring Jesus Christ? As I reread the third chapter of Habakkuk, I

---

122. Ken M. Penner, gen. ed., *The Lexham English Septuagint* (Bellingham, WA: Lexham Press, 2019), 1046.

see wrathy stuff about Yahweh taking out some historic opponent. But as prefigurement, I can see Christ's victory over satan, sin, and death leaping through verses 13 and 14:

> You crushed the leader of the land of wickedness,
>     you stripped him from head to foot.
>     With his own spear you pierced his head....
>
>                                     (Habakkuk 3:13–14 NIV)

These lines remind me of Paul's description of Jesus's victory in Colossians:

> He stripped the rulers and authorities of their armour, and displayed them contemptuously to public view, celebrating his triumph over them in him.                       (Col 2:15 NTE)

This *Christotelic* or *Emmaus Way* of reading does not discount authorial intent, historical context, or any of the other concerns of the patristic literal sense. All of that matters and should not be bypassed, but it's not *all* that matters. It just means we're not done until we've unveiled the moral (discipleship) and spiritual (gospel) sense intrinsic to the passage.

For those who are unimpressed by how the early church fathers read Scripture ("I don't care about the patristics; just give me the Bible"), okay. Let's now turn to John's Gospel, which is not only *read* as "historical allegory" but, as we shall see, was actually *written* as *historical allegory*.

### CHAPTER 10

# TRUE MYTH: C. S. LEWIS AND JOHN THE BELOVED

## WISE MEN AND BIRDSONG

*D*uring the summer of 2020, I was mainly locked down by the COVID-19 pandemic. While many people suffered and died from the disease, others experienced the pandemic's oppression mentally, emotionally, and socially. One of my kids likened it to the madness of Jack Torrance in Stephen King's *The Shining*. But, for me, the outbreak was also an intervention—a reset. The coronavirus shut down my overbooked travel schedule, and I was able to renew healthier rhythms. This included weekly strolls around Willband Creek Park with my mentor, Ron Dart. I was treated to regular quality time with my personal wise man and the cheerful birdsong of 139 different species.

The loop around this peaceful bird sanctuary was occasion for reflection, confession, and exploration. One of our most fruitful talks focused on C. S. Lewis, John's Gospel, and the idea of "true myth." The reflections to follow were gleaned from Ron's expertise.[123]

---

123. For an online lecture by Ron on this topic, see Ron Dart, "Water to Wine: Johannine Hermeneutics & the Alexandrian Tradition," *Clarion Journal for Religion, Peace & Justice*, July 27, 2020, https://www.clarion-journal.com/clarion_journal_of_spirit/2020/07/water-to-wine-johannine-hermeneutics-the-alexandrian-tradition-ron-dart.html.

I was recounting to Ron my journey out of biblical literalism while retaining my conviction of the historicity of the Christ story, lamenting how some of my friends remain stuck in the letter while others overcorrect and reduce the Gospels to fairy tales. Not that this is a new problem. Ron reflected on how, in John's Gospel, Jesus is constantly running into people who are tripping on literalism and, at the same time, John is arguing for the flesh-and-blood reality of Jesus Christ. Meanwhile, even as John roots his story in historical events, he constantly allegorizes the story to unveil the life of Christ as an embodied revelation of eternal truth. John sees the life of Christ as factual and mythical—or, as C. S. Lewis puts it, "true myth."

Halfway around the loop, Ron quoted C. S. Lewis at length:

> Now as myth transcends thought, Incarnation transcends myth. The heart of Christianity is a myth which is also a fact. The old myth of the Dying God, *without ceasing to be myth,* comes down from the heaven of legend and imagination to the earth of history. It *happens*—at a particular date, in a particular place, followed by definable historical consequences. We pass from a Balder or an Osiris, dying nobody knows when or where, to a historical Person crucified (it is all in order) *under Pontius Pilate.*[124]

> Now the story of Christ is simply a true myth: a myth working on us the same way as the others, but with this tremendous difference that *it really happened*: and one must be content to accept it in the same way, remembering that it is God's myth where the others are men's myths: i.e. the Pagan stories are God expressing Himself through the minds of poets, using such images as He found there, while Christianity is God expressing Himself through what we call "real things."[125]

After our walk, I was able to fact-check these precise passages, and I discovered that it was J. R. R. Tolkien who led Lewis to have this perspective:

---

124. C. S. Lewis, *God in the Dock: Essays on Theology and Ethics* (Grand Rapids, MI: Eerdmans, 1971), 66–67. Lewis's emphasis. See also James W. Menzies, *True Myth: C. S. Lewis and Joseph Campbell on the Veracity of Christianity* (Cambridge, UK: Lutterworth Press, 2014).

125. C. S. Lewis, *The Collected Letters of C. S. Lewis, Vol. I. Family Letters 1905–1931,* ed. Walter Hooper (New York: HarperOne, 2004), 977. Lewis's emphasis.

...[Tolkien] had shown [Lewis] that pagan myths were, in fact, God expressing himself through the minds of poets, using the images of their "mythopoeia" to reveal fragments of His eternal truth. Yet, most astonishing of all, Tolkien maintained that Christianity was exactly the same except for the enormous difference that the poet who invented it was God Himself, and the images He used were real men and actual history. The death and resurrection of Christ was the old "dying god" myth except that Christ was the *real* Dying God, with a precise and verifiable location in history and definite historical consequences.[126]

From Ron Dart's point of view, the Gospels, like all good myths, teach us perennial truths, including death and resurrection, and all they symbolize spiritually. There have been many "dying god" and resurrection myths, ancient and modern, that likewise call us to metamorphosis. But Jesus's story is unique because we're simply not going to give our lives to or for Adonis, Baal, Marduk, Gandalf, or Harry Potter. We may recognize and appropriate their timeless lessons, but something—Someone—is missing, whom these fictions can only anticipate or echo. Those who argue that pre-Christian resurrection myths somehow invalidate the life, death, and resurrection of Christ or reduce him to pure metaphor have missed Lewis's revelation—and miss the more-than-literal point.[127]

## JOHN'S HISTORICAL ALLEGORY

The Gospel according to John is our densest biblical example of the literal, moral, and spiritual sense on full display. John's mythopoeic history of Christ appeals both to practicing synagogue Jews and Hellenistic Gentiles trained in classical Greek.

On our second loop around Willband Creek Park's twin lakes, Professor Dart schooled me on some key elements of John's first few chapters that I had overlooked—aspects directly relevant to John's method of interpretation.

---

126. Joseph Pearce, *Tolkien: Man and Myth: A Literary Life* (San Francisco, CA: Ignatius Press, 1998), 59. Pearce's emphasis.
127. See, for example, Tom Harpur, *The Pagan Christ: Recovering the Lost Light* (Markham, ON: Thomas Allen Publishers, 2004).

John begins, "In the beginning...."

"Wait," Ron says. "Beginning? Beginning suggests temporal time. There's a Greek word for 'time' as such—*chronos*. At the beginning of time was God? No, for the triune God is eternal, transcends time, and created time. The word here is *arche* [as it is in the LXX of Genesis 1:1]. Why *arche*?"

Ron described how Greek language is first of all highly pictorial—it is not abstract concepts, as is often supposed. It is modernists who read Greek through Cartesian lenses (Rene Descartes' rationalism), who misread "Greek thinking" as conceptual. "No," says Ron, "the word *arche* goes back to the *archons*—the guardians or magistrates of city-states such as Athens."

Later, sects of Gnosticism and Manichaeism would mythologize the *Archons* as spiritual rulers over seven planets, semi-hostile powers, often demonic. In the New Testament, the word *archons* is often translated as "principalities" or "powers."[128]

Connected to this sense of governance, *arche* is not a temporal "beginning" but includes the idea of "origin" or "source" or "ground of being."

In John 1:1, the word is used in connection with the *logos*. Here again, the modern rationalists generally abstract a rich and ancient word tradition down to "reason." And in the biblical tradition, because God *spoke* the cosmos into being, *logos* is most often translated as "word."

Yet "word" just doesn't carry the weight of meaning that *logos* had borne for centuries since the philosopher Heraclitus (c. 535–c. 475 BC) or what it would have meant to the rabbis who adopted it for use in Judaism.

As Ron and I paused to scan the lake for kingfishers and herons, Ron continued: "For Greek-speaking Jews and Christians, *logos* speaks of the 'I AM'—so prevalent in the Torah and in John—the *logos* is the eternal presence that 'presences' (verb); it is the ground of all being. This *logos* is also present before God and is God. The *logos* is the first principle and source of all that is. Apart from the *logos*, nothing that is would exist, for our being derives from and participates in the *logos* as Being (I Am) itself."

---

128. See Romans 8:38; 13:3; Ephesians 3:10; 6:12; Colossians 1:16; 2:15; Titus 3:1.

This *logos* became flesh. The Eternal (from the *arche*) entered *chronos* time. Being itself became a being—the Creator a creature—myth and history united in the God-man.

So far, so good. The birds were still singing, and I was still tracking. But now it was time to get hermeneutical.

## THE BEGINNING OF SIGNS

In the second chapter of John, we come to the wedding at Cana. John has already been flooding us with metaphors—baptismal waters, the descending dove, the Lamb of God, the fig tree, a reference to Jacob's ladder. But then we arrive at the wedding at Cana.

Dart asks, "So it begins, 'On the third day, a wedding took place'.... Why 'on the third day'? For John, it's an all-too-obvious pointer to the resurrection 'on the third day.' Perhaps the wedding actually was three days along, but is that John's point? Do the details of the story mean something more-than-literal to John?"

As we walked, Ron showed me how John gives us a tantalizing preview of where his Gospel is heading. Why a wedding? Because the new wine speaks of the new covenant, a biblical metaphor for our spousal relationship with God (as in Song of Songs)—the union of Christ and his bride!

And why the water-to-wine miracle? Yes, I happen to believe Jesus actually "spiked the punch"—but why detail the fact that the water was drawn from ceremonial jars that Jews used for ritual washing? What do the water and wine signify? Is Jesus making a point? The "new wine" foreshadows the cross, the blood of the new covenant, and our own participation in that "cup."

Certainly, John calling this miracle a "sign" is suggestive—it's a *"sign"* after all. A "sign" of what? That *this One* has come to bring God's people a miraculous, transforming upgrade—a transfiguration from law to grace[129] that will completely reshape both their collective faith and their individual lives.

Again, these ideas weren't new to me. But then came the mindblower: John says, "This event, in Cana of Galilee, was the first of Jesus's signs. He displayed his glory, and his disciples believed in him" (John 2:11 NTE).

---

129. See John 1:17.

So? Nope, can't see it yet. How about a more literal translation? "This *beginning of His signs* Jesus did in Cana of Galilee, and manifested His glory, and His disciples believed in Him" (NASB).

John says this is the *arche*—the beginning, the ground—of the *semeion* (signs) that Jesus produced to reveal his glory. So rather than reading this as "Jesus's first miracle," we have Jesus *grounding* all his signs in this sign— third-day, water-to-wine transformation—and in this way. In effect, John identifies his guiding hermeneutic from this point as historical allegory. That is, the "signs" of John are unlike the "miracles" of the Synoptic Gospels. Whereas the Synoptic miracles were performed by Jesus of Nazareth (and his apostles) as a human dependent on and anointed with the power of the Spirit, John's "signs" are manifestations of Christ's glory. Or, as Ron put it, "the signs" are portals to a typological reading. They actually occur, but they also always *mean* something. They act as allegories in time.

Sometimes, Jesus simply tells us the allegories: the healing of the blind man in chapter 9 is a lesson about spiritual blindness and spiritual sight. Other times, we need to think through the narratives for ourselves. The raising of Lazarus, removing his stone, unwrapping his linen—how does his resurrection serve as a sign or type of our renewal?

## WATER-TO-WINE HERMENEUTICS

This water-to-wine analogy applies to Jesus's transformation of both the Jewish faith and of individual lives—but it also signifies the transfiguration of our hermeneutics. As Jesus's grounding sign was water turned to wine, so also reading by "the letter" (literalism) became "reading by Spirit," so that all Scripture directs our eyes to Christ and his mission to make all things new.

Immediately after that story, we encounter three examples of water-to-wine or letter-to-spirit interpretation:

1. "The Temple": In John 2:19, Jesus tells the temple leaders they will "destroy this temple" but "in three days" (note the symbolism again), he will raise it up. The leaders stumble over their own literalism, befuddled at how Jesus could claim to rebuild the building so quickly. But John tells us that Jesus was referring to the temple of his own body. He adds that after

Jesus's resurrection, his disciples recalled what he had said and "believed the Scripture and the word which Jesus had spoken" (John 2:22 NASB). To what Scripture is he referring? The Old Testament texts that had concealed but now reveal the Messiah's suffering, death, and resurrection.

By the way, John alone mentions the fashioning of a scourge,[130] perhaps also prefiguring Jesus's own scourging a few years down the line.[131]

2. "Born again": In chapter three, Jesus again runs into a literalistic block when Nicodemus cannot sort out what He means by being "born again."

> "How can someone possibly be born", asked Nicodemus, "when they're old? You're not telling me they can go back a second time into the mother's womb and be born, are you?" (John 3:4 NTE)

Nicodemus needs to *overcome*[132] his literalism if he hopes to become a disciple—and thank God, he eventually does.

3. "Living water": The same dynamic is repeated in Jesus's encounter in John 4 with the Samaritan woman[133] at the well—and not just *any* well. It's specifically "Jacob's well," named for its historical, religious significance. In that sense, it strikes a parallel with the religious jars at the Cana wedding. Here, the woman encounters a Rabbi who offers her living water that will forever satiate her thirst. Her literalism trips her up at first (vv. 11–12), but then she begins to catch Jesus's meaning. The water he's speaking about is not $H_2O$. It's the spiritual spring of life he's going to plant in her innermost being (v. 14). Further, Jesus tells her he's come to transcend competing temple systems and religious segregation. He speaks of a common heavenly Father who is looking for the true worship offered "in spirit and in truth" (vv. 20–24).

And so it goes, with sign after sign, in conversation after conversation, John replays this water-to-wine, letter-to-spirit hermeneutic. In virtually

---

130. See John 2:15.
131. See John 19:1.
132. Nicodemus surely existed in history, but would John also expect us to perceive a pun on his name, since *nike* means "overcome" and *demos means* "people"?
133. The Roman Catholic and Eastern Orthodox churches identify her by name as Photina, "the enlightened one." In the East, they have given her the designation "equal to the apostles." Tradition says she and her sons (Joseph and Victor) were later martyred in Rome.

every chapter, Jesus's acts and speeches are typological windows, drawn from familiar stories and images, unpacked as types, and then applied to Christ.

Off the top of my head, in the Gospel of John, Christ is the fulfillment or anti-type of the following:

*Significant acts of provision in Israel's history, especially the exodus:*

+ The paschal (Passover) lamb
+ The manna that came down from heaven
+ The miraculous spring of water in the wilderness

*The tabernacle, temple, and all their furnishings, including:*

+ The holy water of the bronze laver
+ The table of showbread
+ The golden lampstands and their seven oil-fed lights
+ The high priest offering up prayers from the altar of incense
+ The mercy seat on the ark of the covenant between the two angels
+ The manna, the tablets, and Aaron's rod in the ark of the covenant

*All the Jewish feasts Jesus attends, which outline John's book,*[134] *including:*

+ Passover (recalling the Exodus) three times
+ Purim (recalling Esther)
+ The Feast of Tabernacles (recalling the wilderness)
+ The Great Day
+ The Feast of Dedication (recalling the Maccabees)

The list surely goes on. The life of Christ—the whole incarnation—recapitulates and fulfills Israel's history and vocation. Jesus's actual life, corroborated by eyewitness testimonies, is so packed with meaning that the Gospels become historical allegory, and the early church read them that way. In addition to reflecting on the meaning of Christ's life and ministry, the water-to-wine miracle also resonates with our own transformation, our exodus from egoism into our true and transformed self in Christ,

---

134. See John Behr, *John the Theologian & His Paschal Gospel: A Prologue to Theology* (Oxford: Oxford University Press, 2019), 142ff.

and our wedding into the new covenant union, toasted with the wine of the new covenant.

Yes, I believe Jesus actually performed a wedding miracle in Cana, met with Nicodemus under the stars, and sat with a Samaritan woman who had been divorced five times. And I *also* believe the water-to-wine miracle is a parable of our transformation, that Nicodemus's born-again transformation and the Samaritan woman's inner spring (Spring) are stories about us. I am/we are the morphing water. I am/we are Nicodemus. I am/we are the Samaritan. I am/we are the woman caught in adultery, and the blind man, rescued and healed by Christ. This dual reality of history and allegory is what Lewis meant by "true myth."

### CHAPTER 11

# TRAINING EMMAUS READERS: PREFIGUREMENT IN MELITO OF SARDIS

*W*e've now seen how the Psalms anticipate their *telos* ("end" or "fulfillment") in Christ, how Paul perceived the gospel in the Torah, and how John's Gospel overflows with typology and historical allegory. We can be sure that these perspectives were not novelties contrived in Alexandria after the fact but were learned by a careful examination of the Scriptures and especially John's methodology.

My discovery of this layered reading came through a ton of research and with the help of scholars and mentors. And I'm still learning. I realize this approach can seem disempowering to the lay reader. Are we making the Bible inaccessible? Do we risk losing the "Bible for normal people"?[135] Not that we would expect an untrained layperson to pilot an airplane or perform open-heart surgery. Studying the Scriptures includes studying how to study the Scriptures. So, how do we train and release ordinary Bible readers onto the *Emmaus Way* without turning interpretation into a private bumper car free-for-all? "Is there a path that's open to everyone?" I wondered.

---

135. Peter Enns thinks not. Please check out his *The Bible for Normal People* podcast, https://peteenns.com/podcast/.

Along came Fr. John Behr. I had the great privilege of taking a summer patristics module with him in 2019. The course was an intensive study that covered primary works by Ignatius of Antioch, Irenaeus of Lyons, Origen of Alexandria, and others. But the game changer for me was Behr's stunning exposition of Saint Melito of Sardis, a second-century Jewish bishop in the Johannine school and lineage. Melito's riveting homily entitled *On Pascha* was composed for the celebration of Christ's death and resurrection during Passover. It is glorious and intense, and you can find it in paperback or free online.[136]

For me, *On Pascha* was particularly powerful when I read the entire homily out loud, while standing, as if listening to Melito himself preach it. I imagined hearing his sermon by candlelight during a midnight Paschal celebration as I awaited resurrection dawn. The homily is incredibly rhythmic—in a cadence befitting my favorite Black preachers.

I believe that Melito's sermon teaches us more about how to read the Bible the *Emmaus Way* than any other work in history. All the information we're *not* given in Luke's account is laid out in detail for us in one short sermon. Call it "Prefigurement for Dummies in 30 minutes"! Melito's gifts to us include:

+ Explaining how biblical typology works using multiple concrete analogies

+ Showing us how to spot "prefigurement" in the Scriptures to unveil the mystical/gospel sense

+ Empowering us to do this for ourselves in a profoundly accessible way

+ Modeling for us exactly the manner in which Christ would have shown his friends how Moses, the Prophets, and all the Scriptures anticipate his suffering, death, and glorification

I used the word *typology* in the above summary. A simple definition of Christological typology is that Christ and his gospel are prefigured or symbolized by things, people, or events in the Scriptures. Bible teachers speak of the "type" and the corresponding "anti-type." The type points to

---

136. Melito of Sardis, *On Pascha*, trans. and ed. Alistair Stewart-Sykes (Yonkers, NY: St. Vladimir's Press, 2001), https://sachurch.org/wp-content/uploads/2017/04/On-Pascha-Melito-of-Sardis.pdf.

the anti-type by analogy (this is like that) and by contrast (the anti-type is greater). So, the type *prefigures* the anti-type. Here's is how Melito explains it:

> 35) Nothing, beloved, is spoken or made without an *analogy and a sketch*;
> for everything which is made and spoken has its analogy,
> what is spoken an analogy, what is made a *prototype*,
> so that whatever is made may be perceived through the prototype
> and whatever is spoken clarified by the *illustration*.
> 36) This is what occurs in the case of a first draft;
> it is not a finished work but exists so that, through the *model*,
> that which is to be can be seen.
> Therefore a *preliminary sketch* is made of what is to be,
> from wax or from clay or from wood,
> so that what will come about,
> taller in height,
> and greater in strength,
> and more attractive in shape,
> and wealthier in workmanship,
> can be seen through the small and provisional sketch....
> 39) So then, just as with the *provisional examples*,
> so it is with eternal things;
> as it is with things on earth,
> so it is with the things in heaven.
> For indeed the Lord's salvation and his truth were *prefigured* in the people,
> and the decrees of the Gospel were *proclaimed in advance* by the law.[137]

Melito goes into greater detail, but you can see his interpretive method laid out. His historical typology is surely a simplified and expanded extension of John, his theological forefather.

Melito dials this skill way up while simultaneously making it eminently accessible. The trick is not to demand too much of this way of reading. Seeing prefigurement doesn't require you to say, "This is what the

---

137. Melito, *On Pascha*, 46–47.

author meant" or even "This is what the Spirit meant" specifically. But neither are we making stuff up willy-nilly. Rather, we hear Christ on the road
to Emmaus boldly tell us that he is prefigured throughout the Law, the
Prophets, and everywhere in the Scriptures, and *that is how we should read
them.* So, as we read Old Testament narrative, we are invited to watch and
see:

+ When the people of God experience suffering, Christ suffers with
  them.

+ When God's people cause suffering, Christ suffers in their victims.

+ When the people of God achieve victory, Christ is the victor.

+ When God delivers his people, Christ is the deliverer.

+ When the people go into exile, Christ goes with them.

+ When the people of God are led out of exile, Christ leads them.

+ When the priest offered a sacrifice, Christ was the priest.

+ When the lamb was sacrificed, Christ was the lamb.

+ When God appeared, that was Christ.

In other words, *Christ was always there among them.* His presence was
not an endorsement or justification of their every act or of their interpretation of God's acts. Christ's presence simply made every step of the journey
a "type" in waiting. His presence in their midst and in their folly, in their
growth and in their disasters *all point* to how the incarnation becomes the
far greater, indeed ultimate, anti-type.

It's best to see how Melito of Sardis does this with your own eyes. Here
are some sample verses from his homily, an inspiring and enticing signpost
for our return to an *Emmaus Way* of reading Scripture:

58) Thus the mystery of the Lord,
*prefigured* from of old through the vision of a type,
is today *fulfilled* and has found faith,
even though people think it something new.
For the mystery of the Lord is both new and old;
old with respect to the law,
but new with respect to grace.
*But if you scrutinize the type through its outcome you*

*will discern him.*

59) Thus if you wish to *see the mystery of the Lord,*
look at Abel who is likewise slain,
at Isaac who is likewise tied up,
at Joseph who is likewise traded,
at Moses who is likewise exposed,
at David who is likewise hunted down,
at the prophets who likewise suffer for the sake of Christ.
60) And look at the sheep, slaughtered in the land of Egypt,
which saved Israel through its blood whilst Egypt was
struck down.
61) *The Mystery of the Lord is proclaimed* through the prophetic
voice.

For Moses says to the people:
"And you shall look upon your life hanging before your eyes
night and day and you will not have faith in your life."
62) David says:
"Why have the nations been haughty, and the peoples
imagined vain things?
The kings of the earth stood by and the rulers gathered
themselves together
against *the Lord and against his anointed one.*"
63) Jeremiah says:
"I am like a harmless lamb led to sacrifice;
they planned evil for me saying: come let us put wood on
his bread and let us rub him out from the land of the
living. And his name shall not be remembered."
64) Isaiah says:
"Like a sheep he was led to slaughter and like a silent
lamb before its shearer he does not open his mouth;
who shall tell of his generation?"
65) Many other things were proclaimed by many prophets
concerning the mystery of the Pascha, who is Christ,
to whom be the glory for ever.
Amen.[138]

---

138. Melito, *On Pascha*, 52–54.

Notice how Melito refers to seeing "the Mystery" of the Lord in the Law, the Psalms, the Prophets, and more. What is this "Mystery"? That our salvation (our redemption from bondage to satan, sin, and death) was a mystery concealed (yet foretold) and now revealed (and forthtold) in the incarnation of Christ, his suffering and death, and his glorious resurrection. Most of all, as a Johannine bishop, Melito sees Christ as the Passover Lamb whose victory comes by means of his passion—whose glorification is achieved via the cross.

To summarize, while we still need to work out the literal and moral sense of Scripture, we've not really read the Bible as gospel until we've read it the *Emmaus Way*. Through Melito, we see that using typology or allegory is not a flaky method. Reading this way is truly legitimate and even quite easy when gathered into three broad categories:

+ *Every Old Testament trial* (however disastrous and prolonged) prefigures Christ's ultimate, brutal suffering and death on behalf of those who suffered the trial—and on behalf of everyone.

+ *Every Old Testament injustice* (by the people, the kings, or the priests) prefigures humanity's ultimate and more wicked betrayal of Christ through Judas, the Sanhedrin, Herod's palace, and Pilate's empire.

+ *Every Old Testament victory* (however dubious in its xenophobic violence) prefigures Christ's ultimate and more beautiful victory over darkness, dread, and death.

That sounds all-inclusive—and it's meant to be. But perhaps you have reservations about the misuse of prophetic typology. Believe me, I've seen it, and I get it. I can testify to how some of our charismatic friends over-spiritualize texts and misapply them to world events in worrisome ways. Look, I believe we can be liberal in saying, "I see Christ foreshadowed here," without claiming, "God told me this verse means that." This is not an "anything goes" hermeneutic. Rather, we're reading with an open ear for intimations of the gospel itself within the Scriptures.

As an exercise, why not think of a story or symbol from the Old Testament and ask yourself which of these three categories it falls into: Is it a trial? An injustice? A victory? How does this story prefigure Christ? What aspect of the gospel does it signify? How does reading this story as gospel (the spiritual sense) address and transform my life (the moral sense)? For John and for Melito, this is the point—this is the *Emmaus Way*. We're not merely *free* to go there. We *must*, if we're to read the Bible as gospel.

### CHAPTER 12

# FAITH AND FUNCTION:
# A CHRISTIAN USE OF SCRIPTURE

## THE JOURNEY THUS FAR

*A*s part I of this book comes to a close, we are due for a brief review and some important critical thoughts on the *function* or *use* of Scripture in a Christian context—what we might call the *community hermeneutic or ecclesial sense* of Scripture. I hope that, so far, I've been very clear that the Bible is precious to me in its faithful witness to Jesus Christ. I hope you recognize that I take the Bible *very* seriously, which includes reading it as *gospel* in a way that never blasphemes the character of God as revealed through Jesus Christ. I hope you see that we can learn and restore apostolic and patristic ways of reading that reveal the inspired genius of these sacred texts. And most of all, I hope we can agree that recovering the *Emmaus Way* will lead us to read the Bible with Christ as our divine Rabbi and the Spirit as our illuminating Guide.

So, in point form, here are some of the highlights:

1. **The Word of God is Jesus Christ.** I believe that the Word of God is inspired, infallible, and inerrant. And when he was about eighteen years old, he grew a beard.

2. **The function of the Scriptures, #1: to point to the gospel.** Our gospel—that Christ came for us, died for us, and rose for us—is known "according to the Scriptures" (1 Cor 15: 3–4, various translations). The apostles refer to our Old Testament as "the Scriptures," and the phrase is picked up in the Nicene Creed to affirm that, for Christians, the Bible's primary role is to witness to the incarnation of Jesus Christ.

   *The whole of the Scriptures testifies to the Word and to his gospel* (what I've called *the Emmaus Way*). John, Paul, Melito, Origen, and others showed us that when we read the Scriptures with reference to the gospel and Jesus Christ, the entire Bible is the new covenant, or, as Paul says in 2 Corinthians 5:18, a "ministry of reconciliation" (various translations).

   *Archbishop Lazar's maxim:* "Every Scripture that claims to be a revelation of God must bow to the living God when he came in the flesh."

3. **Function of the Scriptures: #2: a mirror revealing the human condition.** In 1 Corinthians 10, Paul describes stories from the Old Testament as cautionary tales depicting our hardness of heart.

   Or as Abp. Lazar says, the Old Testament is often not about God but about us. It is a *mirror* that reveals the human condition, including our toxic misunderstandings of who God is and what God wants. The Old Testament people of God demonstrate our growing need for God to come in person and set us straight.

4. **What is worthy of God?** We found that the early church, even before opening the scrolls, had made a faith commitment that God is good (indeed, the Good).

   God is Good, and all he does is goodness. God is Light, and in God is no darkness at all.[139] When a passage describes *un-Christlike* images of God, we must not read them *literalistically*, because attributing moral darkness to God's nature or deeds is *not worthy of God*.

---

139. See 1 John 1:5.

5. **Interpreting the Scriptures with the fathers.** The same early church apostles and teachers who composed and collected the Christian Bible also train us how to read it. We do well to recollect their interpretive approach, which carefully draws out the *literal*, *moral*, and *spiritual* sense of the biblical text and functions to reveal a Christlike God who is forming Christlike disciples.

## A CHRISTIAN USE OF SCRIPTURE

In addition to all of the above, I will conclude this section of the book by identifying three further, important practices in the historic church's use of Scripture, all derived from our spiritual roots in Judaism.

**The Bible read in the community.** The Jews practiced what is called a *minyan* (not a minion) that consisted of no less than ten Jewish males, thirteen years or older. A *minyan* established the required minimum for a "congregation" to fulfill certain tasks, including the study of Scripture. This meant that whatever individual Bible *reading* one might do, the *interpretation* of the text involved a community hermeneutic. On one hand, this shows the great importance of working together to understand the Scriptures. On the other, it shows the importance of an individual when needed to fill out the tenth member to form a *minyan*. If we only have nine congregants present, your voice matters and needs to be included.

My godfather, David Goa, was walking down the street one day when a door swung open, and he was beckoned by a Jewish man. Though he was a stranger, David was urged to join their Torah study because they were short one body for their quorum—they even ignored the fact that the tenth seat was filled by a gentile! So it was that David found himself in the world of Jewish community interpretation. Multiple perspectives may be confusing to modernists in our lust for certitude and conformity, but a certain quality control is introduced when ten voices are free to debate the meaning of a passage. One of these qualities is the humility of hearing *the other* and agreeing that we're not able to box the Bible, much less God, into our own individualistic modes.

**The Bible read in the liturgy.** Again, in the high-church traditions, the "liturgy" refers to a service of prayer and Scripture reading with a pattern established through centuries of worship in community. The *liturgies* are bathed in ancient hymns, prayers, and Bible readings that work together as a sort of interactive passion play that choreographs the gospel story as a *drama of redemption.* That redemptive saga is retold each week, from creation through the fall to Christ's death and resurrection, culminating in the Eucharist, where we partake of the body and blood of Christ. The Scriptures for each week have been selected by the broader church and find their proper place in that drama.

What are the advantages to a liturgical approach to Scripture?

1. *It helps the pastor or congregation to avoid meandering off* into the swamps of their pet doctrines and hobbyhorses (i.e., heresies).

When I first started working with Rev. Peter Bartel at Bethel Mennonite, he introduced a four-year lectionary and asked me to stick to it when I gave my monthly sermon. At first, I balked at this idea, but he challenged me to try it, reminding me that I had a whole month to prepare. "Surely, God will speak a message through the text when you have that much time. And if you're really stuck, okay, then preach something else. But I want you to try." Well, I did try, and you know, he was right! I believe that, with just one exception in six years, I was able to hear God's voice and preach a message through the prescribed lectionary reading. More importantly, it kept me from regurgitating my own supposedly "fresh" themes month after month.

2. *It helps congregants to see connections between the Old and New Testament readings.* When readings from the Psalms, the Gospels, and the Epistles are gathered around a particular theme or fast or feast, the liturgical use of Scripture helps us see the continuity and the point of the biblical texts. The liturgists saw parallels and connected dots across centuries of written revelation. We often wouldn't have noticed these correlations on our own.

3. *It helps us understand the place of otherwise "problem texts" in the bigger picture.* Rather than privately reading chapters of the Bible in isolation from the grand scheme, we come to the liturgy and see how various biblical passages are episodes in the story, expressing the tone proper to that moment in the liturgy and anticipating their fulfillment in Jesus.

For example, when I read an angry or despairing psalm on its own, I may think that it justifies how angry I feel, or I may be repulsed by how un-Christlike it sounds. Or I may not personally relate to it at all. Are the lament psalms or the imprecatory psalms giving me words for my own journey through wrath or sorrow? Maybe. If I am willing to voice my honest anguish in God's presence, rather than repress or deny it, God can exchange those burdens with his peace. What if they seem irrelevant to me because I happen to feel joyful today? Perhaps someone else in my world is feeling pain, and I can intercede for them through the Psalms. I address all these questions to God.

But in the context of the liturgy, where we are hearing not only a psalm but also other Scriptures from the Old and New Testaments, we're walking through the drama of redemption, and I find myself *as Adam* locked out of the garden of Eden, or *as the myrrh-bearing women* grieving outside the sealed tomb of Christ. And in that moment, that psalm makes perfect sense, and it also becomes personal to me. I enter the world of the psalmist, and it exposes where I too may still feel locked in shame or blocked by grief. But the story carries on—carries me—toward resurrection victory and shouts of joy (also found in the Psalms) that prefigured it. When, for example, I read a lament psalm during our morning service, I also know that, in less than two hours, the priest (representing Christ) will emerge through the now-opened gates of the altar—a symbol of Paradise and the tomb—and offer me the fruit of the Tree of Life in the communion chalice.

Thus, each Scripture is selected and embedded to fit the context of the gospel saga as it's played out. I'm confronted, comforted, exhorted, and invited by the Scriptures, which have been carefully arranged like puzzle pieces within the greater framework of the gospel.

**The Bible read in prayer and song.** Much of the Bible is written as poetry—you can see that by the formatting in your Bible. When it's formatted as verse, we know that the congregation (*minyan*) probably used it together liturgically. But the Psalms were also used as a personal prayer book.

I don't know for sure when this began, but I am fascinated by the fact that Saint Macrina the Younger (fourth century) kept a Psalter from which she prayed five times a day. I wonder if her practice was widespread enough in the East to have a later influence on Islam two hundred years later. I'm not sure. We know from the Psalms that David was meditating and praying through the Scriptures day and night. At some point, families began to read, memorize, and pray the Psalms daily. Praying, singing, or chanting the words of Scripture was a Jewish and Christian way of internalizing the truth down to the depths of one's heart.

When I went from *reading* David's prayer of confession in Psalm 51 to *praying* it from my own heart, out loud, in the assembly, I was at first surprised by how deeply I felt the words. They came from my heart, sometimes with tears and a lump in my throat, my spirit convening with God's Spirit in a moment of repentance and reconciliation. I was no longer studying the journals of a three-thousand-year-old fallen king. Praying the Scriptures was brokering a living connection between the all-merciful One and my own wounded spirit.

And, of course, it's likely that in your own worship tradition, you've sung Scripture to music in the congregation, then hummed it to yourself at home and perhaps woken up to it playing in your heart. That counts. And in those moments, the human words of God are heard through the living Word of God—Jesus Christ.

## SCRIPTURE AS THE MUSIC OF GOD

Chris Green, a Pentecostal scholar and friend, describes the Christian use of Scripture in the language of Origen: as the music of God interpreted rightly through blessed peacemakers. I will quote his preface to the second edition of his work *Sanctifying Interpretation* at length, and I urge you to obtain his book as an essential companion volume to this book:

> In his reflections on the seventh Beatitude, Origen argues that peacemakers are blessed because of the way they handle the Scriptures (*Philocalia* 6.1–2). First, peacemakers discover the peace *of* the Scriptures, which are at peace in the sense that they manifest one unified witness to Jesus Christ. Second, peacemakers know how to make peace *with* the Scriptures, reconciling the seeming contradictions within the texts—and the real contradictions between themselves and the texts—as well as discerning the

deeper, hidden significances of seemingly meaningless passages. That is why, peacemaking interpreters find that they are also making peace with and for their neighbors, discovering and helping others discover the peace of God. Paraphrasing Paul, we might say that for Origen it is because there is one text that there is one body.

In the middle of this passage, Origen takes up a striking analogy. He describes Scripture as "the music of God," and says it is a composition with strange, unexpected, and perplexingly intricate harmonies that bewilder and frustrate ill-equipped and untrained readers (*Philocalia* 6.2). This is why, Origen says, that unskilled hearers hear in the Scriptures only dissonances, as if the Old Testament conflicts with the New, or the Prophets with the Law, or the apostolic writings with the Gospels. If readers hope to appreciate the divine harmonies of the Scriptures, then they have to be trained for it. The required sensibilities and skills must be seeded into them.

At this point, Origen transposes the analogy into a new image: Scripture is also the *instrument* of the Spirit. But, crucially, Origen insists that believers can only "hear" the scriptural harmonies that they can "play," and so they have to be made "like another David," gifted with the abilities necessary "to bring out the sound of the music of God." Such readers develop over time and under guidance the necessary skills for performing the divine sound; they know "the right time to strike the chords," playing the Law, the Gospels, the Prophets, and the Apostles so as to make the "certain sound" that is the "one saving voice" of God's Word. In this performance, peacemakers become like David whose music "laid to rest the evil spirit in Saul, which was choking him," "implanting" in the spirits of their neighbors the very peace of God that all so deeply desire (*Philocalia* 6.2).

Origen's hermeneutic makes it clear that Scripture must be interpreted, made beautiful. And that depends on believers having the Spirit-given, Spirit-led skills to create good readings, readings which are good because of their effects (and not just their exegetical rigor). Good readings, as opposed to merely correct ones, actually bring the peace of God to bear in the world. Here, Pentecostals fully agree with Origen and the Patristic hermeneutical tradition: the reading of Scripture has a purpose, and that purpose is the making-present of the works of God. And that can only be done as readers are led by the Spirit beyond the "letter" of Scripture to discover its "spirit."[140]

## SCRIPTURE AS AN EPIC SAGA

When the Bible is actually read as Scripture—as the music of God—it functions as an act of worship illumined by the Holy Spirit and interpreted in community. In that threefold, interdependent confluence of text, body, and Spirit, we see the Bible as a whole, as the radiant narrative of salvation—an epic saga, driving toward, climaxing in, and revolving around the gospel of Jesus Christ. It testifies to Christ and is itself transfigured by Christ into a luminescent witness and *a more Christlike word*.

We're now ready to study how the Bible's polyphony of voices, multiplicity of perspectives, and variety of literature churn together into one story—our coherent and beautiful drama of redemption.

---

140. Chris E. W. Green, *Sanctifying Interpretation: Vocation, Holiness, and Scripture*, 2nd ed. (Cleveland, TN: CPT Press, 2020), xii–xiv. Green's emphasis. Used with permission.

PART II

SCRIPTURE AS EPIC SAGA

# INTRODUCTION TO PART II

*W*hether or not you track with my journey toward a more Christlike word, I hope you'll see that my agenda is faithfulness to God. The cultured cynics who ridicule the Bible's most difficult passages no longer phase me. They're just secularized versions of the same old literalism I left behind. By reading the Bible the *Emmaus Way*—that is, with Christ and his gospel, the Spirit's illumination, and the counsel of the historical church—I no longer experience "triggers" of anger or fear when I honestly read the Bible's most difficult texts.

Yet a great many details of our sacred text still surprise and bewilder me. I can't get my head around great chunks of it. But I trust that God is good, that Jesus is Lord, and that the unsearchable ways I read about are riches to be cherished. For me, being stumped has become an invitation to worship and to perpetual discovery.

In part II, I invite you to seven specific elements of biblical interpretation. These are areas that might have been marked "restricted section" if the library at Hogwarts carried books on hermeneutics, and the librarian was a biblical literalist. I'm only partly joking, because in the fundamentalist wing of the Evangelical world, these topics are generally out-of-bounds. But I believe that reading the Bible on Christ's terms—as a Christotelic volume of wonders—means learning new skills that are difficult and beautiful, if sometimes troubling.

There wasn't an easy way to organize these topics into a sequential flow, so we'll have to take each chapter as an independent article on advanced hermeneutics. However, we can gather them under two broad umbrellas:

Chapters 1–3 address three narrative realities:

1. That the Bible is *"a text in travail"*—that is, where inerrantists would try to force contrary points of view into unison, we can, instead, frame conflicting messages as labor pains of a conflicted community that lead to the birth of Christ, who *is* the Message of God.

2. Similarly, that the Bible is a *polyphonic narrative*—a chorus of at least four voices, two foci of revelation, and one story that unifies the many-stranded subplots.

3. Within that epic saga, the story is told through some crazy characters and "unreliable narrators" (a technical term) whose divine Author inexorably weaves storylines toward a climax even while letting his children tell the story.

In chapters 4–7, we take a hard turn into three specific literary features of biblical writing that, if overlooked, sabotage not only our understanding of Scripture but, potentially, even our knowledge of God.

1. The first of these is the use of *rhetoric*, especially in Jesus's preaching and in the New Testament Epistles. Christ and his apostles were masters of oration, and we'll see how their use of *logos, ethos, and pathos* drive their message from head to heart to hands...IF, that is, we can resist literalizing their speeches with gospel-denying conclusion.

   We'll also chat in some depth about a subgenre of rhetoric called "diatribe," the common ancient practice of citing a hypothetical opponent and then retorting. A dilemma arises over texts like Romans 1, for which there's debate about whether Paul is speaking his mind or parroting a hater.

2. Next, we'll briefly consider *phenomenology* (descriptions of things as they appear). We may find that, when the Bible describes God's acts from a character's point of view, God no more "changes his mind" than "the sun sets." As with the language of sunsets,

sometimes biblical descriptions of God convey a perspective that exists in the eye of the beholder rather than in the nature of what they behold. And what if that's perfectly okay?

3. Likewise, we'll look closely at the use and misuse of *anthropomorphism* (projecting human emotions and actions onto God). Again, our literalism can become so severe as to descend into idolatry or blasphemy. For that chapter, we'll need the help and authority of the great saints of history, whom I will cite at length along with some commentary.

### CHAPTER 13

# A TEXT IN TRAVAIL: TIM TALKS

## TRAVAIL

*I* believe it was René Girard who first aptly called the Bible a "text in travail":

> In the Hebrew Bible, there is clearly a dynamic that moves in the direction of the rehabilitation of victims, but it is not a cut-and-dried thing. Rather, it is a process under way, a text in travail...a struggle that advances and retreats. I see the Gospels as the climactic achievement of that trend, and therefore as the essential text in the cultural upheaval of the modern world.[141]

Travail connotes intense labor, especially the labor pains of a woman entering the final stages of childbearing. The word *travail* evokes in me anxious memories of my wife, Eden, as she panted and pushed our three boys into this world—11 pounds, 11.5 pounds, and 10.5 pounds at birth. The awe-inspiring miracle of labor and birth signify the cruciform intersection of affliction and beauty that restores life to this world.

---

141. Robert G. Hamerton-Kelly, ed., *Violent Origins: Walter Burkert, René Girard, and Jonathan Z. Smith on Ritual Killing and Cultural Formation* (Redwood City, CA: Stanford University Press, 1987), 141.

Indeed, every such delivery reminds me of the cross, where blood and water, joy and sorrow "flowed mingled down" from our Savior's side, a fountain of love for the life of the world. *The crucifix as cervix.* Triumph in travail. That'll preach, if you dare.

The whole drama of redemption represents the love and anguish through which *Abba* (or *"Amma,"* in this case) bore salvation's children. Isn't it appropriate, then, that the *story* of divine travail be reflected by a *text* in travail? What Girard describes is *how* the story is told, and I will add, how the story is *read*.

Salvation history was not delivered smoothly, without labor, pushing, or pushback. The prophets and rabbis who produced our Bible were not conspirators who kept their stories straight or shared a common point of view. They strove with themselves, with each other, and with God over what to say and how to say it. The text features the groans of labor and the laughter of new birth, divergent strands finally meeting in the gospel finale.

I also see how *reading* the Bible faithfully involves the same process. It's analogous to the confusion that may overcome a first-time mom when the ordeal she faces finally dawns on her—and there's no going back. Reading what's actually in the text can be shocking and repulsive to those who had flippantly viewed the Bible as heaven's happy Hallmark card, understood so easily because "the Bible clearly says."

What shall I offer but the advice of a child overheard by Augustine: "Take up and read; take up and read."[142] But beware. Maybe every Bible should include this warning: "Beware. Adult themes (violence, nudity, sexuality, etc.). Some scenes graphic in nature. Not suitable for all viewers." When taken seriously, reading the Bible can become traumatic. I'm not joking. I'm in conversations every week with Bible readers in labor, giving their Bibles a second look, either because they had never before noticed the travail or because, having witnessed it, they had previously slammed the Book shut. Maybe desensitizing themselves by binge-watching *Breaking Bad* or *Game of Thrones* prepared them to give "the real Bible" a second look.

The best way to talk about this is to show you. The following is a real conversation between my friend Tim and me. Watch how Tim's commitment

---

142. Augustine, *Confessions*, trans. Edward B. Pusey (Grand Rapids, MI: Christian Classics Ethereal Library), 186, https://www.ccel.org/ccel/augustine/confess.ix.xii.html>.

to the goodness of our Christlike God and his beautiful gospel enables him to wade courageously into the so-called toxic texts (some of which I referenced or alluded to in part I of this book). Perfect love has driven out his fear...but doesn't allow him to bypass the travail.

## TIM TALKS: A REAL CONVERSATION

Dialogue has been an important style of pedagogy from ancient times. From the works of Plato to the narrative of Jesus to the great works of Gregory of Nyssa, Justin Martyr, Cyril of Alexandria, and Anselm of Canterbury, conversations have proven helpful to those who are privileged to listen in. I remember how helpful I found Brian McLaren's dialogues in his book series The New Kind of Christian.

My own experience has placed me at the feet of marvelous mentors and spiritual directors whose best insights came via live exchanges. And as a teacher, I enjoy participating in Q & R, whether in person or by correspondence. It pushes me to answer real questions people are asking and shows me what I need to articulate more clearly.

In that spirit, I'd like to proceed by recounting an actual dialogue I had with Tim (even his real name!).[143] Tim isn't a hypothetical construct I'm using as a foil. He's a real person, and the questions are his. Maybe they're yours too. I hope my responses don't come across as decisive answers. When in dialogue, I like to become a collaborator, exploring ideas together, looking for truth together, even as I'm sharing authentic convictions.

Hey Brad,

You've started me on what I'm sure will be a long journey of discovery, and there are so many questions along the way.

I'm working (I've chosen that verb carefully) through Romans right now because I really want to understand Paul's theology. In addition to my own reading of the text, I am also reading [N. T.] Wright's simple For Everyone commentary and John Stott's commentary on Romans.

In my reading, I am trying to step outside my twenty-first-century North American understanding of justice (and justification), instead

---

143. This correspondence has been lightly edited for this publication and is used with Tim's permission.

looking at the text as God's plan for setting the world back to the way he designed it to function, which will culminate in a new heaven and a new earth.

In reading Stott on Romans 2:6, "God will give to each person according to what he has done," I was directed toward Hosea 12:2.

Now the LORD is bringing charges against Judah.
He is about to *punish* Jacob for all his deceitful ways,
and *pay him back* for all he has done.                    (NLT)

I was instantly curious because you so often reference Hosea. But what I found in Hosea 12–14 was kind of scary. I was careful to read through to the end because I wanted to see God's ultimate plan, which is certainly revealed in Hosea 14:4 (NLT):

The LORD says,
"Then I will heal you of your faithlessness;
my love will know no bounds,
for my anger will be gone forever."

But what is a poor guy to do with Hosea 13:16 (NLT)?

The people of Samaria
must bear the consequences of their guilt
because they rebelled against their God.
They will be killed by an invading army,
their little ones dashed to death against the ground,
their pregnant women ripped open by swords.

I recognize the prophetic utterance in 13:14, which Paul quotes in 1 Corinthians 15:55, but that verse actually ends with, "I will take no pity on them." Obviously, the work of the cross ultimately contradicts this.

But the angry (I would say completely crazy, indecisive, perhaps schizophrenic) God that Hosea presents in these chapters is so completely different from the perfect revelation of *Abba* as seen on the cross. So, was Hosea wrong? If so, how can I trust/quote the things that Hosea says that do reflect *Abba*, such as 14:4?

This is an important question that can be applied to much of Scripture. I think (but am willing to be corrected) that this is different from how I would approach Psalm 22, which was more of an indirect prophecy, poetry expressing his personal feelings toward God and working out his own understanding of *Abba*.

I hope that makes sense. Thanks for always being gracious and patient. I sure appreciate you.

Cheers,<br>Tim

Hi Tim,

Good question. And Hosea is a great place to start. To begin with, we are *not welcome* into Hosea without Jesus as our Rabbi, nor can it be read without reference to the big picture of what Hosea is *doing* (not just saying), and how this fits into the broader context of the twelve Minor Prophets as a recognized collection.

I see these dynamics at work:

1. Big picture, part 1: Hosea is one of our clearest revelations of the radical *freedom of God* to forgive sin without punishment, payment, sacrifice, or even repentance. How do you emphasize such unilateral mercy prior to any response? You do what Hosea does:

a. *You dramatically emphasize how wicked they are.* The Hebrew text in chapter 1–2 is blunt and intense, even choppy. There's no justice in the land. Just corruption, abuse, exploitation, and violence. The whole nation is rotten, adulterous, wayward. She's a whore, and her citizens are unwanted bastard children.

b. *You dramatically emphasize the retributive judgment such sins deserve.* Under their covenant (Deut 28, for example), such sins are worthy of invasion, exile, and eradication. Under the Law, their condition is terminal—beyond hope and without mercy.

c. *This sets you up for the shocker of all shockers:* What is God to do? Watch Hosea.

> Go, take to yourself a wife of fornication
> And children of fornication;
> For the land will surely go a-whoring
> By departing from the Lord.                    (Hosea 1:2 LXX)

Why? Because that's what God will do! He will take the whore back
(whether it's a marriage or a remarriage) and adopt her children. God will
remember them as toddlers to arouse his compassion, and his heart will
turn within him. If they will not repent, God will (Hos 11:8–9)! Meaning
he will trump the Law's demand for retribution to freely show them his
unfailing love, the mercy that endures forever, even prior to their repentance. And then? God will send prophets with such good news that their
hearts will be won (14:2–9), and like God, their hearts will freely turn (a
transformation the Law had failed to coerce).

d. *Ultimately, this series of events is fulfilled in Jesus Christ.* That's the
gospel in Hosea.

2. Big picture (part 2): Hosea describes God as they had known him
through the Law, and even announces his edicts from that God's perspective. He paints us a picture of the ugly, retributive monster-God of their
understanding and even prophesies in that God's name according to their
limited Mosaic expectations. With that image of wrath clearly before their
eyes, Hosea unveils an entirely new and radically different image of God.
His prophetic acts of marriage and adoption are a *major* advancement in
Yahweh's self-revelation. Hosea's little book bridges the image of God seen
in Moses and the revelation of God-in-Christ. You see the transition (travail!) in just a few short chapters of Hebrew poetic drama. Hosea turns his
gaze from Moses and fixes his eyes on the cross, where he sees Christ forgiving and reconciling the wayward race—just as Hosea has already embodied
God's love by forgiving his partner and restoring her children to his family.

3. You asked how we can trust Hosea when so much of what he says is
contradicted in the message of the gospel? How is this:

a. By never reading it apart from the gospel lens of Christ as our
Emmaus-Road Rabbi.

b. By seeing how those ugly pictures of God fit into Hosea's broader
rhetorical-redemption scheme.

c. By seeing how even God's judgment of the nations is subsumed in his intent to redeem the nations.

Regarding that last point, that's where the twelve Minor Prophets come in: Nahum prophesies destruction on Nineveh; Jonah prophesies Nineveh's redemption. There's a trajectory at work, transitioning (travail!): God's people from a tribal network with local warrior-deity into the global blessing whose God created all things to redeem and bless all nations.

Then why these fearful judgments to their neighbors? They are for the people of God to overhear: the judgments against their oppressors function to remind Israel/Judah that they are not ultimately abandoned and that their vindication awaits. And the redemption of their oppressors reminds them of their role as Abraham's seed to fill and bless the world until all the nations stream into the new Jerusalem. This outcome is especially highlighted in Isaiah and in Micah.

How can both be true? Wait for it. Watch for it. There's a Messiah coming who will fulfill these prophecies in himself.

And while the immediate context of Hosea 6:1–3 may be read as the people's cynicism, *in Christ*, it is fulfilled with utmost sincerity:

¹Come, let us return to the LORD.
He has torn us to pieces
    but he will heal us;
he has injured us
    but he will bind up our wounds.
²After two days he will revive us;
    on the third day he will restore us,
    that we may live in his presence.
³Let us acknowledge the LORD;
    let us press on to acknowledge him.
As surely as the sun rises,
    he will appear;
he will come to us like the winter rains,
    like the spring rains that water the earth.   (Hos 6:1–3 NIV)

Selah.

Hi Brad,

Thank you, my friend. I'm going to read and reread Hosea and this email. Then maybe the rest of the Minor Prophets. With Jesus as my Rabbi.

So, if am I understanding you correctly, could I summarize the tension of the ugly bits of Hosea as: God, through Hosea, engaging in rhetoric (as a condescension to man's distorted view of *Abba*) in order to get their attention and then point them to the ultimate reconciliation that will come through Christ?

Hi Tim,

I think that's right.

And it's not just *empty* rhetoric.

This IS what they've done. This IS what they deserve. And they will NOT get what they deserve.

There is a dilemma: we have a divine Author who is not the monster depicted, so in that sense, it must be rhetorical from heaven's point of view. But also, we have the human community (and maybe Hosea himself at first) in whose worldview God really is like that. The only way to sort that out is by reading it as revealing both God (where it's Christlike) and us (where our vision of God is not Christlike). You're watching that distinction unfold right within the book!

Hey Brad,

Cool! I think the language I'm struggling with is "Getting what they (we) deserve." It is a difficult phrase because it conjures up this concept of punishment, which is what leads to the penal substitutionary argument that "Jesus got what we deserve." I was feeling great about a fresh revelation of Romans 1:18, that God's wrath is poured out on ungodliness and unrighteousness itself, rather than those who perform the ungodliness; but then this morning I couldn't escape Romans 2:2–3, which seems to be saying that, ultimately, we must face his judgment (what we deserve) for our unrighteous behavior.

Do we deserve death because it is the natural outcome of sin (the wages of sin)? Is "deserve" less of a punitive thing, and more of the way God made things to work?

Good question, Tim,

I suspect that "what they deserve" is not how God's nature truly works. We're talking about God undoing the human conception of justice as "deserving" with a message of grace.

But that undoing has to engage "deserve" to shatter it.

Where did "deserving justice" come from? From the Law, as it sought to impose limits on vengeance and then move beyond law to grace. That change is not in God as such but marks the path as our gracious God walking us forward.

Here's the progression:

+ Vengeance: 70 x 7 (Lamech)
+ Law: 1 x 1 = eye for an eye (Moses)
+ Grace: 70 x 7 = forgiveness (Christ)

So, by "what they deserve," I think Hosea is referring to what the Law, with its legalized and limited vengeance, would have doled out. But Christ shows us (through Hosea) a better way, a counterintuitive way in which divine justice (the restoration of a just society) is accomplished through grace and mercy. How can that work? Because grace wins the heart rather than restrains (by coercion) the behavior.

Thanks, Brad

I love that progression from Lamech to Christ!

But didn't the Law come from God? Doesn't the Law reflect who God is or how he operates?

Hey Tim,

Which Law?

The Ten Commandments?

The instructions for ceremonial worship?

The ordinances commanding enslavement and death of enemies?

The Torah sometimes includes statements like, "These are the statutes and ordinances and laws which the LORD established *between* Himself and the sons of Israel *through Moses* at Mount Sinai" (Lev 26:46 NASB)[144]

I tend to think of "God's Law" quite narrowly, referring specifically to the Ten Commandments, delivered by angels[145] to Moses on Sinai, inscribed in tablets of stone. These summarize and apply the call to love God and love our neighbors as a simple and just community covenant.

And then we have "Moses' ordinances"—Israel's voluminous, nitty-gritty social contract with all its civic and religious details. I'm inclined to picture God *authorizing* Moses to *author* these detailed ordinances for a people in transition (travail!). Perhaps these statutes reflect Moses's training in Egypt, his worldview, and the culture of the day. God gives Moses freedom, wisdom, and responsibility for this, though the outcome includes some pretty awful stuff. Why?

Because Moses himself composed these ordinances in the name of God. How so? What if God gave Moses the task, not the laws themselves? That seems completely legit to me—more so than imagining God dictated merciless violence and retribution into the Torah directly. But since God has Moses's back, the narrator sees them as God's laws.

And then there are all those laws that Jesus says reflected Israel's hardness of heart and rejection of a direct relationship with God. They also reflect an initial accommodation to sacrificial religion, common across the globe. And we also see the Spirit weaving in the typology that will lead people out of that system toward a new covenant. Isaiah, Jeremiah, Micah, and Christ are all super clear...the temple establishment of ritual slaughter was never God's heart or God's idea. God repeatedly asks instead for justice and mercy—he has no need for a temple or sacrifices, etc.

Hey Brad,

I think you just rattled my cage with that concept that Moses's laws were adopted in the name of God, but not written by God directly. Does it

---

144. See also Exodus 24:3; Leviticus 10:11; Numbers 36:13; 1 Chronicles 22:13; Nehemiah 1:7; Malachi 4:4.
145. See, for example, Acts 7:53.

actually say that? Isn't the book of Leviticus all in quotations as a transcript of what God told Moses to write down?

Yo, Tim,

It's worse than you think.

Re: Levitical Laws

I don't want to rattle your cage, but I don't mind if Jeremiah does. In chapter 7. Brace yourself:

> ²¹Thus says the LORD of hosts, the God of Israel, "Add your burnt offerings to your sacrifices and eat flesh. ²²*For I DID NOT speak to your fathers, or command them in the day that I brought them out of the land of Egypt, concerning burnt offerings and sacrifices.* ²³But this is what I commanded them, saying, 'Obey My voice, and I will be your God, and you will be My people; and you will walk in all the way which I command you, that it may be well with you.' ²⁴Yet they did not obey or incline their ear, but walked in *their own* counsels *and* in the stubbornness of their evil heart, and went backward and not forward." (Jer 7:21–24 NASB)

I'm using the NASB for accuracy here because the translators who created the NIV were likewise so rattled that they had to throw in the word "just." They write, "I did not *just* give them commands..." (v. 22).

They simply cannot believe that what Jeremiah says can be true. They can show you the quotations in Leviticus. But can you see how adding "just" perverts Jeremiah's meaning (without even indicating they've added the word)? Do you hear a difference between these two statements?

+ "I did not beat my wife."

+ "I did not *just* beat my wife."

But don't shoot the messenger. Oops. The Israelites did. They threw Jeremiah down a well and later stoned him to death. And then they declared him a prophet. And then they included his words as Scripture.

Here is Scripture in travail—and now, in your reading, you face the labor of realizing that the *Bible says* God *did not say* what *the Bible says God did say.* That is a problem for us. It was a problem for Jeremiah's opponents. But, apparently, it's not a problem for Jeremiah, the book that records his words, or a problem for the Spirit who inspired him.

Before catching your breath, I'll add one more hiccup. MOST Jewish rabbis and Christian scholars now believe the final form of Leviticus was completed between 538–332 BC...*a thousand years after Moses,* by Jews in exile! *After the death of Jeremiah.* The book of Jeremiah was likewise composed over time, some of it overlapping the composition of Leviticus. What are the implications? For one, we're holding two texts in travail and better not touch them without the Rabbi's guidance:

> "'You study the Bible,' Jesus continued, "because you suppose that you'll discover the life of God's coming age in it. In fact, it's the Bible which gives evidence about me!" (John 5:39 NTE)

Re: Deuteronomic Ordinances

I find Deuteronomy even more difficult. When I slowed down my reading to a digestible pace, I found myself choking on the problems its instructions posed to basic human morality. Could the *Abba* revealed by Christ issue these commands (from Deuteronomy 20–21, still from the NASB)?

> [20:10]When you approach a city to fight against it, you shall offer it terms of peace. [11]*If it agrees to make peace* with you and opens to you, then all the people who are found in it *shall become your forced labor* and shall serve you. [12]However, if it does not make peace with you, but makes war against you, then you shall besiege it. [13]When the LORD your God gives it into your hand, *you shall strike all the men* in it with the edge of the sword. [14]Only the women and the children and the animals and all that is in the city, all its spoil, you shall take as booty for yourself; and you shall use the spoil of your enemies which the LORD your God has given you. [15]Thus you shall do to all the cities that are very far from you, which are not of the cities of these nations nearby. [16]Only in the cities of these peoples that the LORD your God is giving you as an inheritance, *you shall not leave alive anything that breathes.* [17]But you shall utterly destroy them, the Hittite and the Amorite, the Canaanite and the

Perizzite, the Hivite and the Jebusite, as the LORD your God has commanded you, [18]so that they may not teach you to do according to all their detestable things which they have done for their gods, so that you would sin against the LORD your God.

[21:10]When you go out to battle against your enemies, and the LORD your God delivers them into your hands and you take them away captive, [11] and *see among the captives a beautiful woman*, and have a desire for her and would take her as a wife for yourself, [12] then you shall *bring her home to your house, and she shall shave her head and trim her nails.* [13] She shall also remove the clothes of her captivity and shall remain in your house, and mourn her father and mother a full month; and *after that you may go in to her* and be her husband and she shall be your wife. [14] It shall be, if you are not pleased with her, then you shall let her go wherever she wishes; but you shall certainly not sell her for money, you shall not mistreat her, because *you have humbled her.*

*Could Abba have commanded this?*

I know Christians who are so hateful to Muslims that if I showed them this passage and said it was from the Qur'an, they would not hesitate to condemn and burn it. But if it's in the Bible? Does the binding and title on the book suddenly make it defensible?

I desperately read backward in the text to find the actual source of these commands, but it remained unclear. Did God really say it? Or are these laws God dictated to Moses? Does Moses say God gave them to him? Or did God say Moses could come up with them? Or does a narrator draw his own assumptions hundreds of years after the fact? And again, when was this written? Some scholars believe Deuteronomy was composed during the time of Josiah, 649–609 BC. Others believe it was composed even later, during the exile.

Sad to say, it gets still worse. Much worse.

Re: Numbers!

[31:13]Moses and Eleazar the priest and all the leaders of the congregation went out to meet them outside the camp. [14]Moses was angry with the officers of the army, the captains of thousands and the captains of hundreds, who had come from service in the war. [15]And Moses said to them, "Have you spared [lit. "let...live"] all the women? [16]Behold, these caused the sons of Israel, through the counsel of Balaam, to trespass against the LORD in the matter of Peor, so the plague was among the congregation of the LORD. [17]Now therefore, *kill every male among the little ones, and kill every woman who has known man intimately.* [18]*But all the girls* [lit. female children] *who have not known man intimately, spare for yourselves....* [30]From the sons of Israel's half, you shall take one drawn out of every fifty of the persons, of the cattle, of the donkeys and of the sheep, from all the animals, and *give them to the Levites* who keep charge of the tabernacle of the LORD." [31]Moses and Eleazar the priest did just as the LORD had commanded Moses. [32]Now the booty that remained from the spoil which the men of war had plundered was 675,000 sheep, [33]and 72,000 cattle, [34]and 61,000 donkeys, [35]and of human beings, of *the women who had not known man intimately, all the persons were 32,000.*

(Num 31:13–18, 30–35 NASB)

Let's summarize: Kill all the men. Sort out the women. Check the female children. Which ones have a hymen? If they don't, kill them. If they do, if they're virgins, keep them for yourselves as booty. Oh, but be sure to give some of the virgins to the Levites.

Could *Abba* have issued these commands? Could *Jesus* (God in the flesh and famous for his liberation of women) say such things?

The problem with the ideology of literalism is that it cannot possibly allow us to read these Scriptures. Or if it does, we must shut off our God-given conscience. Or we have to read them as cartoon material. The skeptics love this stuff because the same literalism arms them as enemies of faith.[146]

Mercifully, the Jewish rabbis (even the Pharisees) and the early church fathers recognized that we cannot read this material literally and still have

---

146. See The Brick Testament's striking depictions of Numbers 31 at http://www.thebricktestament.com/the_wilderness/massacre_of_the_midianites/nm31_01p25_16p31_02.html.

a good God. The big exception was the infamous heretic Marcion. His literalism caused him to reject the Old Testament altogether because he knew such stories do *not* describe the God revealed through Jesus.

But if we don't toss these stories aside, how do we read them? And how could Jesus say the following?!

> In everything, therefore, treat people the same way you want them to treat you, for *this is the Law and the Prophets.*
>
> (Matt 7:12 NASB)

Or…

> 36"Teacher, which is the great commandment in the Law?" 37And He said to him, "'You shall love the Lord your God with all your heart, and with all your soul, and with all your mind.' 38This is the great and foremost commandment. 39The second is like it, 'You shall love your neighbor as yourself.' 40*On these two commandments depend the whole Law and the Prophets.*" (Matt 22:36–40 NASB)

The problem is not the Bible. It was always the literalism that inerrancy demanded. And now I must relearn how to read it in such a way that submits the whole of Scripture to the revelation of Jesus Christ. That's not easy work, as you can see. But it's also not impossible. We just need to learn how to read it with the Spirit who shows us the deeper spiritual meaning that is not accessible to the flesh (1 Cor 2), to have the veil of the letter that shrouds our hearts removed (2 Cor 3), and to see how these disturbing stories stand as cautionary tales of what not to do (1 Cor 10).

Blessings on you, Tim,
Brad

Brad, that is really helpful stuff.

The [Brick Testament depiction] is amazing because the juxtaposition of form and content helps one see how absolutely ridiculous it is.

One final question (for now). Then why the heck is all this crap in there, and why did God allow it to be in there in such a way that it would fool millions of people into thinking that *Abba* is actually like that? And what do stories like that tell us about Jesus?

Hi Tim,

Why the heck is all that in the Bible?

I defer to Pete Enns's wonderful one-liner:

"Because God let his children tell the story."

...The Bible is what happens when God allows his children to tell his story—which means the biblical writers told the story from their point of view, with their limitations, within the cultural context in which they wrote.[147]

What I wanted Tim to see in our correspondence was that God gave his children the freedom to tell their story from their point of view. Or points of view (plural)! That's an observable feature of our sacred Scriptures. That doesn't exactly answer why. But there it is. A stubborn fact.

How, then, can we say the Bible is inspired? Because as their storytelling proceeds, the Holy Spirit weaves redemption into the grand narrative by his presence in their polyphonic journey. It's now time for me to explore the polyphony in detail.

---

147. Peter Enns, "'God Lets His Children Tell the Story': An Angle on God's Violence in the Old Testament," *Pete Enns.com*, https://peteenns.com/god-lets-his-children-tell-the-story-an-angle-on-gods-violence-in-the-old-testament.

### CHAPTER 14

# A GRAND POLYPHONY: ONE STORY, TWO REVELATIONS, FOUR VOICES[148]

"I actually do read the book of Amos, but I also read the book of Job. And I do read Lamentations, but I also read Psalm 44. And I started to think about the way in which the different strands of the Old Testament jangle against each other, and they are only resolved when you get to Jesus himself. So, then it becomes part of the larger theological project to say, 'If you want to talk about God and what God is doing, please don't dream of doing that until you've looked very carefully at God incarnate.'"[149]

—N. T. Wright

## BIBLICAL AUTHORITY REVISITED

Earlier in the book, I introduced the question of how the Scriptures exercise *practical* authority in our lives and churches. Now we need to

---

148. An earlier draft of "One Story, Two Revelations, Four Voices" was originally posted on *Clarion Journal for Religion, Peace & Justice*, August 28, 2014, https://www.clarion-journal. com/clarion_journal_of_spirit/2014/08/one-story-two-revelations-four-voices-reading-biblical-narrative-christologically-brad-jersak.html. That presentation was inspired by and adapted from ideas and conversations with Richard Beck and Michael Hardin.
149. N. T. Wright, "God and the Pandemic," Interview, *100 Huntley Street*, YouTube video, 14:14, July 6, 2020, https://youtu.be/sAPgzyR6qLU/.

revisit the question of biblical authority with a historical overview from 30,000 feet. Back in the day, when the early church first came to faith in Jesus as Messiah but still relied entirely on the Hebrew Scriptures as their only "Bible," gospel preaching focused on the myriad of Old Testament texts fulfilled in Christ. They saw Jesus everywhere in their Scriptures, before any apostle or evangelist put quill to parchment. Indeed, we read how Jesus himself perceived his life as woven across the whole fabric of Jewish narrative, hymnology, and prophecy.[150] For decades, the continuity and correlations between the Jewish narrative and the Christian revelation were a continuous wonder of discoveries.

But by the end of the first century, believers were also noticing some disturbing discontinuities as well. They noted the disparity between the image of the Father revealed in Christ with the violent images, actions, laws, and judgments associated with Yahweh on display throughout the Law, the Writings, and the Prophets. It seemed impossible that the God whom Jesus called Father could be responsible for the pattern of hatred and atrocities often described in the text and ascribed to his name.

The issue was so acute that potential solutions triggered schism. Believers attempted three major, contrary approaches. The Gnostics preserved the perfection of the Creator God by assigning Old Testament destruction and retribution to lesser gods and demiurges—distortions of God's will. They included Yahweh among this secondary, violent company. Others, like the Marcionites, whom I discussed earlier, could not bear the discontinuity and ultimately abandoned the Old Testament altogether as sub-Christian and unfit for continued use as authoritative Scripture in the church. It's uncanny how these old (and failed) solutions are being recycled today as a rejection of the "Old Testament God."

The church fathers and mothers who represent orthodox Christian belief rigorously anathematized these answers...*but* they did not ignore the question. They only came to peace with the Hebrew text by nodding to its literal origins but interpreting its *meaning* spiritually or allegorically, as I've described in part I of this book. Spiritualizing the Bible was deemed necessary in light of the obvious (to them) discrepancy between God as "a man of war" (Exodus 15:3 KJV, NKJV, RSV) and Jesus as the "Prince of Peace"

---

150. See Luke 24:13–35.

(numerous translations). Up until the imperial reign of the Holy Roman Empire, the great conquest texts of the Bible stood as real contradictions to the cross of Christ *unless* interpreted figuratively as spiritual battles with an unseen enemy, as in Ephesians 6:12 ("Our battle is not against flesh and blood") and 2 Corinthians 10:4 ("Our weapons are not the weapons of this world").

With the adoption of Christian faith by the Roman emperor Constantine, the church was, for the first time, soon in the awkward position of being sanctioned by the state *and* expected to return the favor. How would the kingdom identified with the cross coexist with the realpolitik of a military empire? Augustine, for one, sought to lay some ground rules via his parameters for "Just War." But in spite of Augustine's agenda for restraint, Christendom soon became comfortable enough with war to employ literal uses of Old Testament violence to justify militarism. The church-state marriage could overlook the discontinuity of sacred militarism with the otherwise clear prohibitions of Jesus, Paul, and John against hatred and violence (not to mention Isaiah's prophecies of the peaceable kingdom). Over the centuries, under those conditions, with rare exceptions (e.g., the Anabaptists, the Quakers, and the Tolstoyans), the church could generally live comfortably with a cross in one hand and a sword in the other. Stained-glass warriors furnished cathedrals without triggering a flinch. In other words, the tension between the violence of God in the Bible and the minority report repudiating such a vision has largely been a nonissue for much of our history. Even questioning the apparent discrepancy appears to fundamentalists like a direct challenge to the authority of the Bible!

Moreover, Western culture itself feels threatened when a biblical call to arms is undermined. As Brian Zahnd has taught me, one can easily rouse young zealots to give their lives for "freedom" (i.e., democracy, capitalism, patriotism), but to convince parents to sacrifice their children on the altar of war, one must convince them that "God is on our side." Once that is established, all manner of brutality can commence "in the name of the Lord." Even invoking the words of Christ's Sermon on the Mount barely slows the momentum of sacred violence. But to those who hear Jesus's "No" to hatred and death, we've only come full circle to the problem

196 A MORE CHRISTLIKE WORD

of the early church: how to hold to biblical authority when Jesus himself seems to challenge it.

Modern solutions like "progressive revelation" or a "canon within a canon" are efforts at retaining a measure of biblicism alongside faithfulness to Christ. I remain convinced that my "progressive illumination" alternative can prove helpful.[151] But a new consensus has been emerging around what we are calling a "Christ-centered hermeneutic." This term describes what we have been discussing throughout this book: that we must read the whole Bible through the lens of Jesus. Christ is the chief cornerstone—the Canon par excellence—so that all Scripture is received as authoritative only after passing through the life, teachings, and gospel of Jesus. He has and is the first and final Word. I believe this type of statement works and will finally win the day.

But it does open a few interesting questions I would like to address for further exploration.

## QUESTION 1: WHY HAS THIS COME UP AGAIN?

How or why has this tension around biblical authority—this discomfort between competing images of God in the text—arisen in this generation?

In part, we can cite a general willingness to question authority, based in disillusionment around abusive leadership and an increasing capacity for critical thinking. Further, the average Christian is now *less* biblically literate, and the average atheist is significantly *more* biblically aware, now than in the twentieth century. Therefore, crass indoctrination or an appeal to "because the Bible says so" is far less credible. And among the most faithful, "final authority" is shifting from the Bible in general to Jesus in particular. But something more is afoot.

My belief is that theologians and teachers are *not* the pharmacists of the church. Maybe we thought that, after a careful study of the Bible and sound theology, theologians would prescribe (via the preachers they trained) what people ought to believe. That is not actually how theology

---

151. See Bradley Jersak, "But I Say to You…," *Clarion Journal for Religion, Peace & Justice*, June 9, 2006, https://www.clarion-journal.com/clarion_journal_of_spirit/2006/06/but_i_say_to_yo.html>.

works in practice, nor should it be. Rather, the best theologians are those who analyze and describe what the praying and worshipping community has come to believe through its corporate experience of the reality of the triune God. In other words, worship precedes theology, often by several decades. As we experience the presence of God in prayer and worship, we begin to compose liturgies and songs that express what we have come to see. Eventually, theologians become observant and follow suit. Teachers may begin to confirm the implications of what the congregation has already been singing and praying (which is to say, *believing*) over the past decades. Ironically, the first generation of these teachers are often regarded as heretical, sometimes even by the very congregants who spawned the original revelation. Why? It may be that the congregation is still under the spell of previous teachers whom they regard as their authoritative prescribers of the truth. A strange brew when you really ponder it.

For example, when I began teaching believers to "open the eyes of their heart," I was using the New Testament to affirm and welcome into practice what the church had been proclaiming for generations in our hymnology. Sometimes even those who faithfully sang, "Turn your eyes upon Jesus, look full in His wonderful face," or "Open the eyes of my heart, Lord, I want to see you," would go on the attack when I showed them the new-covenant passages that confirmed their songs. In spite of what we were confessing openly in worship, the old teaching continued to condemn any form of Christian mysticism as "New Age." My sense is that our theology is finally catching up to what we already believed in our worship.

Beyond that simple example, I see another revelation at work, spreading like yeast across the church. *We've rediscovered the Father's heart of intimate and infinite love.* This revelation may bring us into a new reformation in Western theology.

For over thirty years, the church has sung, prayed, and preached on "Father's heart" texts, such as the parable of the prodigal son (or sons... or prodigal Father, depending on your angle). *Millions* of people are truly experiencing God's deep affection for them, just as they are, for the first time. We the church *knew*, once again, as we had *not known* since perhaps the early church, that God is Love and that God's love in Christ can change us from the inside out.

As I watched this revelation capture us, the corollary questions became increasingly obvious, even down to the order in which the dominoes must fall. I will state the following as questions to be raised if the Father's-heart revelation is taken as true.

*Revelation*: God is love. God, in his very essence, is love, expressed as the Father's heart revealed through Jesus.[152]

1.  If God is love and has revealed Godself through Christ, what happened on the cross? Was the Father truly punishing the Son and pouring out his wrath? Or what does it mean that God was *in Christ*, reconciling the world to himself by forgiving us?[153] This is the question of the atonement.[154]

2.  If God is love and has revealed himself through Christ, what's the deal with hell? Is hell really eternal conscious torment in a lake of fire, torturing unbelievers for all eternity? Is there no opportunity for repentance when we face Christ as our Judge? Or could the final judgment somehow be redemptive and restorative, part of the blessed hope where mercy, not torment, endures forever? This is the question of postmortem judgment.[155]

3.  If God is love and has revealed himself through Christ, what's the deal with Old Testament violence? Why the commands to slaughter whole nations, including their children, especially for the sins of their grandparents? Why the proclamation of compassion coupled with swift and merciless judgments? This is the question of Old Testament genocide.

4.  If we challenge retributive justice and divine violence at the cross, at the final judgment, and in the Old Testament, what becomes of biblical inspiration? Is the Bible no longer taken as "our final authority for faith and practice"? Or is there a practical way in

---

152. See Bradley Jersak, *A More Christlike God: A More Beautiful Gospel* (Pasadena, CA: CWR Press, 2016).

153. See 2 Corinthians 5:19.

154. See Bradley Jersak and Michael Hardin, eds., *Stricken by God?: Nonviolent Identification and the Victory of Christ* (Grand Rapids, MI: Eerdmans, 2007).

155. See Bradley Jersak, *Her Gates Will Never Be Shut: Hope, Hell, and the New Jerusalem* (Eugene, OR: Wipf & Stock, 2009).

which Jesus Christ becomes our final authority? This is the question of biblical authority, which this book is at least beginning to address.

Remarkably, I have been asked these questions over and over, in this exact sequence, in private and public conversations over the past thirty years. Whether in the late-night whispers of a Nicodemus or in the heat of Q & R sessions, these questions are the natural response of the body of Christ to the good news that God is Love, revealed through the Christ, crucified and risen. Beyond my own ministry, I see these questions swelling across Christian publishing houses, in articles in scholarly journals, and at conferences.

## QUESTION 2: WHAT IS THE WAY FORWARD?

The following presentation is a particular Christocentric approach to the Bible that resonated with my congregation while we wrestled through the messianic psalms together. Week after week, we struggled to get our hearts and minds around Davidic hymns that simultaneously testify to the coming Messiah while demanding and even glorifying merciless violence that our Messiah, Jesus, would later directly forbid. How does one engage gruesome images and acts of God from the very psalms in which New Testament authors recognize Jesus as the referent?

We return to these salient questions: Even if we use Christ's words and life as a filter, what do we do with the remaining rather embarrassing passages? Do we conclude they are uninspired? Should they be discarded? Shall we just pick and choose what we like, taking our scissors to the pages, as others have done in the past? Or is there a way to acknowledge and embrace the whole story as a narrative told by the *polyphony of voices*, without affirming every verse as revelation? Or is it *all* God-breathed revelation? And if so, of what nature?[156]

---

156. My inspiration (but no blame) for what follows is derived, distilled, and tweaked from conversations with Walter Brueggemann, Ron Dart, Lazar Puhalo, Brian Zahnd, René Girard, Lorri and Michael Hardin, Kevin Miller, and Derek Flood.

## INTRODUCTION

In 2020, I cowrote a novella with Wm. Paul Young, author of *The Shack*, outlined in three parts according to the pose of a clenched fist, a limp wrist, and an open hand. Each of these pictures represents a character in our story, contrasting the three postures of *striving, despair, and surrender*. All three voices are essential to the truth we wanted our story to convey, as they interact around the role of the human will. The clenched fist portrays the protagonist's self-will and striving; the limp wrist shows the broken will of his defeated character; and the open hand represents his need to become willing if he hopes to be healed. The question is whether or not the protagonist can make this journey.

We could use the same outline—willfulness, brokenness, surrender—to track three phases in the life of anyone who embarks on a journey of recovery.

By including the first two voices, Paul and I are obviously not endorsing stubbornness or hopelessness. Rather, the voices are allowed to speak so that readers who relate to them might begin to see a third way, drawing them out of "stuckness" into freedom. A good story contrasts perspectives, and a great story holds up a mirror[157] in which readers might see themselves and hear truth calling. After reading such a story, the perceptive reader would distinguish between the voices. They would not take each voice as equally helpful or true. Neither would we go back through the novel to highlight only the voice of the open hand and censor out every speech that expresses a clenched fist or a limp wrist. Reducing the story to a decontextualized booklet of wise aphorisms would cheapen, not improve, the delivery of the whole truth.

### THE BIBLE TELLS OUR FAITH STORY THROUGH A POLYPHONY OF VOICES

I want to join the expanding chorus of scholars who read the whole Bible as our faith story while also recognizing it as a polyphony of interacting voices. These voices come in the form of speeches by characters in the narrative; written records of lawmakers, liturgists, and prophets; and even the perspective of the immediate narrator.

---

157. See Lazar Puhalo, *The Mirror of Scripture*.

## THE BIBLE TELLS OUR FAITH STORY THROUGH A POLYPHONY OF VOICES.

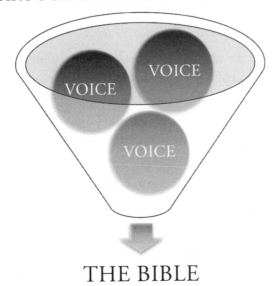

## THE BIBLE

### THE BIBLE TELLS OUR FAITH STORY—IT CONTRASTS TWO REVELATIONS

As we have seen, inerrantists cornered themselves into affirming that every word of the Bible is true, thus having to gloss over or twist passages that are in serious tension or even straightforward contradiction. But Old Testament scholar Walter Brueggemann assures us that the nature of Jewish Scripture is to report conflicting perspectives and competing voices without any embarrassment.[158] The redactors who gathered the Hebrew canon consciously incorporated texts that challenge and subvert other texts across the Scriptures...without imagining that this might undermine or threaten the authority of their Bible. The narrative is allowed to stand as is, confirming the integrity and genius of the story of God and God's people.

So, of course every word of the Bible is "true," but in a richer and less wooden way than the inerrantists could stomach. But *how* is it true?

First, the whole Bible is true as it tells *one* ongoing faith story of the people of God through this polyphony of voices. Second, the whole of

---

158. Walter Brueggemann, *The Prophetic Imagination* (Minneapolis, MN: Fortress Press, 2001).

Scripture is true because it faithfully contrasts *two* revelations. Namely, the Bible reveals:

+ The fallen state of humanity and its broken images of God

+ Humanity restored in Jesus, who incarnates the true image of God

The simplest way to say this is that the Bible is a revelation about us and about God. What the Bible reveals about the fallen human condition is our "sin." This includes the depth of our "death anxiety,"[159] the nature of "mimetic desire" and the "scapegoating mechanism,"[160] and our human propensity to demand retributive justice and then sacralize retribution through sacrificial religion.

## THE BIBLE TELLS OUR FAITH STORY— IT CONTRASTS *TWO REVELATIONS.*

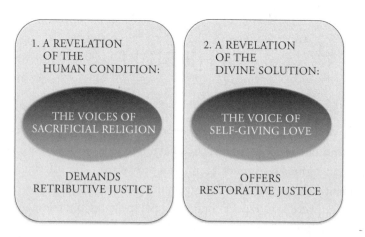

| 1. A REVELATION OF THE HUMAN CONDITION: | 2. A REVELATION OF THE DIVINE SOLUTION: |
| --- | --- |
| THE VOICES OF SACRIFICIAL RELIGION | THE VOICE OF SELF-GIVING LOVE |
| DEMANDS RETRIBUTIVE JUSTICE | OFFERS RESTORATIVE JUSTICE |

The cycle of violence established and perpetuated by such systems is laid bare in the Bible like nowhere else. Conservatives may think we need to justify the violence texts. Progressives may think we need to erase them. Rather, we gaze in wonder at how God brilliantly exposes and diagnoses the mess we are in. For this chapter, I am calling this mess "the voice of sacrificial religion."

---

159. See Ernest Becker, *The Denial of Death* (New York: Simon and Schuster, 1973); Richard Beck, *The Slavery of Death* (Eugene, OR: Cascade Books, 2013).
160. René Girard, *The Girard Reader*, ed. James G. Williams (Chestnut Ridge, NY: Crossroad, 1996).

I am using the word *sacrificial* to describe religion and *self-giving* to describe Christ's love, both for symmetry and for subversion. I am resisting the word *sacrifice*, even though Christ is our Pascal Lamb who offered himself for us. I do this partly to avoid any hint of pagan appeasement and partly in response to this wise warning from Lorri Hardin:

> I believe it's essential that we use the word "self-offering" in place of "sacrifice" when referring to Jesus's love, work etc., lest we also play back into the sick notion of being doormats or putting ourselves in positions to be harmed, just as the early Christian martyrs were warned against. This is carried out very nicely in Hebrews, in that the author has chosen to use *phero* (offering) rather than *thuo* (sacrifice), which is unfortunately not followed through in the translations.[161]

The broken voice of sacrificial religion demands *retributive* justice, and so do its gods. By contrast, the Bible also reveals the surprising and counterintuitive response to our spiritual and social malady: humanity redeemed in Christ, the true image of God. God-in-Christ counters retribution with restoration, justice-as-punishment with justice-as-mercy, wrath with forgiveness, and death anxiety with resurrection life. Jesus's messianic victory is not through military conquest but through radical, kenotic (self-emptying) service. Thus, the voice of Christ forever abolishes *sacrificial religion* through the supreme act of *self-giving love*.

The Bible preserves God's revelation of fallen humanity not because it harmonizes with the voice of self-giving love, but because the former revelation begs for and points to the latter. It is therefore nonnegotiable that we read particular texts in the context of the whole story, so we don't mistake specific retributive invectives or religious injunctions as "the word of the Lord" to followers of the voice of Jesus.

## THE BIBLE TELLS OUR FAITH STORY—SACRIFICIAL RELIGION HAS THREE VOICES

Moreover, we study the voices of sacrificial religion because we recognize ourselves in them and, according to Paul, will see their negative examples as warnings.

---

161. Lorri Hardin, email message to author, summer 2012.

The voices of sacrificial religion that permeate the story of Scripture *are at least threefold* in tone and content. Sacrificial religion speaks to readers as "the voice of the accuser," "the voice of the victim," and "the voice of the law." Each voice makes particular claims and demands.

## THE BIBLE TELLS OUR FAITH STORY— SACRIFICIAL RELIGION HAS *THREE VOICES.*

**The voice of the accuser** is convinced that someone is guilty and must be punished. Judgment (including violence), to the accuser, is both necessary and deserved. It must somehow be *paid down*, whether through natural consequences or direct wrath. We hear that voice frequently within ourselves when watching the news and rendering our own verdict of deserved judgment on the accused. We feel outrage if those who appear guilty to us are acquitted. We feel that voice as *schadenfreude* (pain-joy) when we think, "They deserved that."

**The voice of the victim** is convinced that they are unjustly experiencing judgment or punishment. Victims feel like they are undeservedly on the receiving end of violence. If another person or system (e.g., insert infamous villain or institution's name here) is inflicting the harm, the voice of the victim wants *payback*, if not through restitution of what was lost, then at least through vengeance against the enemy—some punishment, hopefully violent. In effect, *the victim becomes the accuser, sharing the felt need for retributive justice.*

**The voice of the law,** seeing the runaway escalation of violence in the vigilante mob or the vengeful blood feud, is convinced that retributive justice must regulate violence in the name of civilization, or sacralize it in the name of God. Whether one's religion is dressed in Christianity, Judaism, Islam, atheism, capitalism, communism, or anarchism, the voice of the law sanctions violence for the sake of the greater good. Even an ideology of "freedom" (for personal rights or national security) makes violence appear necessary, a sort of blood sacrifice in the name of our god of choice. So civilized! So spiritual! But...

### THE BIBLE TELLS OUR FAITH STORY—SELF-GIVING LOVE HAS ONE VOICE

...a fourth voice emerges in the biblical text, corresponding to the revelation of sacrificial love. I call it "the voice of the Lamb." The voice of the Lamb—the voice enfleshed in Christ as self-giving love—proclaims the way of the cross vis-à-vis the worldly religious way of the sword.

## THE BIBLE TELLS OUR FAITH STORY— SELF-GIVING LOVE HAS ONE VOICE.

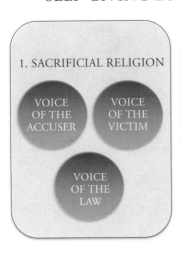

In Christ, God nullifies punishment, vengeance, and sacred violence in favor of mercy, forgiveness, and surrender. The cross publicly exposes the voices of the accuser, the victim, and the priest-judge as masks behind which we cover violence as the coping mechanism for our deep-seated powerlessness.

Through the passion narrative, we see Jesus assume, experience, and redeem human powerlessness. His is the *voice of the forgiving victim*, who breaks the cycle of violence by inviting God's mercy on behalf of his enemies, welcoming restoration and reconciliation into the suffering heart of the human condition.

### THE BIBLE TELLS OUR FAITH STORY—THE VOICES MUST BE DISTINGUISHED

In the end, those who gathered our Scriptures—both the Jewish rabbis and the early church fathers—saw the wisdom of retaining the whole story, the two revelations, and the four voices. The entire narrative tells the whole truth because it includes conflicting perspectives rather than only retaining the divine, messianic solution.

## THE BIBLE TELLS OUR FAITH STORY— THE VOICES MUST BE DISTINGUISHED.

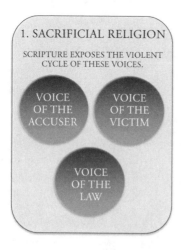

1. SACRIFICIAL RELIGION

SCRIPTURE EXPOSES THE VIOLENT CYCLE OF THESE VOICES.

VOICE OF THE ACCUSER

VOICE OF THE VICTIM

VOICE OF THE LAW

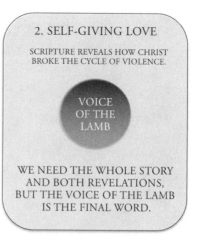

2. SELF-GIVING LOVE

SCRIPTURE REVEALS HOW CHRIST BROKE THE CYCLE OF VIOLENCE.

VOICE OF THE LAMB

WE NEED THE WHOLE STORY AND BOTH REVELATIONS, BUT THE VOICE OF THE LAMB IS THE FINAL WORD.

### THE BIBLE TELLS JOB'S FAITH STORY—THE VOICES MUST BE DISTINGUISHED

An analogous microcosm is obvious in the book of Job. In this epic poem, we can easily discern the voices of the accuser (the devil and possibly Job's wife), the victim (Job), the law (Job's three friends), and the Lord (via Elihu and God himself).

Satan would have God curse Job rather than give him undeserved blessing. Job's wife would have Job curse God in response to undeserved catastrophe. Job's friends would have Job admit to having sinned to justify catastrophe as deserved. Job justifies himself in the face of undeserved catastrophe. Elihu suggests letting go of justification, praying for an advocate, and invoking God's mercy and restoration. God, at last, delivers Job when Job offers a sacrifice of mercy (not payment) on behalf of his friends.

## THE BIBLE TELLS JOB'S FAITH STORY— THE VOICES MUST BE DISTINGUISHED.

Here is the point: would the story have been better if we had simply skipped the first thirty-one chapters? After all, God himself tells us that virtually everything to that point was folly! Then why not just delete it? Why fill our minds with flaws?

I used to flip right to the "good stuff" in Job until I started seeing how "good" the foolish counsel seemed to me. Some of it appears to make good sense. Exactly! The important function of the friends' speeches is to shine a light on our own idiocy. The friends' speeches are an inspired revelation of our own error, *not* a divine thumbs-up to their error.

It was a risky act of wisdom for the biblical compositors to retain voices that would later be revealed as incomplete, distorted, or completely mistaken. It's risky because we might take "the word of the Lord" *about* us as if we were hearing God's heart *for* us—as if an inspired record of the violence of sacrificial religion were a revelation of God's will and ways.

But it was wisdom because God gave us the cipher for distinguishing the revelations in contrast and the voices in competition. We are not left to pick and choose authoritative texts according to the whims of personal preference or cultural trendiness. Rather, the living Word—the living Canon to which every voice claiming revelation must bend and bow—came in person to establish the voice of the Lamb and the way of the cross as our plumb line, our filter.

This means that when we read the story of Abrahamic faith, we are required to read the entire narrative in light of Christ. We will need to render due diligence to the often difficult work of distinguishing between the image of God portrayed by *sacrificial religion* and the image of the Father revealed by the *self-offering Lamb*. We will need to filter through portrayals of God as retributive punisher, bearing in mind that God has delivered *all* judgment into the hands of Jesus, our redeeming and all-merciful Savior.

This discernment process may sound risky, but I would argue that it is *less* perilous to make these distinctions consciously with mindful criteria than to pretend we don't do it unconsciously all the time *or* ignore them altogether.

### THE BIBLE TELLS ISRAEL'S FAITH STORY—THE VOICES MUST BE DISTINGUISHED

For example, when we read the psalmist's blessing on infanticide in Psalm 137:9, no sane person who has experienced the Father's love honestly believes this is a revelation of God's will. We know instinctively that we have here a revelation of the psalmist's real but misguided demand for justice.

## THE BIBLE TELLS ISRAEL'S FAITH STORY— THE VOICES MUST BE DISTINGUISHED.

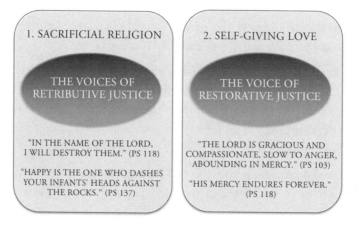

| 1. SACRIFICIAL RELIGION | 2. SELF-GIVING LOVE |
|---|---|
| THE VOICES OF RETRIBUTIVE JUSTICE | THE VOICE OF RESTORATIVE JUSTICE |
| "IN THE NAME OF THE LORD, I WILL DESTROY THEM." (PS 118) | "THE LORD IS GRACIOUS AND COMPASSIONATE, SLOW TO ANGER, ABOUNDING IN MERCY." (PS 103) |
| "HAPPY IS THE ONE WHO DASHES YOUR INFANTS' HEADS AGAINST THE ROCKS." (PS 137) | "HIS MERCY ENDURES FOREVER." (PS 118) |

I'm bewildered, then, when the same spiritual instinct doesn't kick in as we read "God's command" to prophets, judges, and kings that they should eradicate their Canaanite neighbors. What makes us need to defend divine provocations to merciless death-dealing as "the Word of the Lord"? Are we to believe that the Father of love revealed in the crucified Lamb harbored violent grudges? Why can't we see the human urge to spiritualize vengeance in those passages as naturally as we do with the psalmist? Indeed, we *must* in light of the revelation of Jesus.

Further, the ethical stakes to discern *which* biblical voice to follow are very high. I recall the 2004 CNN news program where Jesse Jackson and Jerry Falwell sparred over how to respond to terrorist attacks. Jackson called America to remember the Christian injunction to peacemaking ("Let's stop the killing and choose peace"). Then Falwell virtually paraphrased the psalmist's wrath in Psalm 118:10–12 (the New Testament's most-quoted messianic psalm!): "Chase them all over the world.... Blow them all away in the name of the Lord."[162]

Was Rev. Falwell responding biblically? Absolutely...if by "biblically" we mean that there exists a voice in the Bible that sanctions retributive violence. Moreover, that voice may be the perspective of God's heroic man or faithful woman as an authentic utterance of faith in the God who saves. It may be the retrospective analysis of the narrator, extolling the victories of God through God's chosen warriors. Those voices are part of the story; they belong. They stand as revelation. But when the text runs counter to the voice of the Lamb, it is revealing religion's idea of God, not Jesus's revelation of the Father.

### BOTH THE OLD AND NEW TESTAMENTS DISTINGUISH THESE VOICES

Nor is the issue as simple as "Old Testament bad, New Testament good." Both testaments problematize sacrificial religion and prioritize self-giving love. The voice of sacrificial love and restorative justice permeates the Hebrew Scriptures—it's the heartbeat of the Law and the pinnacle of the Prophets. The revelation of God as "gracious and compassionate" comes through loud and clear early in our story with God's preservation

---

162 See "Jesse Jackson Debates Falwell About Terrorism," *Late Edition with Wolf Blitzer*, CNN, YouTube video, 3:28, Aug. 29, 2006, https://www.youtube.com/watch?v=UY71nzkZHKQ.

of Hagar and Ishmael, in his self-disclosure to Moses, and on through the praises of the Psalms and into the Prophets, such as Isaiah, Jeremiah, Hosea, and Micah.[163]

Among Jesus's major agendas as teacher and prophet were his indictment of the temple establishment and its corrupt priesthood, his revelation of the Father heart of God in the Jewish tradition, and his personal claim to be the authoritative criteria by which we behold that God within the Bible.

## BOTH THE OT AND NT DISTINGUISH THESE VOICES.

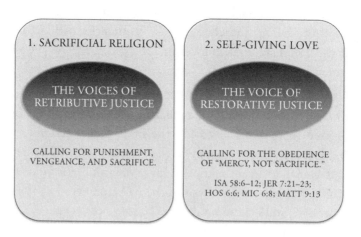

1. SACRIFICIAL RELIGION

THE VOICES OF RETRIBUTIVE JUSTICE

CALLING FOR PUNISHMENT, VENGEANCE, AND SACRIFICE.

2. SELF-GIVING LOVE

THE VOICE OF RESTORATIVE JUSTICE

CALLING FOR THE OBEDIENCE OF "MERCY, NOT SACRIFICE."

ISA 58:6–12; JER 7:21–23; HOS 6:6; MIC 6:8; MATT 9:13

I will leave it to nervier teachers to explicate ways in which the various voices make appearances in the New Testament.[164] My role, for now, is to raise questions. For example, is the polyphony I've described part of the tension between Paul and Peter, or Paul and James? The text tells us they were sometimes at odds, but are their texts at odds too? Maybe more than we thought? Maybe less? And how does the voice of the Lamb bring the final word? What we know for sure: Paul's battles with the Judaizers

---

163. See Genesis 16; Exodus 34; Psalm 103; 145; Isaiah 25; 35; 40; Jeremiah 31–33; Hosea 11; Micah 4.
164. I recommend starting with Michael Hardin, *The Jesus Driven Life: Reconnecting Humanity with Jesus*, 2nd ed. (Lancaster, PA: JDL Press, 2015).

suggest that the early church continued to struggle with issues of sacrificial religion.

So, do sacrificial religion and retributive justice retain a foothold within the New Testament writings? Perhaps not, but shouldn't we ask? How might the four Gospels address or reflect these voices as the evangelists address persecuted faith communities in the first century? We see evidence that Paul knew his readers clung to a desire for vengeance. Derek Flood has written with clarity about how Paul responds to this temptation.[165] I wonder where the voice of the wrathful victim also peeks through certain passages? Have we just assumed that it hasn't, or that it's God's revealed will?

I believe we need to retreat again and again to a Christotelic study of the Bible, *including* the post-resurrection reflections—the book of Acts, the Epistles, and the Apocalypse. We ought to bear in mind that just like Abraham, Moses, and David, so too the apostles of Christ and the authors of the New Testament were people in the *process* of transformation and discovery, not omniscient angels with magical pens. Their works, too, reveal both the human condition and faith culture of their era...*and* the divine solution—Jesus Christ, to whom all Scripture (before and after) points.

## CONCERNING THE CROSS

Derek Flood's book *Healing the Gospel*[166] applies the distinctions I've been making to atonement theology. He offers fresh insights to our understanding of the cross and draws a clear distinction between the cross as divine retribution (the appeasement of an angry deity), which he rejects, and the cross as a healing work of restorative justice. In his clear-minded reading of Romans and Hebrews, he leads the reader to see how wrath is averted by justification rather than satisfied by violence.

For my part, I would largely echo Flood in this way: Evangelical theology since the Reformation has predominantly interpreted the cross through the old lens of sacrificial religion (on steroids). We articulated

---

165. See Derek Flood, "The Way of Grace and Peace," *Sojourners*, January 2012, http://sojo. net/magazine/2012/01/way-peace-and-grace.
166. Derek Flood, *Healing the Gospel: A Radical Vision for Grace, Justice, and the Cross* (Eugene, OR: Cascade Books, 2012).

its meaning according to the juridical voices of retributive justice. And as Isaiah 53 foretold, we would consider the crucified One "stricken by God." We thought God was pouring out wrath on the Christ to satiate God's own need for retribution. We thought that Jesus's sacrifice was offered to appease the anger of God against the sin of the world.

### IN OUR THEOLOGY OF THE CROSS, DISTINGUISH THESE VOICES

However, as I've said many times in this book and elsewhere,[167] the cross is not so much the ultimate religious sacrifice as it is the ultimate revelation of self-giving love. God is not reconciled to us through retribution; we are reconciled to him through forgiveness. In other words, God was *never* our enemy![168]

## IN OUR THEOLOGY OF THE CROSS, DISTINGUISH THESE VOICES.

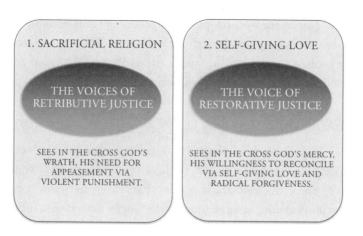

Once again, the cross does *not* reveal the violence of God against sin, but rather reveals both the violence of the human condition and the love of God toward sinners. In fact, the cross of Christ does not change *anything* about God or God's orientation toward the world; it reveals the gracious

---

167. See, for example, Jersak and Hardin, *Stricken by God?* and Jersak, *A More Christlike God.*

168. See, for example, Brian Zahnd, *Unconditional? The Call of Jesus to Radical Forgiveness* (Lake Mary, FL: Charisma House, 2011) and Brian Zahnd, *Beauty Will Save the World: Rediscovering the Allure and Mystery of Christianity* (Lake Mary, FL: Charisma House, 2012).

heart of the Father who has always been, is now, and will always be perfectly revealed in Jesus.

And that, my friends, is our Story.

### CHAPTER 15

# UNDER RECONSTRUCTION: CRAZY CHARACTERS, UNRELIABLE NARRATORS, AND THE DIVINE AUTHOR

## AFTER DECONSTRUCTION

*T*he last years have seen a grand deconstruction of Scripture reading and interpretation—some would say of Scripture itself. Of course, this has been an ongoing, centuries-long project, but two unique elements dominate the past decade: first, as I mentioned previously, the New Atheists are actually reading the Bible—carefully and, *unlike* liberal scholars, they have read it literally with a view to destroying faith. "The Bible says it; I *reject* it; and that settles it." And second, their dance partners in this deconstruction have been Christians who are finally questioning the modernist lingo of inerrancy and its narrow literalist interpretations. They're ready to either toss Scripture or to reconstruct their reading on sturdier foundations.

As I've shared in this book, the deconstruction, so-called, has run along very specific lines in my own life. I have come to believe that Jesus Christ revealed the fullness of God in the incarnation and, thus, he—not the Bible—is the only divine Word and our final authority for theology, faith, and Christian practice. His primacy as the revelation of God challenges doctrines like inerrancy when they elevate "every word of Scripture" as the "infallible word of God." The latter phrase was reserved by the church fathers for God the Son alone. And so, while I do believe in the inspiration and authority of Scripture, I'm among a burgeoning crowd of quite conservative theologians who reject Evangelical bibliolatry in favor of the Christ to whom Scripture faithfully points.

For those who've made that trek, the niggling question remains, "What now? How do we read the Bible, if at all, after the deconstruction?" That's the question we're exploring here. The answer will require many authors to contribute umpteen volumes, a task well on its way.[169] What I'll offer here is one more gesture toward reconstructed Bible reading. Ironically, my suggestions were elementary standards in the early church, but they were often marginalized by Protestant assumptions and the co-opting of Evangelicalism by modernity...and now by the fashionable cynicism of post-modern critics. You'll see how a counterintuitive reconstruction may be helpful.

## AN EPIC STORY HEADING SOMEWHERE

People used to read the Bible as if it were one big book, composed by one big author. Then, partly to acknowledge its many genres and our need to be flexible interpreters, we talked a *lot* about how many books, authors, genres, and years it took to create and compile this little library. After fundamentalism, our pastors and teachers began to deemphasize the unity of Scripture. Our commentators and theologians emphasized the discontinuity of the two Testaments (Old versus New, law versus grace, even "Old Testament God" verses Jesus). I get that. I've just laid out my case for a four-voiced polyphony. The prophet Jeremiah, the apostle Paul, and of course Jesus himself did some serious religious deconstruction within the pages of Scripture. Their radical rereads were disorienting to the status quo. But there's another side to this.

Having many books from many eras gathered into one volume can remind us of something important in terms of *reconstruction*: this is

169. A shout-out here to one great example, Gregory A. Boyd, for his two-volume work, *The Crucifixion of the Warrior God: Interpreting the Old Testament's Violent Portraits God in Light of the Cross* (Minneapolis, MN: Fortress Press, 2017).

ultimately one story—the epic Story (capital *S*, indicating the Big Story or gospel). Heading somewhere. Focused. On purpose and on point.

Behind the many characters, perspectives, narrators, and compositors—none of whom saw the grand plan—stands the Author and Architect who not only weaves together an impossible convergence of storylines and genres, but also actually enters the Story as the surprising climax and reorients every subplot such that they all point to him.

So, when Granny on her rocking chair thinks that she's holding *The Good Book*, inspired and written by God, there is something brilliantly true happening that I propose can be reconstructive and helpful in dealing with problematic particulars.

In theological parlance, I am referring to the *canonical shape and context* of the Bible in its final form. On one hand, proponents of inerrancy imagined a kind of miraculous perfection in the first authors' original "autographs" (completely ignoring the inspiration involved in development, compilation, and redaction). On the other hand, much of modern biblical criticism perpetually re-fragments the Bible through speculative reconstruction of imaginary source material.

The alternative I am describing in popular terms is something like Brevard Childs's "canonical contextual approach."[170] This allows for a high view of divine authorship of the *Story*, the real participation of human authors in the *writing*, and the importance of the church in *authorizing* the Good Book, but also locating the authority of the Bible *in its final form*.[171] That is, the canon of Scripture as a whole becomes a context of its own, far greater than the sum of its parts, because the final product congeals into the one Story. Moreover, a developing canon or differing canons or even various translations need not cause us to stumble because it's all about serving the inspired Story…the *story* (or message) really is the word of God about the Word of God.

Let me break it down even further.

---

170. See Brevard Childs, *Introduction to the Old Testament as Scripture* (Minneapolis, MN: Augsburg Fortress, 2011) and Brevard Childs, *Old Testament Theology in Canonical Context* (Philadelphia, PA: Fortress Press, 1990).

171. I am indebted to my Old Testament professor, Dr. Vern Steiner, in my MDiv program for training me in the canonical-contextual approach. He now serves as founding president of The Emmaus Institute for Biblical Studies in Lincoln, Nebraska.

## 1. THE BIBLE IS AN EPIC STORY OF GOD'S LOVE...

The arc of the Story is about how love creates a beloved cosmos for love's sake. Or as my friend Fr. Kenneth Tanner says, "God loves the world that God made, including humanity. And then God became what God made."

The plot features calamity and redemption, but it's even broader than that, beginning with self-giving Love that will ultimately direct this beloved universe into the *telos* of union with divine love, where God is "all in all" (1 Cor 15:28, numerous translations). At the center of the whole Story, divine Love is enfleshed as Jesus Christ, climaxing in his crucifixion and resurrection as the punchline and *axis mundi* (world axis) that draws the whole saga together.

If we don't see that Christ is the point, then the *whole* Bible remains Old Testament, but if we do, then the *whole* Bible becomes New Testament. Rather than tossing out any of the Scriptures that don't look Christlike, Christians must think of the *whole* Bible as a Christian book, or not at all. This allows for some helpful moves, some obvious, some surprising and exciting.

## 2. ...WITH MANY CHARACTERS
## (SOME RIGHTEOUS, SOME WICKED, MANY MESSY)

We can make an obvious start with the characters of the Bible. The staunchest inerrantist would never defend the actual words of Job's foolish friends, the ravings of Israel's wicked kings, or the castigations of Judas to Jesus as inerrant revelations of the nature of God. They are only "true" in that they are seen as accurate descriptions of a character's line in the Story. We recognize that their actual words are *not* direct revelations per se; we don't treat them as truths to embrace. But neither do we expunge them from the Story. Their roles and their lines are essential, not only as elements of the plotline, but also as moral mirrors before which Scripture asks us to stand. Scripture includes Bildad and Jezebel and Judas precisely so that we will clearly see their rebellion reflected in ourselves, our churches, or our nations when the shoe fits and take heed of their negative example.

## 3. ...WITH MANY PERSPECTIVES
## (MULTIPLE COMPOSERS AND [UNRELIABLE] NARRATORS)

I know that almost no readers stumble over the wicked characters within the Story. But many are still baffled because, even while they can distinguish the Author (God) from the book's problematic characters, biblicism regularly fails to delineate between the omniscient Author and the limited or unreliable narrator. However, there are many examples in literature where we are required to do just that.

For instance, in *Don Quixote*, Cervantes constructs an epic tale of a very strange protagonist—but he also writes the tale through multiple genres, stories within stories, and a famously *unreliable narrator*. That is, the true author (Cervantes) knows exactly what he is doing, but he tells the story through a narrator who does not. Thus, the author is not truly the narrator. *Narrators are actually extensions of the character they're describing* or even an independent character who speaks from a particular perspective.

This method became more obvious to me while I was cowriting (with Paul Young) my first little novella, *The Pastor: A Crisis*, which I described in chapter 14 as allegorizing the three postures of *striving, despair,* and *surrender*. I began to notice how our narrator's voice spoke from the primary character's point of view, not Paul's or my own. Even when the narrator was describing "the Pastor" in the third person, I could hear an echo of the Pastor's personality, perspective, and tone.

When my friend and favorite narrator Boyd Barrett assembled a cast of voice actors to read the novel for the audiobook, there was no doubt about it. The Pastor's bitter thoughts came out through the narrator in bitter inflections. The thoughtful stability of Doctor Hope, the streetwise gruffness of Sage, and the vitriol of the Visitor...all were expressed in the narration. Whatever limitations of vision the characters were bound to was likewise expressed through the narrator—even when that meant they were wrong. Indeed, even Boyd—the actual narrator—did not always know where Paul and I were heading or why. Hence, "the unreliable narrator."

Understanding how an unreliable narrator works in literature can bring perspective to how a particular biblical writer and/or narrator may be as limited as the characters they are describing, while the Grand Architect alone knows how any given book (episode) fits into the larger scheme.

For example, when Saul is "commanded by God" to commit genocide through the prophet Samuel, we might dismiss Saul's actions as sinful but struggle to critique Samuel's prophetic instructions because "the Bible says that God told Samuel." But wait, that's not quite true. Actually, *the narrator says* that Samuel says…the narrator's point of view is indistinguishable from Samuel's, as inseparable as you are from your shadow.

The compositor of 1 Samuel writes as if the narrator is all-knowing (which he isn't), but because this book is in the Bible, we mistake the narrator for God himself.

Another illustration of the narrator's limited perspective comes via Hollywood. Take, for example, a movie series like *Star Wars*, *Star Trek*, or *Aliens*—movies that have an overall architect but whose particular episodes are delegated to writers and directors who are often focused on their own contributions to a single film in the series but don't see the big scheme of things. Prequels and sequels come out that not only may surprise the viewer but also expose the limited perspectives of the previous writers and directors. Only the series architect knows the grand plan (or we hope they do).

TV dramas also have a variety of writers and directors for individual episodes, and they flavor the programs with their own styles, applying their own ways of seeing the world, trademark camera angles, and cinematographic filters. And similarly, even though the series writers, in particular, may have some input into the arc of a character's storyline, only the head writer or "showrunner" is ultimately in control of where the big picture winds up.

So it is with the Bible. Individual characters, narrators, and compositors have a limited field of vision. This becomes obvious when we see them contradicting each other. If only we knew what the divine Author was thinking….

## 4. THEN GOD HIMSELF APPEARS IN THE FLESH

When God arrives in the person of Christ, we get the Author's perspective through his own mouth, and that right within the Story! The only divine Word-made-flesh has a very different perspective from the character

Samuel *or the narrator* of 1 Samuel. When the omniscient Author speaks directly about mercy, about love for one's enemies, about forgiveness, we must radically reconstruct our reading of 1 Samuel and reorder our understanding of what's happening in this new light.

Two corollaries are very important here: on the one hand, this phenomenon means that both the narrators and the characters of Scripture must always bow to the revelation of God the Word when he came in the flesh—and sometimes their perspectives are completely inadequate. Okay, I'll say it: errant. And Jesus says it too.

On the other hand, let's remember that this does *not* mean the story is now unimportant or dispensable. Not at all. I might not approve of George Lucas's writing or the character of Jar Jar Binks or half of the Star Wars episodes, but I can simply dismiss them as irritating diversions. However, unlike them, I *need* the culprits in the book of Judges, and I *need* the disturbing narration of 1 Samuel. Why? Because behind and through the book, the Story Architect is indeed communicating (breathing) an important revelation—not about himself, but about me and my church and my nation.

Through the lens of Jesus, I can now read these books as part of the mega-series in which God's people did and said horrific things *in his name*—things that God himself debunks when he arrives. God wants to show us how *we still do and say awful stuff in his name all the time.* Again, my godfather David Goa says it better than I:

> If God is "one and undivided" with Jesus Christ,…then we are invited by the mind of Christ to read the First Testament through the example and teaching of Christ's love and the spousal covenant it fully expresses. *This spousal covenant runs through the whole of Scripture and is the counterpoint to the idolatry that anchors many of its narratives.* If we claim the Trinity, then it is impossible to see in God the Father anything that we do not see in God the Son. Jesus never killed anyone but allowed himself to be crucified precisely to end the cycle of mimetic contagion. And all of his judgments that we read about in the Second Testament, when read with care and freed from our passions, are descriptions of the kind of alienation

and loss of being that results from death-dealing and missing the mark.[172]

In other words, through the incredible plot twist of the incarnation, the divine Author comes to clue us in: we are *not* to read books like Joshua or Judges as our justification for holy wars and religious violence. Rather, the Author shows us how his people have always justified hatred, bigotry, and violence against the express wishes of an enemy-loving, sin-forgiving God. Moreover, once Jesus has shown us that such crusades and death-dealing are wrong, we can be given eyes to see how the books of Joshua and Judges have *already done so too!* What if they were written to problematize religious warfare, not to glorify it? Then we've never needed those books so badly as we do today!

## SO WHAT?

There are other keys to reconstructive Bible reading, but I've found that this one Author, one Story perspective can free us from the tyranny of a "flat-Bible" mentality. Rather than treating the whole book as univocal, all the voices in the book arrange themselves around the pinnacle of the Story (the incarnation) and its main and only infallible Character. It is then up to readers (in community, by the Spirit) to perceive how each part of the Story leads to and follows from that Center. And how the Center critiques the individual chapters, characters, and narration.

This principle is best reduced to Jesus's words in John 10:10: according to the Author himself, when you see life-giving in the Bible, you are seeing the Good Shepherd at work; when you see death-dealing, you're seeing something or someone else at work—the spirit behind the system (i.e., the thief, the murderer, the destroyer). It remains, then, to see how the Shepherd lays down his life for the sheep to make all things new...the trajectory set in motion for the cosmos by the incarnation toward its *telos* in Christ.

## CHECK-IN

As promised, we now need to take a sharp turn from Scripture as narrative to four specific stylistic devices, equally important and perhaps more

---

172. David Goa, *Reading the Bible as Life-giving Word,* 46–47.

difficult than what we've encountered so far: rhetoric, diatribe, phenomenology, and anthropomorphism. Understanding these stylistic devices is critical to interpreting Scripture in a way that honors the character and nature of God. If we stumble here, we may even lose our faith. So, bear with me as I try to make the technical delectable.

### CHAPTER 16

# NO EMPTY RHETORIC: PARENTAL LOVE AND FRIGHTENING WARNINGS

"Bradley, don't touch!
You'll burn your little hanny [hand] right off!"
—Irene Jersak

"The Lᴏʀᴅ God commanded the man,
'You are free to eat from any tree in the garden;
but you must not eat from the tree of the knowledge of good and evil,
for when you eat from it you will certainly die.'"
—Genesis 2:16–17 (NIV)

"If your right hand causes you to stumble, cut it off...."
—Jesus Christ (Matthew 5:30 NIV)

## "HOT!"—MOM'S WARNING

*J* was perhaps six years old, visiting with my parents at Uncle Henry and Aunt Florence's house. I remember fixating on Auntie Flo's red-hot stove element. I recall my mother's dire warning: *"Bradley, don't touch! You'll burn your little hanny right off!"*

Spoiler alert! I touched the stove but still have two hands.

Mom wasn't lying, though. She was using rhetoric. And while what she said was not literal, it was anything but "empty." That's where we're heading in this chapter. But back to Mom right now.

I know these memories are vivid visual reconstructions of early childhood emotions rather than video footage of exact events. I know, for example, that the oven was never in the location where I see it in my head. And it's very likely that Irene Jersak, my beloved mother, said nothing of the sort. But while the facts may fail to find their way through the haze of five decades, the truth is a clear-flowing stream. Here is the truth:

+ I knew beyond any doubt that my mom loved me and that I loved her.

+ I knew what her warning meant. I knew she meant that touching the stove would burn me—and NOT that if I touched the element, *she* would burn me.

+ Even as a young literalist, I knew that the stove would burn my hand— and NOT that it would burn my hand right off. Even at that young age, I could intuit the hyperbole.

It is therefore surprising to me how often adults who read Scripture stumble into these common errors:

+ We have often imagined that when we disobey a divine warning, God, rather than our own disobedience, becomes the threat and the source of harm. We confuse the wages of sin (intrinsic consequences) with the wrath (violent anger) of God.

+ Similarly, we often mistake God's dire warnings against disobedience for personal threats of divine violence rather than the loving care of our heavenly Parent who seeks only to dissuade us from self-harming choices.

+ And then, we habitually literalize hyperbole of temporal self-destruction into divinely sanctioned, universal, permanent, and even eternal catastrophes. For example, we've equated passages announcing the fiery destruction of Jerusalem (which happened repeatedly) with the end of history, the scorching of the universe, and the beginning of eternal conscious torment.

How did we ever get from "Don't burn yourself today!" to "I'll burn you forever!"?

I'd like to blame colonial revivalist Jonathan Edwards, with his "insects roasting over an open fire" evangelism, but honestly, these disastrous inferences emerged much earlier in the human drama.

## "WHERE ARE YOU?"—HIDING FROM MOM

**God:** *"Where are you?"*
**Adam:** *"I heard you in the garden, and I was afraid because I was naked; so I hid."*

—Genesis 3:9–10 (NIV)

**My wife, Eden, calling our son Dominic:** *"Dominic!"*

**Dominic, age four:** *"Nothing!"*

Back to my memory of the hot stove and my burned hand. Later that day, I committed both a mistake and a sin.

My mistake was in assuming the stove would only burn me when it was set to "On," and only while the element was red. My sin was that I presumed to touch it at all after Mom had said, "Don't." When I ventured the forbidden touch, it was my first experience with a burn. I had no previous reference for how deep a burn goes, and that it doesn't stop burning when you stop touching. This type of pain was a new reality to me—and I was shocked and terrified.

Beyond the pain, I also must have experienced guilt and shame, because my first instinct was *NOT* to cry out or to run to my mother. Instead, I forced myself into silence and ran off to hide. Why would I do that? Had Mom ever given me the impression that when I was suffering, she was someone I needed to hide from—someone who would harm me?

And yet, we see this was precisely how Adam and Eve reacted after eating from the wrong tree. They had only ever known God as the Friend who provided them with Paradise and walked with them as an intimate Companion in Eden.

But when they grasped for autonomy and ate the poison of illicit knowledge through self-will, what happened? Their eyes were opened, they saw that they were naked, and they felt shame. And from that shame emerged a false image of God. No longer their loving Father, Yahweh now assumed the character of someone to fear and to hide from—and, no doubt, the source of impending death.

Had God ever done anything that even remotely warranted such a blasphemous inference? Not at all. Adam and Eve fabricated their new conception and hideous projection of divine punisher from God's loving warning tainted by their *shame* and the dust of death (i.e., their *fear*). In their deluded minds, alienated by shame and self-deception, under the curse of death of their own making, they imagined that God himself was now the death-dealer.

## "WHILE STILL A LONG WAY OFF"

Eventually, I came to my senses and ran to my mother. She scooped me up into her arms and quickly took me to the kitchen sink, where she ran cool water over my fingers for a long time. It felt SO good. She then carefully applied a beautiful healing balm that may have come via Auntie Flo's new discovery of a miracle cure—freshly cut aloe vera. Then came swathing bandages of clean, bright white gauze, healing cuddles from my affectionate auntie, and consolation from Mom. No shaming, no rebuke. Any "I told you so" escapes my memory.

In the Gospels, when the Prodigal Son finally ventured home after being burned on his own self-centeredness, he did not find what he expected either. He did not need to plead for pity or settle for servitude. He had disowned his father, but his father had never disowned him. He discovered the joy of being embraced by his father, who *ran to him* "while he was still a long way off" (Luke 15:20, various translations).

This is the truth about *Abba* that Jesus came to show us. The God we imagined in our guilt and shame was a slanderous misrepresentation, an idol constructed out of human fear. The Prodigal Son not only recovered his place in his father's house, but his broken image of Dad was also repaired, and he was reconciled to his father's welcoming arms. No need to run, no need to hide, no need to fear.

Parental compassion for little Bradley says, "Don't hide from Mom! Run to her as quickly as you can!" And while Jesus's listeners were probably scandalized by his parable, we can imagine Papa calling, "Adam! Eve! All of my children! Don't hide from Papa! Run to me as quickly as you can!" And then, even in our first impulse to head home, we find that Papa is already running toward us—ready to apply a kind parent's cleansing water, aloe gel, and fresh gauze—and extending a warm and generous embrace.

## THE DILEMMA OF PARENTAL DRAMA

Does it offend us that Jesus issued frightening warnings about the consequences of our rebellion? When we are rushing into destruction, is it enough that he said, "Woe to you! This insanity will be the death of you!"? Do we always have to repeat the error of inferring that a parental warning makes him an angry and punitive ogre?

Or do we think he should have said, "Look, it's really no big deal. In the end, you'll find your way back home. I'll forgive your sins and heal your wounds, and all will be well." He often does hint at exactly that (as in the parable), but I will leave you with these principles for interpreting divine warnings:

- The One issuing them is your heavenly Father, whose agenda is your protection and restoration. He's not a retributive tyrant king. He's your loving *Abba*.

- The warnings are *not* threats that God will harm you. In his love, his dramatic and hyperbolic warnings are *not* a measure of how angry he will be, but of how dangerous our defiance can be to ourselves and to others.

- The warnings that end in judgment are stern because the judgment intrinsic to our sin can indeed be terrible. But even if that's how the warning ends, that's not how the Story ends. "Mercy triumphs over judgment" (Jas 2:13, numerous translations). It's just that God's heart for us is not judgment at all. He'd rather we heed the warnings and experience fullness of life now.

## READY FOR RHETORIC?

With that important foundation, we're nearly ready to dive more deeply into the fascinating (but most difficult) New Testament genre we call "rhetoric." As we'll discover, understanding the biblical use of rhetoric is crucial if we're to reconcile its sharp edge with Christ the Word's living revelation of *Abba* as the infinite Good—immutable love, light, and life. Rather than racing to the technical details, let's prepare ourselves with *why* we must go there.

Peter, a Facebook friend of mine, sent me this pertinent question:

> I'm continuing to wrestle with the idea of God as nonviolent. I feel like I see the truth of God's nonviolence through Christ and his teachings, particularly on forgiveness. However, then I also read passages elsewhere that refer to God's punishment.
>
> What do we do with that? Is it our wishful thinking that God really is as loving as we want him to be? Or do we pass off Peter or Paul's writings (for example) as men trying to encourage a church in persecution with God's justice, in order to give meaning to their suffering? Are there different translation possibilities? What does their use of words like "punishment" mean for us?[173]

I responded in the following way, and I hope overhearing my thoughts will help others.

I have spent years thinking over and digging through these questions, as did the great church fathers, such as Clement of Alexandria (AD 150–215). First, he pointed out that the biblical authors never use the Greek words we associate with retributive "punishment" in reference to God. Rather, when speaking of God, they always use words best translated as "correction." Let's start with Clement. The following is an excerpt from my book, *Her Gates Will Never Be Shut*:

---

173. Facebook direct message to author, February 11, 2014. Used with permission. This correspondence has been lightly edited for this publication.

Clement's importance, in my mind, is that he clarifies the New Testament language for "punishment" (see esp. *Paedagogus* 1.5; 1.8 ANF 2). Clement insists that God's "correction" (*paideia*[174]— Heb 12:9) and "chastisement" (*kolasis*—Matt 25:46) is as a loving Father, only and always meant for the healing and salvation of the whole world. He denies that God ever inflicts "punishment" (*timōria*—Heb 10:29—vengeance) in the vengeful sense, a word Jesus never used. Watch how Clement ties judgment to correction with a view to redemption:

> For all things are arranged with a view to the salvation of the universe by the Lord of the universe, both generally and particularly.... But necessary corrections, through the goodness of the great overseeing Judge, both by the attendant angels, and by various acts of anticipative judgment, and by the perfect judgment, compel egregious sinners to repent (*Strom.* 7.2 ANF 2)....

> ...One can see how Clement read God's corrective acts through the parental love emphasized in Heb. 12:5–11, where we read that God disciplines those he loves as dear children. For Clement, Providence uses corrections (*padeiai*) or chastisements (*kolasis*) when we fall away, but only for our good, only for our salvation. But God does not punish (*timōria*), which is retaliation for evil (*Stromata* 7.16 ANF 2).[175]

God deals with sin through correction, not punishment. That's Clement, that's Hebrews, that's Hosea. The chastisements of God are disciplinary—not because divine justice demands satisfaction, payback, or wrath, but because a patient God is raising beloved children who tend to learn the hard way. The hardest lesson we learn is the lesson of the cross: the jarring revelation that somehow each of us is complicit in the crucifixion of perfect Love,[176] yet, in love, God forgave us.[177]

---

174. *Paideia:* John Behr tells me that *paideia* doesn't actually mean correction, except by way of extension. It primarily means education (pedagogy), which, yes, involves or is "correction," but implies so much more.

175. Bradley Jersak, *Her Gates Will Never Be Shut: Hope, Hell and the New Jerusalem* (Eugene, OR: Wipf & Stock, 2009), 121–22.

176. See Zechariah 12:10.

177. See, for example, 1 John 4:9–10.

So, if we're reading the Bible according to the Spirit, as gospel, as the drama of redemption, the cross is a revelation of God's love, our violence, and Jesus's power to forgive and redeem—all at once. Don't miss this point, because it marks a major fork in the theological trail. I fear that, for centuries, we have veered off track when Clement already had it right.

And yet...we do see some pretty heavy-handed threat-rhetoric at play even after the cross—dire warnings trend across the New Testament meta-narrative that require careful consideration. Here are a few starting points.

As we noted earlier, throughout the Bible, including the New Testament and even within the language of Jesus, there are, at times, competing images and conflicting voices. Some of these voices (whether the voice of the accuser, the victim, or the law) call for retribution and promise vengeance. But that other voice—the voice of the crucified Lamb (or self-giving love)—rejects retribution and renounces vengeance. All these voices are a sure fact of the text.

What becomes clear in the broad arc of biblical narrative is a *trajectory* where the language of vengeance and retribution is repeatedly trumped by the Lamb's voice of forgiveness and restoration. This is the deeper, richer, and more weighty voice within the Prophets, Jesus's teachings, and the apostolic writings.

For example, "Vengeance is mine, I will repay" (Romans 12:19 NET, RSV) bows to "Father, forgive them, bless them, don't hold their sin to their account."[178] James's epistle, as mentioned earlier, summarizes this principle as "Mercy triumphs over judgment" (Jas 2:13, various translations). In Paul, the "kindness of God" trumps the "judgment of God."[179] And, in Christ, the perfection of the Father is seen in graciously granting sun and rain on the crops of the wicked and the righteous[180]...clearly negating the exclusive covenant promises and ominous threats of Deuteronomy 28. Perhaps one could even say the *vengeance* language (what is due under the law) leads to the *restoration* language (what is promised under grace), as

---

178. See Luke 23:34.
179. See Romans 2:2–4.
180. See Matthew 5:43–48.

in Romans 6:23: "For the wages of sin is death, but the gracious gift of God is eternal life in Christ Jesus our Lord" (NASB).

Still, how shall we read texts like 2 Thessalonians 1:3–10? (*Don't skim this part—watch for the difficulties in italics*):

> ³We ought always to give thanks to God for you, brethren, as is only fitting, because your faith is greatly enlarged, and the love of each one of you toward one another grows ever greater; ⁴therefore, we ourselves speak proudly of you among the churches of God for your perseverance and faith in the midst of all your persecutions and afflictions which you endure. ⁵*This is a plain indication of God's righteous judgment* so that you will be considered worthy of the kingdom of God, for which indeed you are suffering. ⁶For after all it is only just for God to *repay with affliction those who afflict you,* ⁷and to give relief to you who are afflicted and to us as well when the Lord Jesus will be revealed from heaven with His mighty angels in flaming fire, ⁸dealing out *retribution* [ἐκδίκησιν, "vengeance"] to those who do not know God and to those who do not obey the gospel of our Lord Jesus. ⁹These will pay the *penalty of eternal destruction,* away from the presence of the Lord and from the glory of his power, ¹⁰when He comes to be glorified in his saints on that day, and to be marveled at among all who have believed— for our testimony to you was believed.      (2 Thess 1:3–10 NASB)

When I read this text, Clement's categories of corrective judgment don't seem as clear. What looks obvious here is that Paul is comforting a persecuted church by promising payback, retribution, and vengeance on those who've afflicted them. Now if Paul elsewhere overrides the language of retributive violence with Christ's call to patiently endure and forgive persecutors (as he had been forgiven!), why appropriate this retribution rhetoric at all? Retributive "*rhetoric*"—yes, that is our first clue.

We are quite used to reading *hyperbole* as nonliteral when it appears in Jesus's parables, aphorisms, or symbols of apocalypse. We know that *hyperbole* is a rhetorical device using exaggerated statements or claims to make a point, and we know they are not meant to be taken literally. For example, we know that Jesus never meant for us to actually cut off our hand or poke out our eye in order to be saved. We know that the judgment passages about sheep and goats refer to nations, not domestic farm animals. And with any maturity in our interpretation, we won't expect Jesus to streak across the sky on an actual flying horse with a Valyrian steel sword surging from his mouth to behead people. I hope this much is evident even for nonacademic readers when reading New Testament prophecy, parables, or apocalyptic speech.

*However,* there is one common genre that is more difficult to spot and that we often fail to interpret. This elusive form is formally called *rhetoric*. We tend to overlook rhetoric because it's often embedded in the didactic (teaching) material of the apostles' letters. Whole schools of rhetoric existed when the Epistles were written, and in the cities where they were written. Further, some of the New Testament authors were well-trained in rhetoric and employed their rhetorical skills A LOT. So, at last, *what is rhetoric?*

## WHAT IS RHETORIC, EXACTLY?

**"Rhetoric"** *refers to the art of persuasion used in speeches or sermons—methods that orators and preachers apply as they seek to change minds, hearts, and behavior.* Today, we cynically describe political speeches as *"empty rhetoric"*—perpetually flowery and passionate but empty of substance and chronically misleading. We identify rhetoric with slick talkers and blowhards. Rhetoric is for those who don't say what they mean or mean what they say. In short, rhetoric amounts to circuitous BS—the "sophistry" Paul condemned in 1 Corinthians 1.

But in ancient times, including the first century, rhetoric was carefully studied as an oratory art form, intended to arouse emotions and to convince and motivate listeners to think and act differently. It was especially important for the birth of democracy in Athens, shifting political regime change from conquest to elections. If you can't coerce the populace through violence, you need to convince them with words. Words that sway votes.

Thus, rhetoric has a noble heritage and was an essential element of Greek education—including first-century, Hellenized Judaism. Happily, key textbooks from that era are still available to us today:

+ *Art of Rhetoric* by Aristotle

+ *On Invention* by Cicero

+ *Institutes of Oratory* by Quintilian

The rhetorical methods in those textbooks appear throughout the speeches and writings of our New Testament. Early Christian authors and preachers wielded those skills expertly, and we'd best learn what, why, and how they did it so we can hear rightly and "accurately handle" their messages.

My primary influences and most of what I know and teach about New Testament rhetoric comes from those ancient books and the following modern sources:

+ David A. deSilva, especially *An Introduction to the New Testament* (pp. 508–09, 572–80, 781–86, 815)[181]

+ Ben Witherington III, especially his article "NT Rhetoric—a Handbook"[182]

+ Meghan Henning, *Educating Early Christians through the Rhetoric of Hell*[183]

+ Douglas A. Campbell's various works on "diatribe" in Paul's letters.[184]

Herein you'll find my distillation of their thoughts. I'm not the horse's mouth, but I do claim to be a faithful fact-checker and tried my best to verify what follows as trustworthy. Here are the basics of what I've absorbed from these ancient philosophers and their modern interpreters.

First, rhetoric attempts to build a persuasive case by appealing to:

+ *ethos* (the speaker's credibility)

+ *logos* (rational appeal)

+ *pathos* (emotional appeal)

---

181. David DaSilva, *An Introduction to the New Testament: Contexts, Methods & Ministry Formation*, 2nd ed. (Downer's Grove, IL: IVP Academic, 2018).

182. See Ben Witherington, "NT Rhetoric—A Handbook," *Ben Witherington* (blog), April 23, 2008, http://benwitherington.blogspot.co.uk/2008/04/nt-rhetoric-handbook.html.

183. Meghan Henning, *Educating Early Christians through the Rhetoric of Hell* (Tübingen, Germany: Mohr Siebeck, 2014).

184. See, for example, Douglas A. Campbell, *The Deliverance of God: An Apocalyptic Rereading of Justification in Paul* (Grand Rapids, MI: Eerdmans, 2013).

*Ethos* was all about establishing the speaker's character and authority. It's the effort to portray themselves as trustworthy and believable. A lot of factors can affect one's ethos. If a speaker's toupee blows off in the agora during an otherwise compelling discourse, he was having a "bad ethos day," and his speech lost credibility. Effective preachers attend to ethos, whether naturally or strategically.

How do I personally "do ethos"? How do I establish credibility as a guest speaker, for example? I am often invited to preach or teach at meetings where the audience members are hearing me for the first time or haven't yet made up their minds about me. I've come to realize that I instinctively use the same skills found in classic rhetoric to lay a groundwork of ethos. Rather than duplicity, my rhetoric expresses my sincere desire to connect with people and to show genuine appreciation for them as I'm about to share my topic:

1.  Build rapport: "Greetings, brothers and sisters! It's great to be with you! I'm so grateful you've chosen to join me tonight, even after a long week. That's so honoring and encouraging—it takes some of the sting out of being away from my wife, Eden, and our kids. But now that we're here together, I'm confident that God is connecting us for a reason."

2.  Create goodwill: "Of course, we come from different cities, cultures, and faith traditions. But one thing we share is our desire to know Jesus better. I'm convinced that your motive for being here is love for Christ. I'm told this is a safe place for me to share my heart because you're faithful."

3.  Build trust and confidence: "And I'm so happy to see your pastor again. Did you know we went to college together? Has it really been thirty years? [Insert funny story about the pastor from the good ol' days.] Anyway, I was happy to hear from my dear friend Paul Young—yes, *The Shack* guy—that this place is one of his favorite venues to speak. Coming from him, it seems like we're in for a good time."

4.  Establish moral character (despite yourself): "I bring you greetings from Archbishop Lazar Puhalo, my spiritual father. And from my friends back home in my recovery community. They would want

me to remind you: there's fresh mercy every day!" [Insert a touching testimony.]

5. Appeal to your credibility as a speaker. "Anyway, I'm just back from St. Stephen's University, where I serve as Dean of Theology & Culture. Our claim to fame is that we're Canada's smallest university with the biggest classroom! That's because we have travel modules and take students to Italy, Greece, Ephesus, and the Isle of Patmos. In fact, why not join me some time?"

What am I doing there? I'm building a healthy ethos. Is what I said true? Yes, it's best to tell the truth. Is it manipulation? That's one way to describe it, I guess. But another way is to say I'm creating an atmosphere of trust that will help them hear the truth with open hearts instead of folded arms. Ethos is about destroying prejudice (or, if you're up to no good, creating it).

The apostle Paul uses ethos frequently, in various ways, reminding his churches:

+ That he's an apostle AND slave of the Lord
+ That he's their spiritual father and actually planted their churches or is one of their foundational teachers
+ That he had never been a burden on them, always providing for himself
+ That they enjoy a previous connection (nostalgically)
+ That he's been bragging about them to other churches (so live up to it)
+ That he loves them and longs for them
+ That he's in prison and has remained faithful

*Logos* refers to the real meat of rhetorical discourse. On one hand, *logos* appeals to the head, to the mind (sort of). This is where you lay out your case:

+ using formal logic
+ providing poignant analogies
+ giving supporting arguments

When Christian preachers do this, they try to use the logic, analogies, and supporting arguments that are most appealing to their target audiences. While Socrates used dialectic and syllogism with his philosophy students, Jesus used different audience-friendly approaches. At dinner parties, for example, he used parables, employing familiar symbols and relatable metaphors. However, like Socrates, Jesus also used questions that led his listeners to self-discovery.

And while *logos* appeals to the mind, note that I used the parenthetical "sort of" because the arguments can be emotionally charged. How so? You've probably seen courtroom dramas where the prosecutor and defense attorney give their opening and closing arguments. They use reason, but their arguments can get very intense—preachy, even. Or think about a debate (formal or not) where we refer to a "mic-drop" or "mind-blown" moment. Or think about an interview where the host leads their guest into a "gotcha" question. Each is an example of *logos*. Logical arguments, but emotionally charged.

And who used logos better than Jesus? Hello! He IS the divine Logos. Dare we say that Jesus was at his rhetorical best when, through parables and disputations, he left the crowd speechless with awe or freaking out with rage?

*Pathos* normally (but not exclusively) comes at the end of a speech, when rhetoricians push hardest into the crowd's deep emotions. The endgame is not to create emotion. The point is to use emotion to evoke a particular response. In retail, we'd say you're closing the deal. In the courtroom, you're vying for an advantageous verdict. In evangelism, you're inviting a response to faith. The appeal to emotions—to love or hate, joy or grief, outrage or empathy—creates *pathos* in the audience, so that they respond *affectively*. If the rhetorician succeeds, they've achieved their aim: winning over the whole person or group—body, mind, and soul.

These strategies of persuasive speech are designed to drive truth through the mind and into the heart in order to stimulate action. There's a proven psychology to rhetoric, with a very long track record. Rhetoric creates an emotional state in the listener/reader that makes them more *suggestible* to the orator's arguments. Sounds insidious, but let's think practically for a moment. Why does a preacher share a funny story? Why does an author share a tear-jerking illustration? Why did Jesus speak in parables? Something about the form affects our willingness to be convinced.

In his *Introduction to the New Testament*, David deSilva recalls Aristotle's work *Rhetoric* (1.2.3–4) and Quintilian's *Institutes* (Quintilian was the master of rhetoric in Paul's day). DeSilva describes the appeal to *pathos* in this way:

> ...A speaker could enhance the persuasive effects of an address by "putting the hearer into a certain frame of mind," that is, arousing emotions in the hearers that will move them in the direction the speaker wishes them to go. These are called appeals to *pathos*, or emotion.[185]

> ...Arousing emotions to move the hearers closer to taking the action or making the decision the speaker is promoting is always part of the strategy of persuasion.[186]

## EPISTOLARY RHETORIC

What does this have to do with biblical interpretation? Knowing the types of rhetoric the apostles used helps us distinguish between calculated emotional appeals and basic instruction. Literalists find this approach troubling and troublesome. I would argue that the number one genre error in biblical interpretation occurs when we mistake epistles for straightforward didactic teaching when, in fact, they are rhetorical sermons, designed to be *preached aloud* in the congregation. By misreading them as instruction manuals, we can miss the tone of the letters, read verses in isolation, and lose the larger point.

The following are examples of rhetorical tone that purposely appeals to listeners' emotions in order to sound more convincing. The ancient textbooks encourage infusing speeches with triggers that induce:

+ anger OR calm
+ enmity OR friendship
+ fear OR confidence
+ shame OR favor
+ rebuke OR pity

---

185. DeSilva, *An Introduction to the New Testament*, 508.
186. DeSilva, 782.

+ indignation OR affirmation

+ envy OR emulation

Do you see how I've paired these words? That's because rhetoric frequently sets conflicting emotions back-to-back, first flattering then bullying the listener, or shouting at them then soothing them. The effect is to throw the reader off balance. Strange but true, the impact actually motivates hearers.

I still recall a 1996 sermon by Jackie Pullinger, a lifelong missionary to heroin addicts in Hong Kong. I remember it well because she is a masterful preacher who left a deep impression on me. She spoke of visiting the poor in Winnipeg's notorious North End. Jackie related the fact that her hosts asked her to pray for their poorest residents—the homeless, the addicts, and the sex workers on North Main. Suddenly, she hollered at us at the top of her lungs, "Pray for *your* poor?! Why would I pray for *your* poor?! They're *your* poor!" I cowered in my seat, and my friend Chad may have wet himself a little. My hair stood on end in fear. I wondered if this was what spiritual abuse felt like. Then, just as suddenly, in the most soothing, honey-sweet tone you could imagine, she smiled and coyly said, "But of course I prayed for them."

What was she doing? She was using rhetoric. Why? Was her purpose to shame us and scare the living daylights out of us? No! That's not the point of rhetoric. It was to arouse action! To love and care for the poor! To see them as *our* poor, as *our* responsibility! To get off our numb and overfed derrieres and *"go out quickly into the streets and alleys of the town and bring in the poor, the crippled, the blind and the lame"* (Luke 14:21 NIV). That moment was pivotal in the call Eden and I felt to plant Fresh Wind Christian Fellowship, whose pillars were those very people.

That's the power of Spirit-filled rhetoric. That's the nature of the New Testament Epistles.

## RHETORICAL CRITICISM

*Rhetorical criticism* is an important element of New Testament interpretation because it identifies these preaching methods when they're being used. Again, the strange thing is that while rhetoric can seem extremely manipulative, it is used all over the New Testament, and some authors are absolute masters. Jesus's sermons and parables are highly rhetorical. The devices I described permeate the books of 1 and 2 Thessalonians, Hebrews, and 1 and 2 Peter (attributed by some to the fisherman's Roman protégé, Mark, in honor of his mentor).

For example, one can see appeals to various forms of pathos throughout the letter sermon to the Hebrews, including the contrasted emotional pairings mentioned above. DeSilva lays out this sample:

+ Hebrews 4:14–16: makes them feel confident

+ Hebrews 5:11–14: makes them feel shame

+ Hebrews 10:26–31: makes them feel fear (and urgency)

+ Hebrews 11:1–12:3: makes them feel praiseworthy[187]

Why does the author of Hebrews do this? Because he's doing whatever is necessary to persuade his readers not to abandon the faith, despite the powerful temptation they were feeling. There it is: *feeling*. They had good *reason* to embrace Christianity, but those reasons are buckling under the pressure of a *feeling*—mainly fear. And now the author must overcome those fears to win their hearts and minds once again. He uses *logos* and *pathos* to the hilt to get there.

I find the apostles' willingness to use rhetoric so brazenly a bit troubling, but there it is. The question is not *whether* or not they "go there"— they obviously do—but rather, *why* they go there and *how* to interpret their pathos-driven messages.

*Since* they do, we are expected to recognize the rhetoric (just as we are meant to recognize poetry, parables, or symbolic visions) and understand the flattery, threats, or pathos at some level as *nonliteral*, while not dismissing their important meaning as "empty." We need to read behind and beneath the rhetoric to identify the authors' intent and God's message. Rather than interpreting their rhetoric woodenly (over-literally), isolating or totalizing a single paragraph, we need to learn how to read *through* rhetorical texts so as not to throw them into direct conflict with the gospel teachings of Christ and his apostles on mercy, grace, and forgiveness—and especially the way of the cross, which God incarnate not only taught but lived as the preeminent revelation of the nonviolent God.

---

187. See deSilva, *An Introduction to the New Testament*, 784–86.

### CHAPTER 17

# THE DIATRIBE DILEMMA

$\mathcal{T}$his seems the best time to mention a specific rhetorical device that's seeing increased attention (and increasingly being debated) these days. I'm referring to the subgenre we call *diatribe*, used by the apostle Paul and made popular by Douglas Campbell's breakthrough works on Paul's letters. Diatribe is a style of rhetoric in the form of vivid dialogues with hypothetical interlocutors. The orator cites his opponent's arguments and objections and then refutes them for their listener. In his *Reading Romans as a Diatribe*,[188] Changwon Song discerns the common markers of Hellenistic diatribe in Paul's epistle to the Romans and the *Discourses of Epictetus* (a second-century Stoic). Among these, I especially watch for:

- The emergence of an imaginary second-person singular—e.g., "Therefore *you* [singular] are inexcusable, O man…" (Rom 2:1 NKJV)

- Apostrophic vocatives—e.g., *ho anthrope,* "O man!" as in "Therefore you are inexcusable, O man…." (Rom 2:1 NKJV)

- Hypothetical objections and rejection phrases—e.g., *me genoito,* "May it never be!" as in "What shall we say then? Are we to continue in sin so that grace may increase [objection]? May it never be [rejection phrase]! How shall we who died to sin still live in it? ³Or do *you* [second person singular] not know…?" (Rom 6:1–3 NASB)

---

188. Changwon Song, *Reading Romans as a Diatribe* (New York: Peter Lang Publishing, Inc., 2004), chapter 2.

Strangely enough, one night, I had a dream about Paul's use of diatribe in Romans—a nice break from my usual diet of tossing, turning and worry-mares. In the dream, I was studying Romans 1–2, with Jesus sitting to my right. Very helpfully, the text was laid out in two colors so I could clearly see where Paul is talking and where his hypothetical opponent is speaking. Like so, with separate paragraphing for each verse, and with italics where I saw a different color:

> ¹Therefore you are inexcusable, O man, whoever you are who judge, for in whatever you judge another you condemn yourself; for you who judge practice the same things.
>
> ²*But we know that the judgment of God is according to truth against those who practice such things.*
>
> ³And do you think this, O man, you who judge those practicing such things, and doing the same, that you will escape the judgment of God? ⁴Or do you despise the riches of his goodness, forbearance, and longsuffering, not knowing that the goodness of God leads you to repentance?                              (Rom 2:1–4 NKJV)

And then, in the dream, Jesus spoke to me and said, "See, you can tell when Paul is responding to the opponent. The signal is when he uses the phrase, 'O man.'"

I woke up at that point and immediately fact-checked in a real Bible what my "dream-Jesus" had shown me. Sure enough, there it was—"O man"—twice.

I realized that verse 2 might not be Paul's point of view at all, even if it's a true statement. Maybe he's quoting a hypothetical member of the Roman church whose self-righteous certitude in God's wrath needs a reminder that it's kindness, not judgment, that changes people's lives. Maybe.

I heard about a real-life version of this type of dialogue from my brother Rodney, a nurse who co-established House of Hesed as a hospice for people suffering from late-stage HIV infections. He had attended the funeral of a gay man who had died of AIDS-related illnesses. He cringed as the minister used Romans 1 to condemn the man for his sexuality and attributed his death to the wrath of God. Gratefully, my friend David Ruis was also present and was expected to close the memorial with a song immediately after the message. He went to the piano and said something like, "We mustn't hear Romans 1 without also hearing the message of Romans 2," and he proceeded to proclaim the radical mercy of God toward all people, including the man who had passed away. That was a form of epistolary diatribe at just the right time.

Once you begin to notice it, Paul's use of diatribe is often obvious. In 1 Corinthians 4:8 (NASB), he says of his opponents, "You are already filled, you have already become rich, you have become kings without us…" [their claim]. And then he responds, "And indeed, I wish that you had become kings so that we also might reign with you" [rejection phrase, with a dash of sarcasm].

Another example is 1 Corinthians 11, in the passage about women's head coverings. One section (vv. 5–10) seems to argue for enforcing women's head coverings during worship, but in the next section (vv. 11–16), Paul seems to be contradicting himself and undoing his own argument. His reasoning is either arcane or asinine. But wait, what if that's not what Paul is doing? What if he's neither a misogynist nor an idiot? Dr. Lucy Peppiatt, in her must-read work *Woman and Worship at Corinth*,[189] demonstrates Paul's genius as he rhetorically eviscerates the Corinthian opponents' misuse of his own teaching. If he's using diatribe, it's actually a brilliant refutation of their practice. Verses 5–10 aren't his position at all. He's laying out a Corinthian error, then expertly unravelling it.

## THE DILEMMA

If Paul indeed uses diatribe, we face a very serious quandary. Our Greek New Testament doesn't record the tones he would have used in preaching his message to the Romans aloud.

Side note: Paul commissioned the female deacon Phoebe to deliver (preach!) his sermon to the Romans in person.[190] He would have prepared her to communicate the tones such that his first audience picked up on the diatribe.

---

189. Lucy Peppiatt, *Woman and Worship at Corinth: Paul's Rhetorical Arguments in 1 Corinthians* (Cambridge, UK: James Clarke & Company, 2017).
190. Romans 16:1–2.

But the New Testament codices don't indicate the opponent's voice by using a different font. That sets us up for one of two critical errors:

+ We might accidentally quote the statements of Paul's opponents as inspired truth when their words are the very heresy he's rebutting.

+ We might accidentally ascribe anything Paul says that we don't like to his opponents. Indeed, some of Campbell's critics claim he *over*-diatribes Romans.

Hopefully, the possibility of diatribe in the Epistles will humble us and heighten our mindfulness. It begs the question of where to draw the line, especially in Romans 1, where debate rages between two opinions:

+ Is Paul a homophobe condemning homosexuality? If so, then he sure seems to contradict himself in chapter 2, where he calls out condemnation and reminds the Roman believers that kindness, not wrath, is how God makes things right.

+ Or is Paul citing and condemning the homophobes in the Roman church? If so, then half of chapter 1 gets written off as the opponent's voice. But is Paul even remotely describing gay love?

I do see a rhetorical strategy at work in this passage, but it's more complex than citation-rebuttal. More likely, Paul is actually, truly condemning the Greco-Roman practices and power structures around pedophilia/pederasty, where boys and slaves were regularly raped as proof of one's "manliness." The extrabiblical literature on this practice is extensive and explicit.[191]

The same despicable practice continues today in nations like Afghanistan (as depicted in Khaled Hosseini's novel *The Kite Runner* [192]). If two men fall in love, they'll be stoned to death. But the good ol' boys can flaunt their machismo by raping underage "dancing boys" for Wednesday night fun.

So, what is Paul's rhetorical strategy? He's definitely *not* going on a rant against homosexual love *nor* is he giving pederasty a pass. Here's what I think:

---

191. See, for example, Sarah Ruden, *Paul Among the People: The Apostle Reinterpreted and Reimagined in His Own Time* (New York: Image Books, 2010), chapter 3.
192. Khaled Hosseini, *The Kite Runner* (New York: Riverhead Books, 2003).

1. First, he is actually condemning the disgusting arrogance of exploitative and frequently violent sex acts against same-sex minors and slaves.[193]

2. Second, he deliberately stirs up the Roman church's disgust against those practices, suggesting how rightly deserving such people are of God's seething wrath. Now he has them nodding.

3. Next, he sort of says, "And now that we're at it..." and goes into a long list of other contemptible sins worthy of divine judgment, including:

> [29]...every kind of wickedness, evil, greed and depravity. They are full of envy, murder, strife, deceit and malice. [Amen, brother!] They are gossips, [30]slanderers, God-haters, insolent, arrogant and boastful; they invent ways of doing evil; they disobey their parents [uh, wait a minute]; [31]they have no understanding, no fidelity, *no love, no mercy* [but, but...?]. [32]Although they know God's righteous decree that those who do such things deserve death, they not only continue to do these very things but also approve of those who practice them.                              (Rom 1:29–32 NIV)

Do you see what Paul does there? He starts with the "big" sin deserving big wrath. Then once they're all stirred up, he includes a host of other sins in descending order so that everyone in the congregation is indicted of something. And the final straw is the greatest sin of all—"no love" and "no mercy"—for which he's just entrapped them. If it's about "deserving death," then we're all in the same boat.

This sets up his argument in Romans 2:1–3:34.

4. Hang on, everyone. Don't you remember that it's God's *kindness* that leads to repentance, not condemnation and wrath? (Rom 2:1–4)

---

193. Full disclosure: Romans 1:26 refers to *women* exchanging "natural sexual relations for unnatural ones." Were women of privilege also involved in pedophilia, promiscuity, or exploitative sexuality? Scholars who emphasize pederasty in Romans 1 tend to focus exclusively on male exploitation but downplay liberal sexuality among women in that era. How might they explain verse 26? I suspect the scarce documentation of lesbianism indicates that it was seen as a violation of gender roles. For primary sources, see Thomas K. Hubbard, ed., *Homosexuality in Greece and Rome* (Berkeley, CA: University of California Press, 2003).

5.   If we're all in the same boat, that includes Jews and gentiles, Christians and pagans. Favoritism is off the table—it's ludicrous.

6.   Thanks be to God, since we're all shut up in the same sinking boat, the grace and mercy of God through the faithfulness of Christ extends to all. (Romans 3:21–31, and again in Rom 11:32)

7.   Phew! That's really good news! But it means letting go of exclusive claims that lock others out while you stand on your moralistic pedestal. We were *all* in deep trouble, and we are *all* saved by grace. Now can we drop the us/them, in/out debates?

That's how I read Paul's rhetoric. He's not refuting the fact that pederasty is a heinous and outrageous injustice. What he's refuting is their self-righteous contempt, as if they're above all that. At least this is one approach to weigh for consideration.

## OBJECTIONS

All right, earlier I said I found the overt use of rhetoric (not only diatribe) in the New Testament "a bit troubling." That's really an understatement. Part of me objects to it. Here's why:

**First, there's an apparent moral problem.** Obviously, there's the charge of manipulation. But it goes deeper than that for me. When the rhetorical device used bates the listener to experience fear, hasn't the means of communication become incongruent with the message? I mean, how can we justify using fear to promote a gospel that drives out fear? And if the gospel frees us from fear, how can our gospel preaching deliberately incorporate threats? Isn't that kind of a lie? Do the ends really justify the means?

I can tell you that when the message I heard at church switched from love for Jesus into fear of hell, I spent the next full decade worshipping God out of expedience rather than love. A crack formed in the foundations of my faith. The emotional pairing of the terror of judgment offset by the relief of escape is effective(ish). But if our message focuses on fear that makes God the cause or agent of fear, we'll either run from God or turn to him but have no desire to draw near to him. Spiritual Stockholm Syndrome.

Was this not a problem in and for the early church? Maybe not. Why not? Maybe because they were all trained in rhetoric (we aren't) and understood how it works (we don't) and didn't slip into hearing it literally (we do), even while feeling "all the feels." But if they knew it was rhetoric, would it still work? Would the message get through? I think so.

Here's an analogy. Let's say I'm watching a zombie show like *The Walking Dead*. The program uses the zombie genre to teach really important lessons about power dynamics, social hierarchies, community building, conflict resolution, and the perils of life under duress. The writers and most viewers don't believe zombies exist. I don't sense that my neighborhood is genuinely under threat. And yet I *feel* the blood-curdling suspense intrinsic to the zombie genre. Meanwhile, I'm picking up the intent of the storyline, especially noting where it's engaging in penetrating social commentary. I'm being led to *feel* and to *think* and to *act*...but I'm able to distinguish the scary zombie entertainment from the truths the story is delivering about strength versus folly or sacrificial love versus selfishness. I let myself *feel* the genre, and it grips me in ways that help me listen attentively to the point.

Skillful orators can move their listeners to feel and to act. But the skill includes careful stewardship because rhetoric has the potential to either motivate people to serve a greater good or transform them into a monstrous and murderous mob. Paul used rhetoric. So did Hitler. Let's make sure we can tell the difference.

That raises the question of *interpretive problems*. Three potential interpretive mistakes come immediately to mind:

**1. Readers may *misjudge the referent*.** That is, we might be swept up in the powerful imagery and mistake what the orator is actually talking about. A common error of this type in biblical interpretation concerns Christ's parables.

Dr. Meghan Henning taught me that the parable of the sheep and goats[194] is a moral exhortation. That should be obvious. What do Jesus (as speaker) and Matthew (as author and pastor) *want*? They want us to be a compassionate community that cares for the poor, the sick, and the marginalized. But to motivate his listeners, Christ sets that social ethic in the context of a do-or-die final judgment. *Why?* To show us that these values

194. See Matthew 25:31–46.

are of ultimate import. They really, really matter. But, what happens? We literalize the parable into an eschatology. And since we can't work out why the criterion of judgment is mercy rather than faith in Christ, we sit around reworking our end-times timeline instead of welcoming the stranger or visiting those who are sick and in prison.

**2. Readers may *literalize the imagery.*** Here's an example: apocalyptic imagery appears in the Prophets, the Gospels, the Epistles, and the book of Revelation. It's a rhetorical form. And the imagery is meant to surprise and shock...but it is *not* meant to be read literally.

Think of 2 Peter 3:10:

> But the day of the Lord will come like a thief. The heavens will disappear with a roar; the elements will be destroyed by fire, and the earth and everything done in it will be laid bare [burned up].
>
> (NIV)

Literally? Are we to believe that Christ is going to consume the entire universe with fire, cause every planet, star, and galaxy to disappear? Will all the elements in the periodic table be destroyed with actual fire?

I remember, as a young dispensationalist, practicing faithful literalism as I tried to convince a man three times my age that this is what the Bible says so it must be true (contradictory passages notwithstanding). Then I doubled down into my hellfire speech, citing Revelation 14:11: "And the smoke of their torment will rise for ever and ever" (NIV).

The old man patiently tried to set me straight and explain the verse figuratively. Ironically, he was a Jehovah's Witness, normally even more vulnerable to literalism. I'm now convinced he held the interpretive high ground...and his tone was better too.

**3. Readers may *confuse rhetorical preaching with didactic instruction.*** As I've explained, the Epistles can be the toughest genre to interpret because, at least with poetry or parables or apocalyptic language, we're used to recognizing rhetoric and adjusting for it. But with the Epistles, I suspect that most readers wrongly assume the authors are only offering instructions in a series of propositions—theological and ethical. And worse, we're prone to take a paragraph literally in isolation from the next, uncoupling

THE DIATRIBE DILEMMA 251

emotional pairs where threat turns to comfort or shame shifts to consolation. Thus, in contrast to the patristic conviction that God is not actually retributive, people think of God as punitive. I field questions every week asking, "What about this verse, where Paul/Peter/James/John/Jude says God is wrathful/vengeful and going to punish/destroy this or that type of sinner?"

Simple answer: It's rhetoric. No, don't read it literally. No, it's not *empty* rhetoric....

More complex answer: Let's take a look at what the author is *doing* between the lines of what he's *saying*....

## FLAGGING RHETORIC

This section on rhetoric began with a question from Peter, my Facebook friend. As we continued with our conversation, he replied with a follow-up question:

> When I read your thoughts on the use of rhetoric in the New Testament, it leaves me with this question: is the only way to know it's rhetoric by the language used (e.g., fear invoking...) or are there other indicators?
>
> I'm imagining telling friends about this who would call themselves Reformed. I feel like they'd tell me I'm twisting Scripture to fit my view of a nonviolent God. Or is it possible to point out clearly where Paul or others are using it?
>
> That established schools of rhetoric are a first-century fact is very significant to explaining the retributive language, but I'm wondering if there are key writing cues or genre flags that highlight a text as rhetoric?
>
> I can definitely feel the push and pull of the vengeance versus forgiveness voices. But the fact that retribution-talk continues after Christ, and even among Jesus's apostles, challenges the merits of your completely nonviolent image of God.
>
> I'm basing this off the fact that most Christians (Evangelicals) read the threat of God's vengeance at face value and completely

literally. Even they pick and choose what texts to read literally and what parts are hyperbole and rhetoric.[195]

Apparently, Peter wasn't letting me off the hook so easily. But what an important question! I chose not to evade the problem. Allow me to use my reply as a good summary of what we have been discussing:

Let me begin with the question of "twisting Scripture to fit my view of a nonviolent God." Yes, that's one way to look at it, and my friendly critics often see it this way. But there is another way of looking at it: *Jesus alone is God's final and only perfect Word about himself.*[196] *All Scripture is inspired as it bows to the revelation of God incarnate.* That is, we must either squeeze Christ into conformity with the violence texts, or we must subject the violence texts to the infallible plumb line of Christ and his gospel. Those are our only options. Those who consider the Bible their sole and final authority feel they must conform all the competing visions and conflicting voices into a monotone unison. How can they honestly claim to do this? I don't believe it's possible or desirable. It's only the cruciform Story that draws the polyphony into a coherent whole. For me, Jesus Christ is the final authority, and every text must be read through his living demonstration of God's true nature.

Jesus himself demonstrates this practice: "*You have heard it said, but I say….*" So did Paul. He even deletes lines of the Old Testament when quoting the prophets in order to bring their message into conformity with Christ's revelation of God. Derek Flood explains this usage clearly with examples in his breakthrough essay, "The Way of Peace and Grace."[197] Paul will actually draw lines from anti-gentile passages and rework them to argue for their inclusion.

As for the rhetorical flags, I'm still working this out with the help of our rhetorical experts (especially as I read David deSilva and Ben Witherington III).

I personally believe the simplest way forward looks like this:

---

195. Facebook direct message to author, June 11, 2014. Used with permission.
196. See Hebrews 1:1–3.
197. Derek Flood, "The Way of Peace and Grace," *Sojourners*, January 2012, sojo.net/magazine/january-2012/way-peace-and-grace.

1. Start by learning to recognize the common ancient uses of rhetoric. I hope you will use chapters 16 and 17 of this book as a starting point.

2. Notice when a biblical text uses one of the common forms AND when that same text does *not* conform to Christ's quintessential revelation of God. Our final authority is the voice of the Lamb slain and the good news of his cruciform victory through self-giving love, indiscriminate grace, and radical forgiveness.

3. When the text seems to use a rhetorical device, and when that rhetoric is in conflict with the gospel of the "Lamb slain," then interpret the text rhetorically rather than literally. Get past what the author is *saying* to search out what he's *doing*, what his intent is.

Notice what I've done here: I deny that a "nonviolent God" is merely a sentimental, liberal ideology that I'm imposing on the Bible. Instead, I'm centering the apex of God's self-revelation in (1) the cross itself (what God-in-Christ accomplished), and (2) the gospel of grace that Paul and the other apostles announced. These dogmas form the heart of our Christ-centered hermeneutic. Our interpretation of rhetoric that is in tension with the message of the gospel must conform to the Word made flesh. Christ is our guiding star and Lord. And if we remember that, the Bible's rhetorical literature will come alive with fresh disclosures of truth.

## SO, THERE'S NO WRATH OR JUDGMENT?

Finally, I'm *not* saying there is no such thing as wrath for sin or judgment in God. Rhetoric is a vehicle for truth, and its actual meaning must *not* be stripped away. When Christ and his apostles use rhetoric, they mean *something*. Our task is to recognize the inspired truth the words convey—e.g., about our suffering under sin and facing God's righteous judgments, which will set everything right.

This requires distinguishing the preachers' bark from their bite—and knowing that God isn't the biter, but sin is. Or in Bishop Robert Barron's words, we read more deeply than "what the Bible says" by discerning "what the Bible teaches," just as I had to learn what my mother *meant* and *didn't mean* through her stove-top warnings.

### CHAPTER 18

# TONGUE TWISTERS AND SUNSETS: PHENOMENOLOGY

*T*he *Late Show with James Corden* introduced me to "the Dame Judi Dench Challenge" (Dench is one of my favorite actors). How many times can you say "Dame Judi Dench" quickly? While it's nearly impossible to say "Dame Judy Dench" multiple times without stuttering, it is totally impossible not to try. How did you do?

I've been working on another tongue twister: phenomenon, phenomena, phenomenal, phenomenology, *phenomenological!* I almost never pronounce that final word correctly—even slowly, even once.

And yet, I bet you speak *phenomenologically* every single day. A *phenomenological description* means simply this: describing things as they appear to us rather than how we know they actually are. A common example is our use of the word *sunset.*

Sunsets never actually occur—but they happen every day! Does the sun actually sink below the horizon? No. We know the earth is rotating and giving the appearance of a sunset to observers. But when we speak of romantic *sunsets*, we are not showing our ignorance of elementary-school science. We are using a *phenomenological description.*

On the other hand, maybe the person who originally coined the word *sunset* really did think the sun was revolving around the earth. Perhaps that was their worldview. We know better now, but even as we recognize that the ancients saw things differently from the way we do, I hope we won't negate the great truths they spoke via their ancient worldviews OR archaic descriptions. We haven't even thought it necessary to expunge *sunset* from our own language. No need.

All of this is important to our understanding of inspired Scripture. The Holy Spirit breathed truth through the authors of Scripture via both ancient worldviews and now-archaic descriptions. This does not make what they said untrue—*unless, again, you force their descriptions to be read literally.*

Note: The Bible is not the problem. The worldviews of the biblical writers may be outdated and/or their language may by phenomenological, but that is not necessarily a deficit. There is no problem until we squeeze their descriptions into a mold that demands we believe the sun actually revolves around the earth because "the Bible clearly says."

Not that the church would ever be so daft. Oops. #Galileo.

## CASE STUDY: DOES GOD CHANGE HIS MIND?

Here's an example of a phenomenological concept: does God "change his mind"?

*The Bible says God DOES change his mind.* Some examples are Exodus 32:12–14; 2 Samuel 24:16; Jeremiah 18:8–10; 26:13, 19; 42:10; Ezekiel 7:22; Jonah 3:9–10; 4:2; and Amos 7:3–6.

*The Bible also says God DOESN'T change his mind.* Examples: Numbers 23:19; 1 Samuel 15:29; Isaiah 31:2; 2 Corinthians 1:19; and James 1:17.

*Does the Bible contradict itself?* Yes, these verses are contradictory if we read them literally. If we forget to account for worldviews and phenomenology, we may insist dogmatically, "'The Bible clearly says' God changes his mind *and* God does not change his mind." To me, that way of thinking seems rather sloppy—it does not take language or the Bible very seriously.

The problem is as easily addressed as the sunset dilemma. Sometimes the Scriptures speak *ontologically*, which refers to how God actually is in his *being* or *nature*. So, at times, the authors of the Bible are revealing this truth: the Holy Trinity of Love never changes. At other times, the authors are speaking phenomenologically; that is, they describe how God appears to be acting from the human point of view. Some people say it like this: "Objectively speaking, God never changes. Subjectively speaking, God appears to change."

I like to imagine a scientist and a romantic poet strolling together on the beach at sunset, each sharing their own perspective on the scientific wonder and breathtaking beauty of the flaming red star they see sinking into the ocean waves. There is no conflict, because they know they're talking about the same phenomenon from two glorious points of view.

## WHEN IT MATTERS

Does this even matter? It matters greatly in real relationships. We may understand that someone loves us dearly, but if we turn from them, we may think they don't love us anymore. We may think they're angry at us. We may want to avoid them, as Adam and Eve avoided God in Eden. We may think they've cut us off and disowned us, as the Prodigal Son in Jesus's parable thought his father had. All because *we* turned away. Have you ever felt that way about God? Is that something you still struggle with? Yet the One who loves us has remained faithful, patient, and loving toward us, longing for us to return, just like the Prodigal's father did. And when we do turn and return, our own circumstances and experiences may change so drastically that it *appears* to us that the One who never left and never stopped loving us somehow changed. As if turning toward God *caused* God to love us.

The change of circumstances through our change of orientation gives the appearance—indeed, the illusion—that what we did changed God's mind and orientation toward us. We feel and act very differently toward God if we think God has turned from us or is angry with us than if we know he is slow to anger and abounding in loving-kindness toward us and has never turned his face away or cut us out of the life of the Trinity.

This truth shouldn't be news to anyone. Anthony the Great, a Christian hermit from ancient Egypt (early fourth century), explained it carefully and clearly: *"To say that God turns away from the wicked is the same as to say that the sun hides itself from those who lose their sight."*[198]

---

198. St. Anthony the Great, "170 Texts on Saintly Life," in *Early Fathers from the Philokalia*, ed. E. Kadloubovsky and G. E. H. Palmer (London, UK: Faber and Faber Limited, 1954), www.trueorthodoxy.info/spir_stanthony_great_saintly_life.shtml.

To those who can see, the sun appears to shine. For those whose eyes are beginning to fail, the sun appears to dim. Or someone who is experiencing deep sadness might say, metaphorically, "The sun ceased to shine." And we would know they meant, "I can't see the sun; even though it still shines, my eyes (or my heart) no longer perceive it." And hopefully, we would not feel obligated to correct them. "*Well, actually….*" With any emotional intelligence, we would allow for descriptive, subjective language.

Speaking of the orbs in the sky, some of the apocalyptic literature says, in effect, "The sun will become dark, and the moon will turn blood red before that great and glorious day of the Lord arrives."[199] As a child, I wondered what would happen if the sun and moon actually did that. I figured all life on our planet would be extinguished within minutes. I was reading the passage as an ontological description. But then I discovered that a season of heavy forest fires can darken the sun and turn the moon bloodred *in appearance.* I realized that Jerusalem under siege and engulfed in flames would experience the same phenomenon.

It seems to me that neither the biblical literalists nor the New Atheists are able or willing to allow biblical authors to speak phenomenologically about God without taking them literally. Both insist on the literal interpretation because they need to *prove something*—one to defend inspiration and the other to negate it. I would suggest they let that go and take a walk together down a beach at sunset.

Who knows? A little romance might inspire them.

It might even be *phenomenal.*

---

199. See Acts 2:20. See also Isaiah 13:10; Joel 2:31; Matthew 24:29.

### CHAPTER 19

# THUS QUOTH THE FATHERS: GOD'S "WRATH" AS ANTHROPOMORPHISM

"This is what the LORD says: 'Stand at the crossroads and look;
ask for the ancient paths, ask where the good way is, and walk in it,
and you will find rest for your souls.'"
—Jeremiah 6:16 (NIV)

## COMMENTARY

*T*he central section of my book *A More Christlike God* explored the developing doctrine of divine "wrath" in the Bible. I showed how the Bible itself comes to view wrath as a metaphor for God's consent to our defiance—as "giving us over" to our willful ways. And thus, his judgments come to be seen as the natural and spiritual consequences intrinsic to our sin. As the psalmist says, we dig our own pit and then fall into it.[200] Or as Paul says, "The wages of sin is death" (Romans 6:23, numerous translations). Thus, what we had once thought of as retributive punishment is actually the pains of a stubborn ox "kick[ing] against the pricks" (Acts 9:5 KJV).

---

200. See Psalm 7:15.

This progressive shift within the Bible distances God from causing harm, doing violence, or directly punishing sinners. That development is both radical and necessary. It is radical because it demands that we transpose direct claims in the Bible that God was meting out punishment into metaphors for indirect consequences. Not all readers are willing to make that scary leap. But it is a necessary leap the authors of Scripture made as they became convinced that God is infinitely good, that he is forever opposed to the dominion of death, and that his mercy endures forever. More to the point, the cruciform revelation of God in the person and passion of Christ led the church to understand that God's judgments are restorative rather than retributive, and that the cross demonstrates how God invites us into self-giving love, radical forgiveness, and the renunciation of wrath as a solution to the human condition. Most simply, God is the life-giver, not a death-dealer, because Christ said so and then revealed that truth definitively on the cross.

What, then, shall we say to those texts that announce God's wrath? I argue that to avoid regressing to pagan images of God, we must read them as *anthropomorphisms*—i.e., figures of speech projecting human characteristics onto God.

I had originally planned to include a simple appendix in this book highlighting the early church's dogmatic convictions on this point, but their conclusions are so important that I've elected to incorporate them within this chapter, adding some commentary of my own for clarity's sake. I will highlight key points in italics.

I begin with Saint John Cassian because I have the longest history with him, and he really represents the entire church. He spent decades as a monk in Palestine, then studied under the desert fathers and mothers[201] in Egypt, was ordained deacon by John Chrysostom in Constantinople, and became a priest in Rome. He went on to head a network of monasteries based in Marseille, and his influence would spread to both Benedictine monastics and Celtic Christians. He's an honored saint (officially), and a perfect representative of the historic faith.

---

201. The desert fathers and mothers were Christian ascetics who lived in the Egyptian desert from the third century onward. They lived as hermits or as monastics, committing themselves to self-denial, prayer, and service.

# SAINT JOHN CASSIAN (360–435)

## INSTITUTES, *BOOK VIII*

Cassian begins by defining anthropomorphisms and highlighting two problems with reading them literally. First, he demonstrates how a "bare literal" reading of anthropomorphic texts sets various Scriptures in contradiction to each other. Second, he shows how literalizing these texts reduces an infinite God to a finite material form. This he finds "shocking" and "must be far from our thoughts."

### CHAPTER III.

Of those things which are spoken of God anthropomorphically.

*For if when these things are said of God they are to be understood literally in a material and gross signification,* then also He *sleeps,* as it is said, "Arise, wherefore sleepest thou, O Lord?" though it is elsewhere said of Him: "Behold he that keepeth Israel shall neither slumber nor sleep." And He *stands* and *sits,* since He says, "Heaven is my seat, and earth the footstool for my feet:" though He "measure out the heaven with his hand, and holdeth the earth in his fist." And He is "drunken with wine" as it is said, "The Lord awoke like a sleeper, a mighty man, drunken with wine;" He "who only has immortality and dwelleth in the light which no man can approach unto:" not to say anything of the "ignorance" and "forgetfulness," of which we often find mention in Holy Scripture: nor lastly of the outline of His limbs, which are spoken of as arranged and ordered like a man's; e.g., the hair, head, nostrils, eyes, face, hands, arms, fingers, belly, and feet: *if we are willing to take all of which according to the bare literal sense,* we must think of God as in fashion with the outline of limbs, and a bodily form; which indeed is shocking even to speak of, and must be far from our thoughts.[202]

---

202. John Cassian, *The Twelve Books of John Cassian on the Institutes of the Coenobia, and the Remedies for the Eight Principal Faults,* trans. Edgar C. S. Gibson, in A Select Library of Nicene and Post-Nicene Fathers of the Christian Church, second series, vol. 11, gen. ed. Philip Schaff (New York: The Christian Literature Company, 1894), 258, Internet Archive, https://archive.org/details/selectlibraryofn11scha/page/258/mode/2up. Public domain. The words *sleep, stands,* and *sits* are italicized in the original.

262 A MORE CHRISTLIKE WORD

Cassian then proceeds to a problem more severe than imagining God as having a bodily form (although he definitely believed in the incarnation). He shows us that it is far worse to ascribe human *passions* to God, "with whom there is no...shadow of turning" (Jas 1:17 NKJV). What are the "passions" according to early Christian thought?

> Passions are the uncontrolled desires that come from our bodily needs. They subordinate our soul to the ego or self-will. They come about because we forget about God and only think of our own needs. The seven passions are: gluttony, lust, avarice, anger, dejection, listlessness and pride. All these passions lead us to sin, but with proper discipline can be offset by virtues.[203]

By this definition, you can see how horrified Cassian would have been to ascribe human passions to God! He specifies how the biblical use of words such as *anger*, *wrath*, and *fury* are passions that, when literalized, replace the one true God with an idol and commit a monstrous blasphemy. He explains:

### CHAPTER IV.
In what sense we should understand the passions and human parts which are ascribed to the unchanging and incorporeal God.

> And so as without horrible profanity these things cannot be understood literally of Him who is declared by the authority of Holy Scripture to be invisible, ineffable, incomprehensible, inestimable, simple, and uncompounded, *so neither can the passion of anger and wrath be attributed to that unchangeable nature without fearful blasphemy.*[204]

Having made such a strong statement, Cassian feels the need to reinforce his case by returning to some of the basic bodily anthropomorphisms and defining their actual meaning:

> ...For we ought to see that the limbs signify the divine powers and boundless operations of God, which can only be represented to

---

203. "Passions and Virtues: What Are Passions?" Saint George Greek Orthodox Cathedral, http://stgeorgegreenville.org/our-faith/catechism/asceticism/passions-and-virtues.
204. Cassian, *Twelve Books*, 258.

us by the familiar expression of limbs: by the mouth we should understand that His utterances are meant, which are of His mercy continually poured into the secret senses of the soul, or which he spoke among our fathers and the prophets: by the eyes we can understand the boundless character of His sight with which He sees and looks through all things, and so nothing is hidden from Him of what is done or can be done by us, or even thought. By the expression "hands," we understand His providence and work, by which He is the creator and author of all things; the arms are the emblems of His might and government, with which He upholds, rules and controls all things. And not to speak of other things, what else does the hoary hair of His head signify but the eternity and perpetuity of Deity, through which He is without any beginning, and before all times, and excels all creatures?[205]

Cassian's readers will get this. God doesn't have a human mouth, but the mention of God's "mouth" in the Scriptures must mean something. What does it signify? Speech. Does God have eyes? No. Then how does God "see"? God's "seeing" stands for his all-encompassing knowledge of all things visible and invisible. God's "hands" represent his works. And so on. Simple enough. He has us nodding. But now back to the harder sell: that the passions, too, are anthropomorphic and not to be read literally:

> ...So then also when we read of the anger or fury of the Lord, we should take it not ἀνθρωποπαθῶς [anthropathetically, human pathos]; i.e., according to an unworthy meaning of human passion, but in a sense worthy of God, who is free from all passion; so that by this we should understand that He *is the judge and avenger of all the unjust things* which are done in this world; and by reason of these terms and their meaning we should dread Him as the terrible rewarder of our deeds, and fear to do anything against His will.[206]

For Cassian, then, references to God's "wrath" or "anger" are a way of affirming God's justice. It's not that God is actually overcome by violent rage and lashes out to do harm. Rather, we need to know that God is a righteous Judge before whom we are accountable, and that we don't

205. Cassian, 258.
206. Cassian, 258–59.

264 A MORE CHRISTLIKE WORD

actually get away with anything. Even the statement that God is a "terrible rewarder of our deeds" is anthropomorphic but by no means meaningless. What we sow, we reap "to the last farthing."[207] Gratefully, God is also a gracious Judge whose mercy triumphs over judgment, so we pray, "Lord, have mercy," remembering how Christ answers that prayer.

Having warned us of a dreadful divine judgment, Cassian has us on our heels. But here we see how effectively he wields rhetoric, for he identifies this fear as a projection of our own hearts rather than an accurate response to the character of the divine Judge. The passions exist in our own minds, and the Judge is only as terrifying as our stricken conscience portrays him:

> ...For human nature is wont to fear those whom it knows to be indignant, and is afraid of offending: as in the case of some most just judges, *avenging wrath is usually feared by those who are tormented by some accusation of their conscience*; not indeed that this passion exists in the minds of those who are going to judge with perfect equity, but that, while they so fear, the disposition of the judge towards them is that which is the precursor of a just and impartial execution of the law. And this, *with whatever kindness and gentleness it may be conducted, is deemed by those who are justly to be punished to be the most savage wrath and vehement anger.*[208]

In other words, to the one whose accusing conscience is terrifying them with judgment, their fear of punishment will paint the Judge as furious. As we learn to live in the love and mercy of God, God's perfect love drives out that fear, and our hearts are assured of God's kindness. What Cassian describes from a negative standpoint, we see in 1 John 3 from the positive side:

> [18]Children, let us not love in word, or in speech, but in deed and in truth.
> [19]Because of this, we know we are of the truth, and *we will persuade our hearts* of this fact before him, [20]because *if our hearts condemn us, God is greater than our hearts.* He knows everything. [21]Beloved, *if our hearts do not condemn us, we have boldness before God,* [22]and we

---

207. See Matthew 5:26 KJV.
208. Cassian, *Twelve Books*, 259.

receive from him whatever we ask, because we keep his commands and give him pleasure when he sees what we are doing.

(1 John 3:18–22 NTE)

This may sound like "If I am good, God is happy. If I am bad, God is angry." But for both John and Cassian, God's disposition never changes. What changes is *our conception* of God according to *our disposition.* Instead, "When I love, I *see* that God is love. When I turn from love, I *expect* that God is angry." I totally relate to this. Even when I believe that God, out of his love for me, truly is convicting me of some sin, it may come across as if he's yelling at me. Cassian identifies that "yell" with our own fear rather than God's tender heart. God compassionately sees through our sins to our broken, confused, or diseased hearts. But because of my willfulness, my fear, and my accusing conscience, the Spirit's still, small voice is amplified *by me* into a barrage of condemnation. You'll notice angry preachers who do the same to their people.

Cassian summarizes his main point: that "wrath" is actually sin to be avoided and that our wrath should never be attributed to God:

> ...It would be tedious and outside the scope of the present work were we to explain all the things which are *spoken metaphorically of God in Holy Scripture, with human figures.* Let it be enough for our present purpose, *which is aimed against the sin of wrath,* to have said this that no one may through ignorance draw down upon himself a cause of this evil and of eternal death, out of those Scriptures in which he should seek for saintliness and immortality as the remedies to bring life and salvation.[209]

## SAINT AMBROSE (339–397)

### NOAH'S ARK, *CHAPTER IV*

Slightly earlier but overlapping Cassian, we have Saint Ambrose of Milan, the city where he was archbishop. He's considered one of the four great doctors of the Latin church and had a major influence on Saint Augustine. Fun fact: he's the guy who coined the saying, "When in Rome,

---

209. Cassian, 259.

do as the Romans do," encouraging liturgical flexibility. He also *may* have believed in ultimate redemption, inferred from these words:

> Our Savior has appointed two kinds of resurrection in *the Apocalypse.* "Blessed is he that hath part in the first resurrection," for such come to grace without the judgment. As for those who do not come to the first, but are reserved unto the second resurrection, these shall be disciplined until their appointed times, between the first and the second resurrection.[210]

In any case, he was certainly convinced that divine "anger" can only be read as an anthropomorphism.

> We read that the Lord was angry.... God's thoughts are not as man's thoughts; in Him there is no such thing as change of mind, no such thing as to be angry and then cool down again. These things are written that we may know the bitterness of our sins, whereby we have earned the Divine wrath. To such a degree had iniquity grown that God, Who by His nature cannot be moved by anger, or hatred, or any passion whatsoever, is represented as provoked to anger.[211]

Like Cassian, Ambrose argues that God does not change. Neither God's mind nor his heart change. His temper doesn't rise and fall like ours does. His love doesn't come or go like ours does. It's not that God is unmoved or unresponsive. For the fathers, the point is that God's *love* is immutable. God loves us with an everlasting love and will never, ever turn from us like the fickle "gods" of pagan religion. God's love runs deeper than wavering human passions. It's an infinite spring that never diminishes. God is not sometimes loving and sometimes angry. God is love. Period.

Ambrose makes a second helpful point. The Bible uses the "wrath" anthropomorphism for a reason. It's not to show us how mad God can get. It's trying to communicate the "bitterness" or seriousness of sin.

210. "The Church Fathers on Universalism," Tentmaker, https://www.tentmaker.org/Quotes/churchfathersquotes.htm.
211. St. Ambrose, *Noah's Ark*, in *The Roman Breviary*, vol. 1: Winter, trans. John, Marquess of Bute (Edinburgh: William Blackwood & Sons, 1879), 338, https://books.google.ca/books?id=SutDAQAAMAAJ&printsec=frontcover&source=gbs_ge_summary_r&cad=0#v=onepage&q=God's%20thoughts.

I was thinking about this one day when dealing with my children. I wanted to move beyond retribution into a consistent practice of restorative justice. But, I asked myself, "If I don't 'punish' in the retributive sense—if I'm gracious and compassionate, slow to anger, and abounding in loving-kindness and don't treat them as their sins deserve—how do I show them the severity of their sin? Or that failing to respect their mother is much worse than failing to mow the lawn?" I realized that, apart from punishment, I was trying to communicate the gradations of their supposed sins with the volume of my voice and the expression on my face. I wonder if biblical authors were up to something similar, expressing God's rage as a way to communicate how bad the people's sin really was. Ambrose seems to think so.

Ultimately, there's a better way. The severity of sin is driven home by *what we did to God*. The cross becomes the simultaneous measure of humanity's great sin and God's perfect love. Beholding and experiencing that vision—the impact of the crucified God—makes a deeper impression and transformation on our hearts than would any yelling or any threat of punishment in this world or the next.

## SAINT ISAAC OF NINEVEH (613–700)

### "ST. ISAAC THE SYRIAN: A THEOLOGIAN OF LOVE AND MERCY"

Isaac of Nineveh, who lived in the seventh century, is one of the great saints and preachers of divine Love in Christian history. He was a monk who was also briefly ordained bishop of Nineveh in the monastery of Beit 'Abe. But after just five months, he abdicated and retreated to a community of anchorites[212] on Mount Matout. Later, he lived in the monastery of Rabban Shabur. He eventually lost his eyesight, but it is said that he had so thoroughly memorized the Gospels that he could "see" the entire story in his mind.

My favorite commentary on Isaac's thought is in a paper by Metropolitan Hilarion Alfeyev (a hierarch in the Russian Orthodox church). The article is entitled "St. Isaac the Syrian: A Theologian of Love and Mercy," and from it I'm drawing excerpts of Isaac's primary writing

---

212. An *anchorite* is a religious recluse, even more isolated than a hermit.

along with Alfeyev's poignant commentary.[213] The sections in quotation marks are Isaac's own voice. Summarizing Isaac, Metro. Hilarion writes,

> To say that the love of God diminishes or vanishes because of a created being's fall means *"to reduce the glorious Nature of the Creator to weakness and change."* For we know that *"there is no change or any earlier or later intentions, with the Creator: there is no hatred or resentment in His nature, no greater or lesser place in His love, no before or after in His knowledge…."* Nothing that happens in creation may affect the nature of the Creator, Who is *"exalted, lofty and glorious, perfect and complete in His knowledge, and complete in His love."*

Here again, we have the notion of God's immutable love. God *cannot* become angry or resentful because God is eternal, unchanging Love by nature. Any depictions of God as angry must therefore be read metaphorically—as anthropomorphisms.

> This is why God loves equally the righteous and sinners, making no distinction between them.…

> Even when God chastises one, He does this out of love and for the sake of one's salvation rather than for the sake of retribution. God respects human free will and does not want to do anything against it: *"God chastises with love, not for the sake of revenge—far be it!—but seeking to make whole His image. And he does not harbour wrath until a time when correction is no longer possible, for He does not seek vengeance for Himself. This is the aim of love. Love's chastisement is for correction, but it does not aim at retribution… The man who chooses to consider God as avenger, presuming that in this manner he bears witness to His justice, the same accuses Him as being bereft of goodness. Far be it, that vengeance could ever be found in that Fountain of love and Ocean brimming with goodness!"*

I remember the first time I publicly declared that "God is not a punisher" and that "there is no retribution in the nature of God." It was terrifying because I was speaking to a "mixed multitude," many of whom

213. Bishop Hilarion Alfeyev, "St. Isaac the Syrian: A Theologian of Love And Mercy," *Syriac Studies*, April 4, 2008, http://www.syriacstudies.com/2013/12/04/st-isaac-the-syrian-a-theologian-of-love-and-mercy-bishop-hilarion-alfeyev.

sported twenty-pound Bibles, crossed arms, and long faces. Their countenances screamed that God's chastisements are retributive and vengeful. Otherwise, how could he be called "just"? For them, justice was an eye-for-an-eye transaction, inflicting pain in equal (or far greater) measure than one's offences. Isaac resounds with an unequivocal "NO!" Far be it that such a God could be called good. In truth, God is an Ocean brimming with goodness, and ALL his chastisements are, as Hebrews 12 declares, the corrections of a loving Father.

In Isaac's view, God the all-merciful Father overshadows the image of God as Judge. He was speaking in a context much like ours—where justice and mercy are deemed as opposites. Justice had been reduced to punishment, and mercy had been reduced to withholding punishment. In that case, says Isaac, they do not and cannot coexist, least of all in the nature of God. Of course, the biblical vision of justice we see in Isaiah or Micah is different. True justice for the prophets is the beautiful restoration of the shalomic state by means of mercy—defined as every manifestation of divine goodness. In that case, justice and mercy kiss.[214] Mercy is the method and means of justice. And these together are demonstrations of the Good, which is to say, of God.

But Isaac must condescend to resist the so-called justice of retribution. That fallen form of justice is not worthy of God:

…Thus one cannot speak at all of God's justice, but rather of mercy that surpasses all justice: *"As a grain of sand cannot counterbalance a great quantity of gold, so in comparison God's use of justice cannot counterbalance His mercy. As a handful of sand thrown into the great sea, so are the sins of the flesh in comparison with the mind of God. And just as a strongly flowing spring is not obscured by a handful of dust, so the mercy of the Creator is not stemmed by the vices of His creatures."*

Now Hilarion takes us to the heart of the matter. What do we make of descriptions of the Creator's wrath, anger, and hatred? They are, for Isaac, anthropomorphic—i.e., figurative.

Thus, Isaac claims, one should not interpret literally those Old Testament texts where the terms *wrath, anger, hatred* and others

---

214. See Psalm 85:10.

are used of the Creator. If such anthropomorphic terms occur in Scripture, they are used in a figurative sense, for God never does anything out of wrath, anger or hatred: everything of that sort is far removed from His Nature....

With God, there is no hatred towards anyone, but all-embracing love, which does not distinguish between righteous and sinner, between a friend of truth and an enemy of truth, between angel and demon. Every created being is precious in God's eyes, He cares for every creature, and everyone finds in Him a loving Father. If we turn away from God, He does not turn away from us: "If we believe not, yet He abideth faithful, for He cannot deny Himself." Whatever may happen to humankind and to the whole of creation, however far it may be removed from God, He remains faithful to it in His love, which He cannot and will not deny.

This is the point of immutable love: *it never, ever turns away.* As Christ taught in the Sermon on the Mount, our heavenly Father is indiscriminate in his kindness, causing the rain to fall and the sun to shine on the crops of both the righteous and wicked alike. His love is unwavering, even for the ignorant and rebellious. And this, for Isaac as it was for Christ, is the perfection of divine Love.

## SAINT JOHN OF DAMASCUS (675–749)

### *EXACT EXPOSITION OF ORTHODOX DOCTRINE, BOOK I*

John of Damascus marks one of the latest theologians that we refer to as a church father, since we're stretching early church history into the mid-eighth century. The original title of his book, *Exact Exposition of Orthodox Doctrine*, sounds intimidating and even presumptuous. Yet, far from spouting certitudes, he ironically begins the book with a statement on the limitations of the human mind and human language to adequately represent Deity. Even the incarnation reflects "unutterables" that should humble us. The implication is that when we do express our thoughts about God, the words we use are only inexact placeholders—that is, *all* human speech is figurative when it comes to God. All theology is fan fiction (in the *Star Wars* sense)[215]—i.e., not canon, but fallible and derivative.

> Chapter 2. Concerning things utterable and things unutterable, and things knowable and things unknowable.
>
> It is necessary, therefore, that one who wishes to speak or to hear of God should understand clearly that alike in the doctrine of Deity and in that of the Incarnation, neither are all things unutterable nor all utterable; neither all unknowable nor all knowable. But the knowable belongs to one order, and the utterable to another; just as it is one thing to speak and another thing to know. Many of the things relating to God, therefore, that are dimly understood cannot be put into fitting terms, but on things above us *we cannot do else than express ourselves according to our limited capacity*; as, for instance, *when we speak of God we use the terms* sleep, *and* wrath, *and regardlessness*, hands, *too, and* feet, and such like expressions.[216]

Do you see what John snuck in there? He inserted "wrath" into the same category as "sleep," "regardlessness" (unmindfulness), "hands," and "feet"! We know God doesn't actually sleep, or clench physical fists, or wander across the heavens on corporeal feet. And we know nothing escapes God's mind—so his being "forgetful" cannot be read literally. But how about "wrath"? For the Damascene (as we affectionately call him), attributing wrath to God is as ludicrous as saying God is absentminded.

## SAINT ANTHONY THE GREAT (251–356)

### *PHILOKALIA*

For our last entry, we return all the way back to the days of the first church council in Nicaea, when the bounds of the New Testament were still being negotiated and our core doctrines (the deity of Christ and the three-personal God) were being contested. In the midst of that golden

---

215. Credit for this metaphor to Caleb Miller.
216. St. John Of Damascus, *An Exposition of Orthodox Faith*, trans. E. W. Watson and L. Pullan., in Nicene and Post-Nicene Fathers, Second Series, vol. 9, ed. Philip Schaff and Henry Wace (Buffalo, NY: Christian Literature Publishing Co., 1899), revised and edited for New Advent by Kevin Knight, www.newadvent.org/fathers/33041.htm.

age of theology—shadowed by both political persecution and ecclesial corruption—stood a few shining stars. One of these was Saint Anthony the Great, a wizened desert sage whose austerity and solitary life was legendary. His story of spiritual warfare with demonic beasts, published by Saint Athanasius, became a best seller. Had he been a first-century saint, doubtless, his words would have been canonized. But surely the gospel he stewarded and lived does represent the "canon of truth" received from the apostolic tradition.

I think he earns the parting shot as I close this chapter.

God is good, and passionless and immutable. If a man accepts it as right and true that God does not change, yet is puzzled how (being such) He rejoices at the good, turns away from the wicked, is angered with sinners and shows them mercy when they repent, the answer to this is that *God does not rejoice and is not angered, for joy and anger are passions.*[217]

If we recall our earlier definition of the passions, it's not as though God is some heartless Stoic in the sky or the "unmoved mover" of Aristotle's philosophy. No, God is LOVE. And God *is* relational and responsive to us—infinitely so. It's just that God's love is not *reactive, subject to* or *contingent* upon our drama, shame, or performance. Rather, God's love flows as the infinite, constant, and unfailing spring of his own nature. Does God grieve with us and rejoice with us? The incarnation reveals God's limitless empathy.[218] Yes, God sympathizes with our weaknesses and knows the human condition from within—but not as one whose character (love/goodness) is jerked around by external forces.

...It is absurd to think that the Deity could be helped or harmed by human deeds. *God is good and does only good; He harms no one and remains always the same.* As to ourselves, when we are good we enter into communion with God through our likeness to Him,

217. St. Anthony the Great, "170 Texts on Saintly Life," in *Early Fathers from the Philokalia,* ed. E. Kadloubovsky and G. E. H. Palmer (London, UK: Faber and Faber Limited, 1954), http://livingorthodoxfaith.blogspot.com/2009/11/170-texts-on-saintly-life-by-st-anthony. html. All excerpts in this section are from text 150.
218. See, for example, Hebrews 2:14–18; 4:15–16.

and when we become evil, we *cut ourselves off* from God, through our unlikeness to Him.

"Cut ourselves off from him"? Yes—subjectively, existentially—from our point of view. But Anthony's point is that cutting ourselves off from God does *not* cut God off from us. The estrangement is one-sided and, in that sense, delusional. Nothing can separate us from the love of God,[219] and yet we were "alienated *in our minds,*" according to Paul.[220] There's that ontological/phenomenological distinction again.

> …When we live virtuously we are God's own, and when we become wicked, we fall away from Him. *This does not mean that He is angry with us,* but that our sins do not let God shine in us, and that they link us with the tormentors—the demons. If later, through prayers and good deeds, we obtain absolution of our sins, *it does not mean that we have propitiated God and changed Him,* but that through such actions and our turning to God we have cured the evil in ourselves and have again become able to partake of God's goodness. Thus, *to say that God turns away from the wicked is the same as to say that the sun hides itself from those who lose their sight.*

## TAKEAWAYS

Today, not all Christians give credence to the authority of the early Christians who gave us the New Testament, the apostolic gospel, the deity of Christ, or the doctrine of the Trinity. Too frequently, I hear, "I don't care about all that; just give me the Bible." Oddly, the same voices tend to get uptight about any theology that differs from theirs, as if theology *does* matter, and as if *their* theology were the measure of orthodoxy. As if they have not inherited their theology from somewhere or learned it from someone. As if they composed it themselves in the privacy of their personal devotions. They may mislabel their literalism as "conservative," conserving nothing of the Great Tradition—merely parroting a version of Evangelicalism scarcely two hundred years old. Ironically, when they hear

---

219. See Romans 8:38–39.
220. See Colossians 1:21.

274 <i>A MORE CHRISTLIKE WORD</i>

the orthodoxy of the early church, they frequently cry, "Heresy." Such are the vagaries of modernist sectarians.

But for those who've soured on the bad fruit of Christianity's self-pruned branches—those desirous of retrieving and conserving "the faith once delivered"—these citations might matter, if only to validate their best spiritual instincts about God. These patristic giants defined orthodoxy and defended it against some of the same heresies that pass themselves off as mainstream Christianity today. Their dogmatic teaching on the Christlike God of unswerving goodness and cruciform love *is* the gospel through which all Scripture must be read. I commend them to you as the pinnacle of biblical interpretation, without whom we would have no Bible at all.

To ignore the way those who gave us the Bible actually read Scripture is folly. We'd best remember their Emmaus Way before the crass biblicism of our times consigns the sacred Scripture to dustbins and bonfires for the hate literature we've made it. The Bible tells the greatest story ever told. How it became bad news is the sad legacy of the new Sanhedrin. So, yes, I'm a huge fan of the "cloud of witnesses" (Heb 12:1, numerous translations) and the help they offer. Once again, Jeremiah's words as outro:

> This is what the LORD says:
>     "Stand at the crossroads and look;
>     ask for the ancient paths,
>     ask where the good way is, and walk in it,
>     and you will find rest for your souls."
>
> (Jer 6:16 NIV)

### CHAPTER 20

# OUTRO:
# TOO GOOD TO BE TRUE?

*T*o summarize part II, this entire book, and the great arc of my *More Christlike* trilogy, I want to emphasize the big picture that drove the whole project.

I care deeply about Jesus and want people to know him. But I see the deconstructionists exiting their churches and walking away from faith by the tens of millions. One reason for this is that they've been indoctrinated with false images of who God is and what God requires. The wrathful God who threatened to burn them in hell forever if they don't believe right or behave right is not the *Abba* whom Jesus revealed—not the gracious and gentle Shepherd who descends into *hades* to rescue lost sheep, who are too entangled in briars to find their way home. The "mighty smiter" of our theology and "absentee landlord" of our experience is *not* the God who ascended a cross to give himself to the world in self-giving, radically forgiving, co-suffering love.

For those who've not already flown the coop in dismay, or maybe especially for them, I've done the best I can to propose the more Christlike God, the more Christlike Way, and the more Christlike Word of the historic gospel. That this ancient orthodoxy sounds like heresy to the Sanhedrin of the modern church tells us how far we have fallen.

No matter. The demand for a beautiful gospel is an urgent pastoral and evangelistic concern. Day after day, I respond to those who are either hindered from faith or about to abandon it because the God they've heard preached is so ugly, so small. And when I share the good news that the one true God is *exactly* like Jesus, and his love endures forever, the world-weary wonder if it's too good to be true. As Saint Cyril once said, "Indeed, the mystery of Christ runs the risk of being disbelieved because it is so wonderful."[221] Or as George MacDonald said,

> But there are not a few, who would be indignant at having their belief in God questioned, who yet seem greatly to fear imagining him better than he is: whether it is he or themselves they dread injuring by expecting too much of him?[222]

No wonder Paul had to assure the Ephesians that such divine love is higher, wider, longer, and wider than we can conceive or imagine! But by the grace of the Holy Spirit, we do catch glimpses.

To press home the pastoral urgency of reading the Bible through a more Christlike Word—Jesus Christ—and interpreting it the *Emmaus Way*, I leave you with a final real-life conversation with a reader named David.[223] His plea and my response gather up and summarize key themes of this book and the broader trilogy.

## QUESTION

Dear Brad,

Just bought and read *A More Christlike God*. I loved the book! I really want to believe your theology of God's love and your interpretation of "wrath"—but how do you explain these New Testament verses that refer to wrath? Is it all explained by "giving over"? For example [from the NIV]:

+ **John 3:36** – Whoever believes in the Son has eternal life, but whoever rejects the Son will not see life, for *God's wrath remains on them.*

---

221. Cyril of Alexandria, *On the Unity of Christ*, trans. John A. McGuckin (Yonkers, NY: St. Vladimir's Seminary Press, 1995), 61.
222. George MacDonald, *The Complete Works*, ill. ed. (Musaicum Books, 2017), n.p.
223. This correspondence has been lightly edited for this publication.

* **Romans 2:8** – But for those who are self-seeking and who reject the truth and follow evil, *there will be wrath and anger.*

* **Ephesians 5:6** – Let no one deceive you with empty words, for because of such things *God's wrath comes* on those who are disobedient.

* **Colossians 3:5–6** – ⁵Put to death, therefore, whatever belongs to your earthly nature: sexual immorality, impurity, lust, evil desires and greed, which is idolatry. ⁶Because of these, *the wrath of God* is coming.

* **1 Thessalonians 2:16** – …in their effort to keep us from speaking to the Gentiles so that they may be saved. In this way they always heap up their sins to the limit. The wrath of God has come upon them at last.

* **Hebrews 3:9–11** – ⁹…where your ancestors tested and tried me, though for forty years they saw what I did.¹⁰ That is why *I was angry* with that generation; I said, "Their hearts are always going astray, and they have not known my ways." ¹¹So I declared on oath *in my anger,* "They shall never enter my rest."

* **Hebrews 4:3** – Now we who have believed enter that rest, just as God has said, "So I declared on oath *in my anger,* 'They shall never enter my rest.'" And yet his works have been finished since the creation of the world.

* **Revelation 11:18** – The nations were angry, and *your wrath has come.* The time has come for judging the dead, and for rewarding your servants the prophets and your people who revere your name, both great and small—and for destroying those who destroy the earth."

Sincerely,
David

## RESPONSE

I'd begin the same way I describe in *A More Christlike Way:* "wrath" (*orge*) is a metaphor for the self-inflicted consequences of defying God. It's not that God literally *wraths* them, but as long as we turn from the light, we will endure the suffering generated by the shadow we ourselves create. The light of Christ's unfailing love shines on all without fail, but our rejection of the light leaves us wallowing in our brokenness. The wrath or the judgment is intrinsic to the sin—i.e., "The 'wages of sin' [not of God] is death, but the free gift of God is eternal life" (Rom 6:23). Reject eternal Life and Light, and what do you have left? The *dire warning* is very real but should not be confused by literalizing it into a *direct threat* of divine violence (even if a literal reading suggests it).

Take someone who falls into a serious drug addiction, supports the addiction through breaking and entering, gets caught, gets arrested, is convicted, and is put in jail. They are undergoing "the wrath" of their own sins. And indeed, some texts use "wrath" as a synonym for satan or "the destroyer" (as per Romans 5 and Wisdom of Solomon 18). God did not cause the addiction, the lifestyle of crime, the arrest, or even the imprisonment. The natural consequences and spiritual bondage are the addiction's own severe and sufficient punishment.

So then, in what sense is the wrath "of God"? The church fathers say, "Only figuratively." We habitually project the consequences of our sin onto the One we are sinning against. If God's law is love, but we act in hate… when we experience the backlash of our own hatred, is God's law the problem? Did God's law *cause* the backlash? The backlash is only associated with God in that our acts were a violation of God's law. But the punishment is the blowback of our own hatred.

The wrath is also "God's" in that, despite our willful defiance and the consequential suffering, God's presence in our lives transforms these outcomes into a means of redemption. In our example, the addict may lose everything…but losing everything may be the very occasion God *uses* (not *sends*) to wake them up and steer them home.

The parable of the prodigal son(s) is the clearest picture we have of what wrath is, how it works, what causes it, and how it is and isn't "God's." The Prodigal Son woke up in a pigpen of his own making and came to his senses. The father did not send him there. Were his days or years or life of misery literally God's wrath (anger expressed as violence)? No. But his trials were transformed by God's grace into the big story of the son's redemption.

The texts you've listed would all generally fit that same model. However…

The other dynamic is that these texts do employ rhetoric. Rhetorical devices are common in the New Testament—a way of communicating with intense *pathos* to move truth from the head to the heart to the hands (action). And New Testament authors skillfully use rhetorical devices all the time (along with hyperbole, etc.). Threats of wrath are used rhetorically as a slap on the face—a wake-up call—but are nearly always paired with contrasting words of comfort, consolation, and confidence. We run into a problem when we literalize and totalize rhetoric, as if those texts contained passionless information to be absorbed at face value. It's the toughest genre to work with because we're prone to think we're reading simple didactic teaching or propositional truth. But rhetoric is like preaching. It's an oratory method for effect.

Sometimes, the wrath language serves as a wake-up call similar to the stench of manure and hunger pangs that finally caught the Prodigal's attention. But, speaking analogously, does the father ever literally shove the pig paddies in the boy's face? Did the father withhold his food until he verged on starvation? Not at all. Indeed, the punchline to his wake-up call comes as the father's scandalous invitation to rejoin the family...the same invitation we see in the immediate context of nearly all wrath rhetoric.

This approach might seem like a stretch to modern readers, but to the early Christians, such an approach is mandatory because the alternative ends up throwing God's character under the bus. To anthropomorphize the "wrath" inevitably creates an idol or commits a blasphemy—a lesser God than the all-merciful *Abba* revealed in Christ.

But we have much better news than that—beautiful news we learned through the life of God-in-the-flesh. Moses, the Prophets, the Gospels, and the apostolic sermons—all the Scriptures—share in this great Story that we've learned by the illumination of the Spirit and through our direct experience of the Spirit's transforming grace.

This beautiful news is that, in Jesus Christ, we have a more Christlike God, a more Christlike Way, and a more Christlike Word than human minds and history's religions could ever conceive. A Word whose voice we hear saying, "Come, follow me. There's a place at my Father's table for everyone. Even you. *Especially* you."

# ACKNOWLEDGMENTS

Acknowledgments pages have become a point of trauma for me, given the hurt I've caused those whom I've failed to remember in the past. Apologies in advance. Your missing name probably should have been at the top of my list. For this book, I'm going to stick very closely to my biblical studies trajectory.

Thanks to my early childhood Bible teachers: to Mom and Dad for my first Bible. To the young lady who showed me "I will never leave you or forsake you" at our backyard DVBS when I was eight. For my first Sunday school teachers, Murray and Enid MacMillan and Stanley Moffat.

Thanks to my college and university Bible teachers: Carl Hinderager, Stephen Bramer, Ken Guenther, Bruce Fisk, and Vern Steiner.

Over the last two decades, those who've specifically mentored me into my current hermeneutic: Ron Dart, Archbishop Lazar Puhalo, David Goa, and Matthew Lynch.

And for my most recent focus, these Open Table colleagues: Fr. John Behr, John MacMurray, Brian Zahnd, Joe Beach, Kenneth Tanner, Cherith Fee Nordling, Paul Young, C. Baxter Kruger, Katie Skurja, Julie Canlis, Chris Green, Felicia Murrell, Scott Erickson, Jonathan Parker, and especially Anna Parker and my beloved Eden.

Finally, thanks to the folks at Whitaker House who helped bring this book to press: Christine Whitaker, Lois Puglisi, Don Milam, Becky Speer, and Elizabeth Vince. I love working with you!

# A SPRING IN MY STEP: RECOMMENDED READING

*A*s a fledgling student and young rookie pastor, such was the imbalance in my life that, if you had asked me what my hobby was, I would had said, "hermeneutics." I know, I know: nerd alert. I was lucky to manage a first kiss in those years. But at least my favorite pastime was consistent with my passion for Scripture and my aggressive (and embarrassing) zeal for defending biblical inerrancy.

Since then, I've read many really helpful hermeneutical works—ancient and recent, conservative and radical—that enlarged my love for God and unshackled my view of the Bible to enjoy its inspired genius. Even books I was warned against, far from demolishing my spiritual hunger, drew me deeper into the epic saga of redemption told across the pages of our sacred text.

Among these, I recommend the following books, which I hope will help you read Scripture more attentively and freely. These authors aren't all on the same page—some wouldn't even identify with Christianity. Others might be horrified by the convictions I've laid out in these pages. All I can say is that their books infused something lively and life-giving into my understanding. They added a spring to my step on the Emmaus Way. I gratefully commend them to you.

Alter, Robert. *The Art of Biblical Narrative.* New York: Basic Books, 2011.

Augustine of Hippo. *On Christian Doctrine.* Pickerington, OH: Beloved Publishing, 2014.

Brueggemann, Walter. *The Prophetic Imagination.* Minneapolis, MN: Fortress Press, 2001.

Byassee, Jason. *Surprised by Jesus Again: Reading the Bible in Communion with the Saints.* Grand Rapids, MI: Eerdmans, 2019.

Childs, Brevard. *Introduction to the Old Testament as Scripture.* Minneapolis, MN: Augsburg Fortress, 2011.

———. *Old Testament Theology in Canonical Context.* Philadelphia, PA: Fortress Press, 1990.

DeSilva, David A. *An Introduction to the New Testament: Contexts, Methods & Ministry Formation.* Downers Grove, IL: IVP Academic, 2004.

Edwards, Dennis R. *What Is the Bible and How Do We Understand It?* Harrisonburg, VA: Herald Press, 2019.

Enns, Peter. *The Bible Tells Me So: Why Defending Scripture Has Made Us Unable to Read It.* New York: HarperOne, 2014.

———. *How the Bible Actually Works: In Which I Explain How An Ancient, Ambiguous, and Diverse Book Leads Us to Wisdom Rather Than Answers—and Why That's Great News.* New York: HarperOne, 2019.

Erasmus. *Erasmus on the New Testament.* Edited by Robert D. Sider. Toronto, ON: University of Toronto Press, 2020.

Fee, Gordon D. *Gospel and Spirit: Issues in New Testament Hermeneutics.* Peabody, MA: Hendrickson Publishers, 1991.

Flood, Derek. *Disarming Scripture: Cherry-Picking Liberals, Violence-Loving Conservatives, and Why We All Need to Learn to Read the Bible Like Jesus Did.* San Francisco, CA: Metanoia Books, 2014.

Goa, David, and Dittmar Mündel, *Reading the Bible as Life-Giving Word.* Camrose, AB: The Chester Ronning Centre for the Study of Religion and Public Life, 2013.

Green, Chris E. W., *Sanctifying Interpretation: Vocation, Holiness, and Scripture*. 2nd ed. Cleveland, TN: CPT Press, 2020.

Greenblatt, Stephen. *The Rise and Fall of Adam and Eve: The Story That Created Us*. New York: W. W. Norton & Company, 2018.

Hardin, Michael. *The Jesus Driven Life: Reconnecting Humanity with Jesus*. 2nd ed. Lancaster, PA: JDL Press, 2010.

Hays, Richard. *Reading Backwards: Figural Christology and the Fourfold Gospel Witness*. Waco, TX: Baylor University Press, 2014.

Henning, Meghan. *Educating Early Christians through the Rhetoric of Hell: "Weeping and Gnashing of Teeth" as Paideia in Matthew and the Early Church*. Tübingen, Germany: Mohr Siebeck, 2014.

Irenaeus of Lyons. *On the Apostolic Preaching*. Translated by John Behr. Yonkers, NY: St. Vladimir's Seminary Press, 1997.

Kugel, James L., and Rowan A. Greer. *Early Biblical Interpretation*. Edited by Wayne Meeks. Philadelphia, PA: Westminster Press, 1986.

Lynch, Matthew J. *Portraying Violence in the Hebrew Bible: A Literary and Cultural Study*. Cambridge, UK: Cambridge University Press, 2020.

Melito of Sardis. *On Pascha: With the Fragments of Melito and Other Material Related to the Quartodecimans*. Yonkers, NY: St. Vladimir's Press, 2001.

Origen. *The Philocalia of Origen*. Whitefish, MT: Kessinger Publishing, 2005.

Puhalo, Lazar. *The Mirror of Scripture: The Old Testament Is About You*. Abbotsford, BC: St. Macrina Press, 2018.

Ruden, Sarah. *Paul Among the People: The Apostle Reinterpreted and Reimagined in His Own Time*. New York: Image Books, 2011.

Sailhamer, John H. *The Pentateuch as Narrative: A Biblical-Theological Commentary*. Grand Rapids, MI: Zondervan Academic, 1992.

Seibert, Eric A. *Disturbing Divine Behavior: Troubling Old Testament Images of God*. Minneapolis, MN: Augsburg Fortress, 2009.

Sheridan, Mark. *Language for God in Patristic Tradition: Wrestling with Biblical Anthropomorphism*. Downers Grove, IL: IVP Academic, 2014.

Witherington, Ben, III. *New Testament Rhetoric: An Introductory Guide to the Art of Persuasion in and of the New Testament.* Eugene, OR: Cascade Books, 2009.

Zahnd, Brian. *Sinners in the Hands of a Loving God: The Scandalous Truth of the Very Good News.* Colorado Springs, CO: Waterbrook Press, 2017.

# ABOUT THE AUTHOR

*B*radley Jersak is the Dean of Theology & Culture, a modular graduate studies program at St. Stephen's University in New Brunswick, Canada. He is also an editor for the Clarion-Journal.com and CWR Magazine (PTM.org). Bradley and his wife, Eden, have lived in the Abbotsford area of British Columbia since 1988, where they served as pastors and church planters for twenty years. Bradley is the author of a number of nonfiction and fiction books, including *A More Christlike God*, *A More Christlike Way*, *Her Gates Will Never Be Shut*, *Can You Hear Me?: Tuning in to the God Who Speaks*, and *The Pastor: A Crisis*. He has an MA in biblical studies from Briercrest Bible College and Seminary, an MDiv in biblical studies from Trinity Western University/ACTS Seminary, and a PhD in theology from Bangor University, Wales. He was also a visiting scholar at the University of Nottingham, United Kingdom, for postdoctoral research in patristic Christology (under Dr. Conor Cunningham).

www.bradjersak.com

# Welcome to Our House!

## *We Have a Special Gift for You*

It is our privilege and pleasure to share in your love of Christian books. We are committed to bringing you authors and books that feed, challenge, and enrich your faith.

To show our appreciation, we invite you to sign up to receive a specially selected **Reader Appreciation Gift**, with our compliments. Just go to the Web address at the bottom of this page.

God bless you as you seek a deeper walk with Him!

WE HAVE A GIFT FOR YOU. VISIT:

whpub.me/nonfictionthx

WHITAKER
HOUSE